D1355713

MODERN NEEDLEWORK IN 600 PICTURES

MODERN
NEEDLEWORK

In 600 Pictures

THE WORLD'S GREATEST NEWSPAPER

A
DAILY
EXPRESS
PUBLICATION
LONDON
E.C. 4

Printed for London Express Newspaper Ltd. by the
Syndicate Publishing Co., Ltd., London, W.C.2
[8/R. 30. 156]

Contents

Contents

Part Two: HOME DRESSMAKING

Contents

7

Contents

PART ONE

Basic
Sewing

Fundamental Stitches

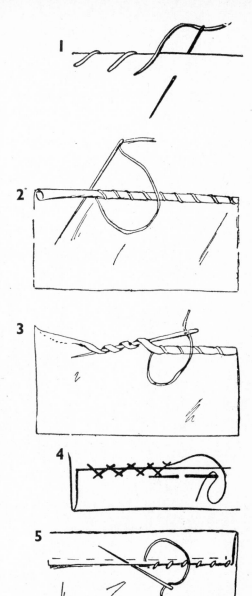

1. OVERCASTING is used to neaten the raw edges of seams to keep them from fraying. The method of working should always be somewhat loose, and not tight enough to pucker up the edge.

2. WHIPPING is used for gathering lace on to material and attaching frills. The edge to be whipped must be trimmed perfectly smooth, and carefully marked with pins or tacks into halves or quarters. Halve and quarter the material to which the frill is to be whipped in the same way, and pin marks together, so that the fullness will be evenly distributed. To whip, with your left-hand thumb roll over the edge of the stuff to be whipped very closely and tightly towards you, a small piece at a time. Point the needle towards you from the top of the roll, bringing it out just beneath the roll. Do not stitch through the roll, but through one thickness of fabric only. Whipping in which several stitches are taken on the needle at once is shown in Diag. 3.

4. HERRINGBONING is used to secure the hems of flannel and other materials which are too thick to turn in twice. Such hems are turned once only and then secured by herringbone-stitch worked over the raw edge in a series of backward stitches taken alternately on the doubled hem and on the material.

5. FELLING corresponds to hemming in plain needle-work, except that it is not usually worked so finely and neatly. It is used for facing or hemming-up purposes and for skirt hems, fixing linings to coats, etc.

6. CATCH-STITCHING. The large, temporary stitches used to fix the canvas to the material. Used in tailoring, to attach canvas and stiffened linings to a garment.

7. CATCH-STITCHING. The smaller, permanent stitches. The needle is taken through the turning of the material, then through the canvas. No stitches may show on the right side.

6

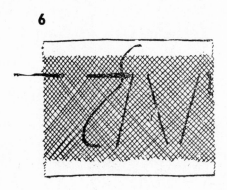

7

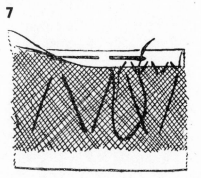

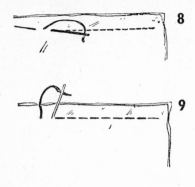
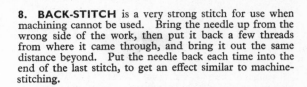

8. BACK-STITCH is a very strong stitch for use when machining cannot be used. Bring the needle up from the wrong side of the work, then put it back a few threads from where it came through, and bring it out the same distance beyond. Put the needle back each time into the end of the last stitch, to get an effect similar to machine-stitching.

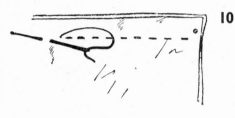

9. STAB-STITCH is back-stitching, worked on very thick material, where it is not possible to take up the stitch on the needle. The needle is brought up from the wrong side and drawn through, then inserted back where the last stitch ended.

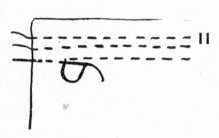

10. RUNNING-STITCH is used for tacking up for fitting, or where there is strain on the tacked edges. The stitches are short and even, and several may be taken upon the needle before pulling through.

11. GAUGING, sometimes used as a trimming, consists of a number of rows of gathers. All the stitches should be made without drawing up the thread, and a long thread should be left by which the gathers can be adjusted when all rows are done. 12 shows the gathered-up effect.

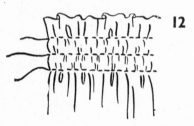

13. SLIP-HEMMING is used for the hems of tailored skirts, coats, etc., and is worked by taking up merely one or two threads of the material, then inserting the needle in the turned-in fold of the hem and passing it along for ¼ in. before bringing it out in the usual way.

14. PAD-STITCH, used for attaching the canvas interlining to tailored collars and revers, is worked upwards and downwards in alternate rows, without changing the position of the work, taking up a tiny stitch through canvas and material, and leaving ½-in. space before taking up the next stitch.

15. FLY-RUNNING is used to gather very thin materials, such as georgette and chiffon. Take five or six small running-stitches on the needle at once, and push the material, as it is gathered, off the needle towards the right hand, instead of drawing the needle out. Move the hands a little farther to the left-hand end of the material and repeat the process.

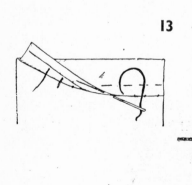

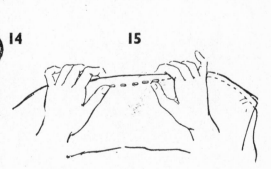

Embroidery Stitches

16. RUNNING-STITCH. The simplest embroidery stitch, consisting of a thread run in and out of the material at even distances. Effective for all-over designs.

17. STEM-STITCH. Used for outlines, etc. The needle is inserted at a slight angle to its direction instead of back along the direction in which the line proceeds ; thus the line gains more width, and each stitch has a tiny space between.

18. SATIN-STITCH. This is a stitch that should be worked very evenly. The needle takes up the width between the lines, thus making flat stitches on the surface. In 19 the stitch is shown with a padding of running-stitch underneath.

20. CHAIN-STITCH. Consists of a series of loop stitches, and the thread coming out of each loop has the needle inserted at side of same, the thread being under the needle.

21. BUTTONHOLE-STITCH. Extremely useful for all kinds of needlework. A running-stitch can first be worked along the line to be covered as slight padding, if desired. The stitches may be placed closer together.

22. SPLIT-STITCH is used for very fine outlines. The needle is taken through the stitch on the right side, thus splitting it.

23. STAR-STITCH. Employed as a powdering, and all stitches begin from the centre. It is as well to pencil out the design lightly, as the stitches must be kept regular as to length and spacing.

24. CABLE-STITCH is worked like chain-stitch, but the needle is inserted at the side of the preceding stitch.

25. CROSS-STITCH is quickly worked. Slanting stitches are first made from left to right, then crossed with others from right to left. Always keep the top stitches in the same direction throughout one piece of work, the crosses coming exactly one over the other.

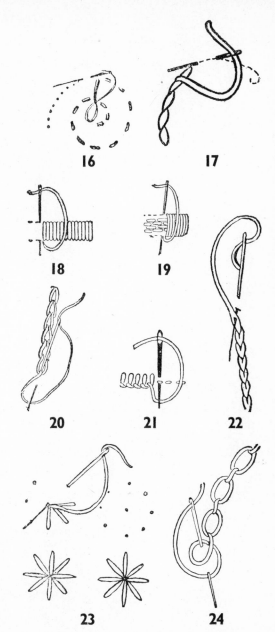

16 17

18 19

20 21 22

23 24

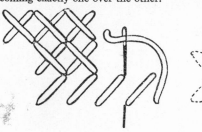

25 26

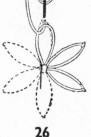

26. LAZY DAISY STITCH. A very quick way of embroidering small daisy-like flowers. The needle is brought up at centre, the thread held down under the left thumb, then the needle taken down again at centre and brought up at tip over the loop held by thumb. To secure loop the needle is taken down at other side of it and brought up at centre again ready for next stitch.

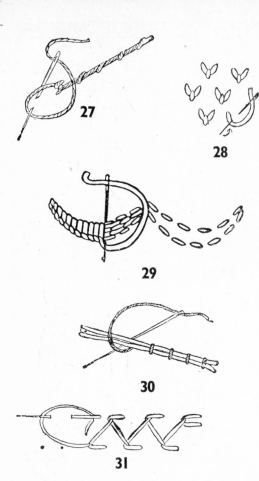

27

28

29

30

31

32

33

27. KNOT-STITCH. Useful for edging purposes, as it has the effect of a braid or raised line. It is worked from left to right, either straight, curved, or according to the design. Bring up the needle from the wrong side of the work, take up a small portion of the material, draw up stitch, then pass needle under same once, twice, or more, according to the size knots required. The diagram shows the thread passed once under.

28. FLY-STITCH. One of the most widely used filling stitches; gives a dainty light effect that is very pleasing. Bring thread up from wrong side, and take it to the back again a tiny distance to the right, bringing the needle out just below the two points with the thread under the needle. To complete, take needle down on other side of the loop.

29. BUTTONHOLE SCALLOPING is popular for finishing both white and coloured embroidery. The scallop transfer should be ironed on the material about an inch from the edge. The stitch is then worked from outline to inner edge of the scallops, the stitches being straight as shown in the sketch. When the stitching is completed the work should be pressed, then the material below the scallops cut away close up under the purl edge of the buttonholing.

30. SIMPLE COUCHING-STITCH. Two threads or more fastened down to the ground material by means of stitches taken across the cords —the stitches being worked straight, as in diagram, or on the slant, as desired.

31-33. CORAL- OR FEATHER-STITCHES. Also known as cat- or osier-stitch. It is illustrated in three forms, single (31), double (32), and treble (33). It is useful for outlining purposes, ornamenting dresses, etc., and can be executed in fine or coarse crochet cotton, turkey red cotton, etc., etc. Keep the work a uniform width, which can be arranged by creasing the material, or running in tacking threads, or marking lightly with a pencil.

All three stitches are worked on the same principle, and consist of a buttonhole loop taken in a perpendicular direction; also each stitch can be taken rather on the slant from right to left if preferred.

34. EMBROIDERED HEMS. When an article is lengthened by having a piece of material joined on to it, or when a hem is turned in or binding applied on the right side of the material, the seam can be embroidered over and thus made into an ornamental seam.

35. NET EDGING made of lingerie net folded double can be joined on by simple stitching or by SCALLOPING. The superfluous net and material are cut away close to the stitches.

34

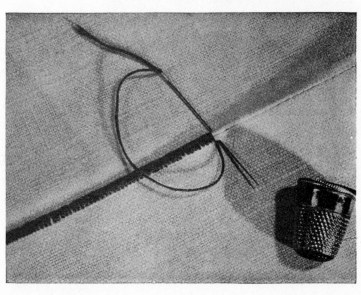

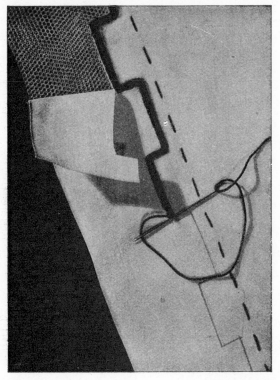

35

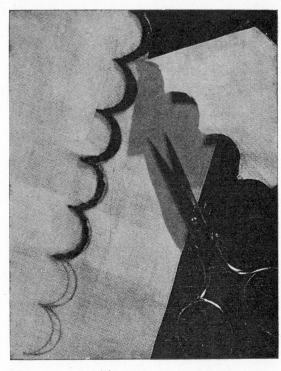

36

37

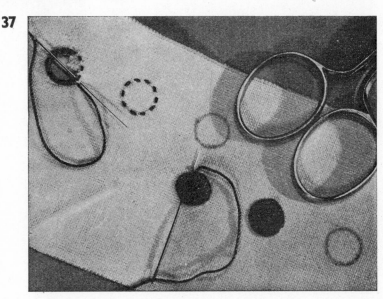

38

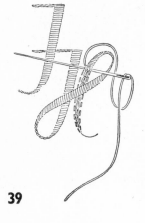

39

36. SCALLOPING. Trace the scallops on to the material with the help of a transfer or a coin. Use chain-stitch to form a padding and finish off with button-hole stitch.

37. BRODERIE ANGLAISE. Draw the circles in pencil on the material. If a prominent raised outline is required, cord-stitch is useful. Make the padding by covering the outline with closely set running-stitches, then work closely across these with short satin-stitches. To make EYELETS begin by outlining the circle with very small running-stitches. Cut the material inside the circle crosswise and overcast round the hole so as to catch in the corners of the material, which are thus made to serve as padding.

38-39. MONOGRAMS. The design must be pencilled or traced and outlined with running-stitch. Outline-stitch is used for the thin "strokes." The thick "strokes" are filled in with chain-stitch to form a padding, and covered with satin-stitch.

Hand and Machined Seams

Very fine silks or delicate velvets should be stitched by hand, as machine-stitching would spoil their graceful "hang." Back-stitching wears particularly well, or a combination stitch consisting of running-stitches and back-stitches applied alternately can be used. Running-stitch is often used for the first row of stitching in the case of a French seam, but it is used chiefly for tacking and gathering.

A hand-sewn seam should consist of very small stitches and must be worked with a fine needle ; in many cases it will wear better than a seam sewn by machine.

The cross-seam (40a, upper) and the oversewn seam (40a, lower) are used to join two selvedges. Both these seams are quite flat and are used mainly for household linen and furnishings. The cross-seam is worked from right to left on the right side of the material. Hold the two selvedges together over the index finger, and take up each selvedge in turn with the needle. The stitches must be very close together and must be drawn tight.

The oversewn seam is used to join two selvedges or turned-in edges which are placed together right sides facing.

Face cloths and velours may be joined invisibly by darning on the wrong side of the material. The darning-stitches, which should be about $\frac{1}{3}$ in. long, must not pass right through the material. They must be drawn tight so that the two cut edges of the material are as close together as possible.

A machine-sewn seam in a thinner cloth may be made invisible by darning over the seam on the right side of the material. The nap is then teased out a little with the needle so as to hide the darning-stitches.

The following instructions apply to all good sewing-machines. There is no need to go into any detail here,

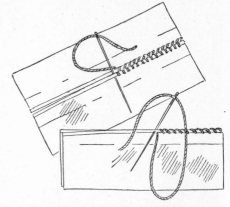

40a

since full instructions are always supplied with the machine. The machine may be operated by hand, treadle, or electricity ; treadle machines being the commonest. Place both feet on the treadle, start the machine by moving the upper flywheel towards yourself with your right hand, and keep the machine in motion by regular even movements of the feet. Keeping the treadle working smoothly is an art which must be learned, so practise on odd pieces of material.

Be considerate to your machine. Frequent oiling and cleaning, perfect needles, and thread of the correct thickness are essential if the machine is to work satisfactorily. When inserting a needle, the flat side of the " head " must face to the right, the long groove of the needle to the left. Needle and thread sizes must correspond.

The cotton from the reel must be threaded into the needle from left to right. The bobbin which holds the lower

40

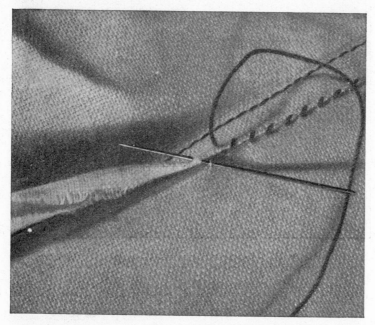

40. RUN-AND-FELL SEAM. Place the two thicknesses of material together, right sides facing each other, and stitch about $\frac{1}{4}$ in. from the cut edges. The lower edge is then trimmed off close to the stitching, while the upper edge is turned in and hemmed down with small stitches.

41. FELL SEAM (machined). Here, too, the right sides of the material must face each other. The lower cut edge can be placed back a little, or it can be trimmed when the first row of stitching has been done. Smooth down the seam, then turn in the wide edge and stitch down over to the narrow one.

41

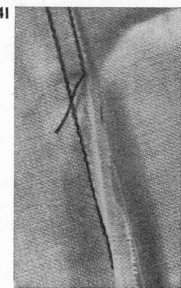

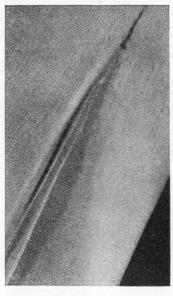

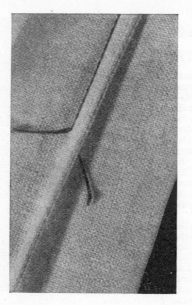

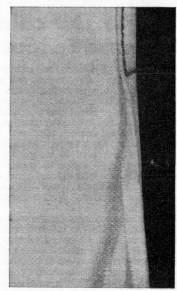

42 **43** **44**

thread must be placed in the bobbin case in such a way that the thread can be drawn out of the bobbin case in the direction of the slit. The tension is regulated by turning the screw which controls the tension spring. When the bobbin has been inserted, the lower thread is brought up in a loop by a single turn of the flywheel. Pass the upper thread through the loop and lift it so as to draw out the lower thread. When beginning to sew, hold the ends of the two threads until the first three stitches have been made, so as to prevent the threads from becoming tangled or the machine from getting jammed.

When the seam is finished, remove the material by pulling it to the left away from you, never towards you, as this would bend or break the needle. Perfect stitching can be obtained only if the upper and the lower threads have the same tension. Tightening the tension nut at the head of the machine increases the tension ; loosening it decreases the tension.

45

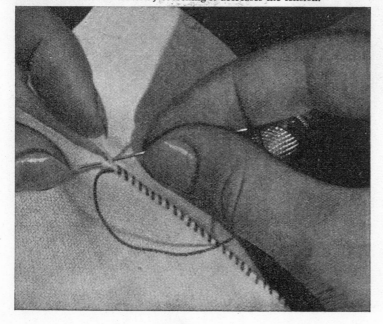

42. FRENCH SEAM. For the first seam, which must face outwards, the wrong sides of the material are placed together. Stitch from the right side, then trim off the edges as closely and neatly as possible. If any loose threads of material are left, the seam will not lie perfectly flat.

43. Fold the seam over and run a second line of stitching beside the first, so as to enclose the turned-in cut edges.

44. SIMPLIFIED FRENCH SEAM. Used for thin materials, or where a clearly defined flat seam is not required. The two thicknesses of material are placed right sides facing each other. The cut edges are then turned in like a hem and stitched down close to the edge.

45. OVERSEWN SEAM. Two even selvedges with no coloured edging threads can be sewn together with close overcasting stitches. Only a very little of the material should be taken up, so that the stitches will remain invisible as far as possible when the seam is pressed.

Single Machine Seam and Fell Seam

In order to facilitate the subsequent removal of the tacking thread, you must stitch not on top of it but beside it—about $\frac{1}{16}$ in. away. Such tacking threads as have been stitched down should be carefully removed in short sections, unless the whole thread can be pulled out. Cut the thread into short lengths; each length can then be removed with a pin or the point of a small pair of scissors. The expert will use a stiletto for the purpose; this is also particularly useful when removing the short tacks used to mark the stitching line.

The finished seam must be pressed on the wrong side. This can be done with the edges opened out or turned over to one side. The latter method is employed if the edges of the seam are to be turned in or sewn together with overcasting stitches, or—as is common in the case of sports clothes—if the seam is to be stitched down. Here the distance of the second row of stitching from the first may be as desired, or the seam may be stitched down twice, the first row of stitching being close to the seam, the second the distance of the presser-foot away. This gives the effect of a lapped seam, but the treble stitching naturally results in a very much stronger seam.

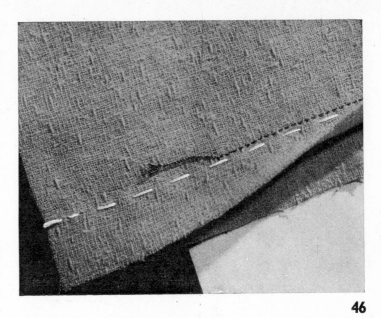

46

47. When pressing, the edges of the single seam can be either opened out or turned down. If a bulky and very apparent seam is to be avoided, the edges should be opened out. Turning the seam down is a preliminary to the next work.

48. Before a seam is stitched down, the seam edges should be tacked. The stitching is carried out on the right side, and can be quite close to the seam or as far away as the width of the presser-foot.

47

48

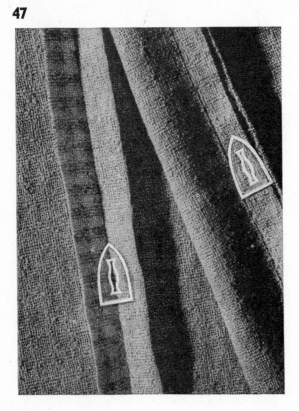

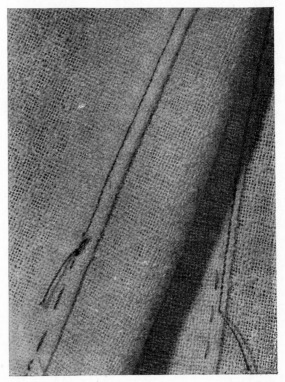

Various Fell Seams.
The French Seam

49

The flat fell seam (49) is used almost exclusively for linen, and can be sewn with the ordinary presser-foot or with the hemming attachment. The two pieces of material, right sides facing, are first stitched together about ½ in. from the edge. Then the left edge is trimmed off quite close to the stitching so that the right edge projects. This turn-in can be taken into consideration when tacking, so that no trimming off will be necessary. The wide edge must now be turned over and in and stitched down close to the fold. If the hemming attachment is being used, the material must be inserted into the opening and it will then be turned down automatically.

The raised fell seam is tacked and then stitched, so as to enclose the cut edge of the material. If the piece of material which is being folded over also has a cut edge, and not a selvedge, then it should be turned in before being stitched down.

Both the raised fell seam and the French seam are suitable for straight seams in thin materials.

For a French seam the cut-seam edges should be trimmed off evenly and fairly close to the first seam, so that a neat second seam can be sewn. No loose threads should be left sticking out, as once the second seam has been sewn it will be impossible to remove any threads showing on the right side.

50. THE RAISED FELL SEAM is used to join and neaten two pieces of material with a single seam. If the edge of material which is to be turned over is a selvedge, it need not be turned in, but can be stitched down flat.

51. For the **FRENCH SEAM** the two edges of material are first stitched together on the right side, wrong sides facing, then enclosed on the wrong side by a second seam.

50

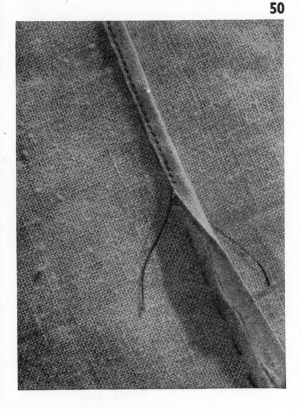

51

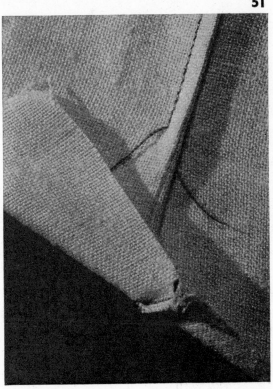

Neatening the Seam

There are as many ways of finishing off or neatening a seam as there are of making one. Here, too, it is important to employ a method which is appropriate to the material and the seam itself.

The simplest finish is by overcasting. It has a somewhat cheap appearance, however, and in good sewing is justifiable only when the stitches are short and lie close together.

By way of compromise between overcasting and rolling, the seam edge may be turned in narrowly and overcast; this method is useful in the case of thin material. As an alternative, where the material is sufficiently thick the edges may be turned in narrowly and hemmed.

Wide seam turnings can be dealt with by turning in both seam edges.

BUTTONHOLE-STITCH, which may be used for many purposes, gives a very secure and hard-wearing seam finish. It is sewn with sewing silk to match the material in colour. The stitches should be as close together as possible. Linen thread or cotton should not be used, since the little knots in the stitches would then be too hard and would tend to press through, especially in the case of thin materials.

Frequently blanket-stitch is used instead of buttonhole-stitch. In working it, hold the seam edge down (58; for the buttonhole-stitch the seam edge should be held up), and for every stitch, loop the thread round the needle.

The neatest-looking seams are those in which the seam edges have been folded back. Various stitches

52

53

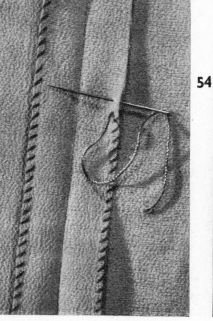

52. SEAM EDGES which are pressed down on one side should be turned in and slip-stitched together.

53. OVERCASTING is usually done from right to left, but may also be done from left to right. The stitches should be as even as possible. As a method of neatening seams, overcasting should only be used for non-fraying materials.

54. The same stitch is used to overcast a rolled seam edge, and is executed as in the case of the roll hem. This method is used to neaten thin silks, chiffon, and net.

54

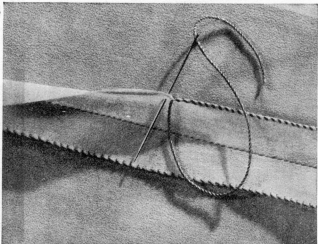

may be used to secure the folded edge. In the case of a hard material, cover the folded cut edge with a very closely worked herringbone-stitch; alternatively the seam edge may be hemmed down narrowly, or—for very quick work—it may be stitched on the machine. Another quick method is to secure the turning with small running-stitches, putting in a back-stitch every now and again for greater security.

A zigzag edging gives a very hard-wearing finish (61), but will be used only when the sewing-machine has the necessary attachment. Both the open edge, which will afterwards have to be trimmed, and the folded edge are suitable for finishing off with a zigzag edging.

55. In making buttonhole-stitch the thread can be looped round the needle, or the loop can be taken up from the back after the needle has been pulled out of the material.

56. SEAM EDGES that have been folded back narrowly can be secured by means of herringbone-stitch. This method is very suitable for hard materials having threads that unravel easily.

57. JERSEY MATERIALS must be dealt with in a special way: The edges of the seam, which must be sewn very loosely, will tend to roll. Herringbone-stitches are therefore used to secure them to the material. The stitches must not be taken through to the right side of the material.

55

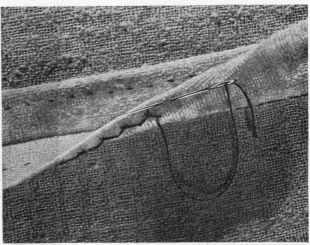

56

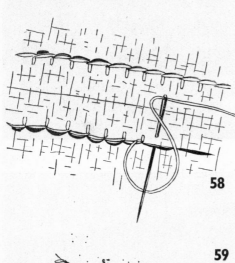

58

57

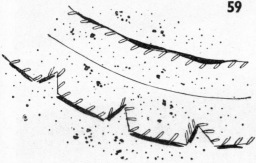

59

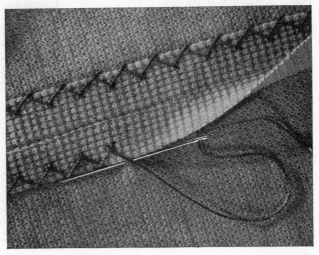

21

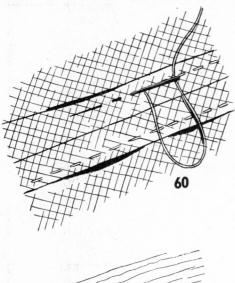

60

62

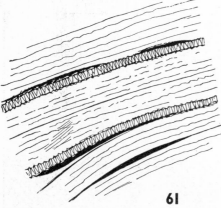

61

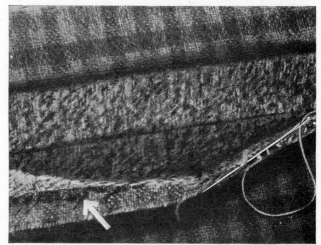

63

64

It is always possible to pink and overcast the edge, if the material is suitable, but hemming the seam turning by hand or by machine should only be done when the edge is left straight. Curved seam edges, particularly when they have been snipped, can only be neatened by overcasting, button-holing, or scallop-stitching (59).

When ironing, the turnings should be dealt with first of all, separately, and then the seam should be pressed by itself, so as to prevent the turnings from marking the right side of the material.

62. CLOTH-LIKE MATERIALS are finished off with pinking. The cuts should be made diagonally first in one direction, then in the other; this makes it easier to obtain a neat appearance. Alternatively, special pinking scissors may be used.

63. COATINGS with a woven lining are never made up with a silk lining. The seam edges must therefore be finished off particularly neatly. The lining is separated and hemmed on to the right side of the material.

64. STRAIGHT SEAM EDGES, where the material is not too thick and does not fray, can be hemmed narrowly on the machine. This is the simplest and quickest method of neatening.

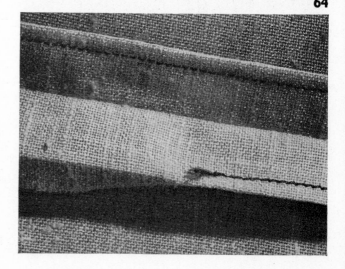

NEATENING THE SEAM. Binding the seam edges
is a method used chiefly in the case of sports wear and
woollen clothing (skirts, divided skirts, unlined jackets,
and coats). Seam-binding is applied only to straight
seams, but braid or bias-binding can also be used to
bind curved seams. If the seam edge is to retain a
certain amount of "give," the seam-binding may be
sewn on entirely by hand, as in the case of braiding.

Seam-binding and braid can be folded in half and
ironed so as to allow one selvedge to project a little.
The edge of the material is then slipped into the
fold and can be secured with a single row of stitching
(by hand or by machine). But it is safer, especially
when one has had little practice, to begin by stitching
or hemming one edge of the binding or braid to the
material, and then to secure the other edge on the left
side by a second row of stitching. This method should
also be used for bias-binding.

65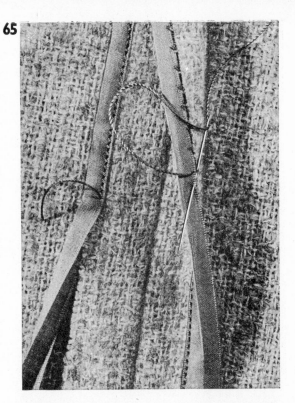

65. SEAM-BINDING, used to neaten a seam, may be applied in
several ways. On the wrong side the binding, folded in half, is secured
with one row of stitching, on the right side by a row of stitching
followed by hemming.

66. BRAID, too, can be used for binding seam edges. The stitches
are passed right through, taking up the slightly projecting lower edge
as well as the upper one.

67. Strips of lining cut on the bias will also produce an elastic binding.
They are stitched on to the seam edge on the right side, then folded
over to the inside and either felled on or tacked and stitched.

66 **67**

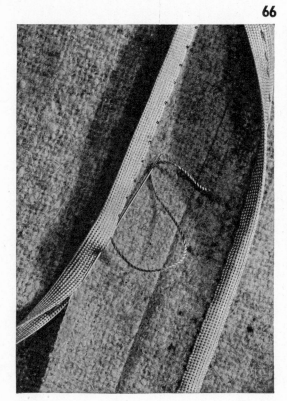 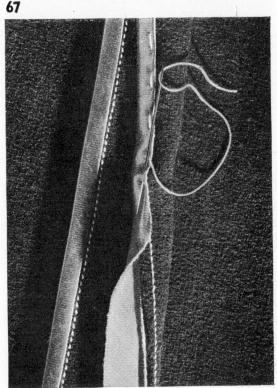

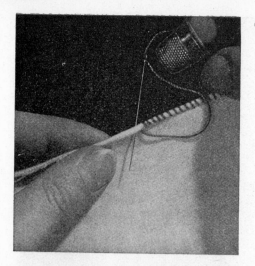

68

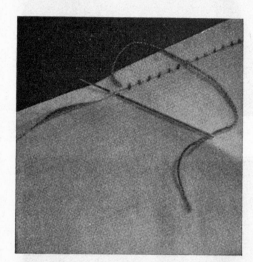

69

70

68. ROLL OR WHIPPED SEAM. With the left thumb, roll over the edge of the material very tightly, a small piece at a time, and whip on with overcasting-stitches. The stitches must not pass through the roll, but only through one thickness of the material.

69. FELL HEM. Turn in the edge of the material and secure with fell-stitches, each of which must take up one cross-thread only. The width of the hem may be as desired.

70. PLAIN HEM. This is used for all household linen. Turn in the edge of the material, press, turn in the cut edge, and hem down with tiny back-stitches.

Tucks and Pin-tucks

Tucks and pin-tucks are always sewn on a straight thread. It is not necessary to tack or mark the material, as an even width can be obtained by using the edge-stitching foot and the rule (71) or the tucker. These attachments are supplied with most sewing-machines. By screwing the rule quite close to the stitching-foot, a very fine pin-tuck is obtained, while tucks are produced by having the rule farther away. Thus, with any given adjustment the width of the tucks and pin-tucks will always remain even, but the distance between the individual tucks should be accurately measured with a tape or cardboard marker.

When sewing fine pin-tucks the greatest care must be taken that the material does not slip away under the stitching-foot, or a few stitches will be missed. If this does happen, the stitching will have to be unpicked for some little distance and begun afresh.

Pin-tucks which are to be sewn by hand may be marked out before beginning the work.

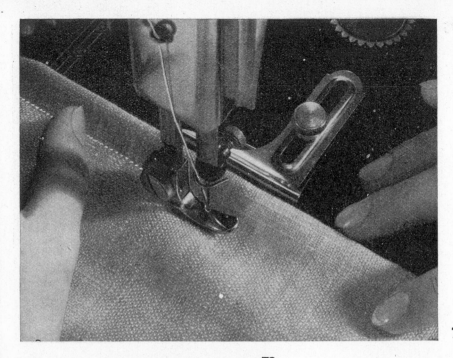

71

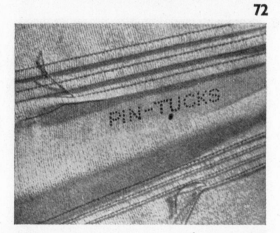

72

PIN-TUCKS

73

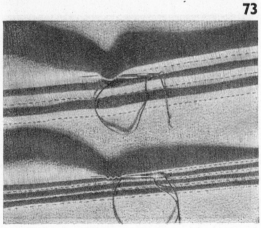

73

72. Pin-tucks may be $\frac{1}{32}$ in. to $\frac{1}{8}$ in. wide; anything above this width is called a tuck or fold.

73. In the case of thin materials the pin-tucks are sewn by hand, since the double thread of machine-stitching, in veiling or netting, for instance, would show up too much.

74. SHAPED PIN-TUCKS, curved or running zigzag, for instance, are difficult to produce. They should be marked out and tacked, and then, with the tacking in the fold, stitched. The width should be about the thickness of the needle.

74

76. If the hem has been well sewn, no stitches should be visible. The needle takes up only one cross-thread of the outside material and moves forward within the fold of the turn-in.

77. THE TURN-IN may be machine-stitched if the material is difficult to work. The slip-stitches should take up the edge of the hem above the line of stitching and must not be drawn tight.

78. THIS ORNAMENTAL HEM, which is suitable for thin materials, consists of a tuck about ⅛ in. wide, which is over-sewn at regular intervals with two back-stitches.

Hems (General)

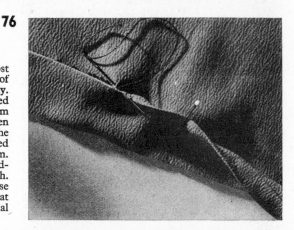

The hemming attachments which are supplied with most machines in various widths are very useful for the hemming of long edges, since they help to do the work evenly and quickly. The end of the work is turned in for about 1 in. to the required width of the hem, and passed into the spiral spring of the hem foot as far as the needle. While sewing, care must be taken that the material does not escape, but runs evenly into the spiral spring, as shown in 75. If the hem is to be slip-stitched the work may be done from right to left or from top to bottom. The hem should first be pinned, tucked, or pressed, a cardboard marker being used to make certain of an even width. Pin the edge of the hem and begin to sew, using fairly loose slip-stitches. The material must not be pulled, in order that neither the stitches themselves nor the threads of material they have taken up may be visible on the right side.

78 **77**

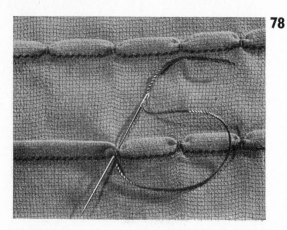

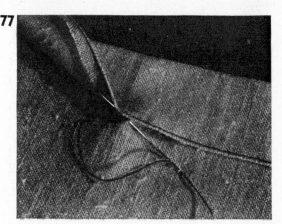

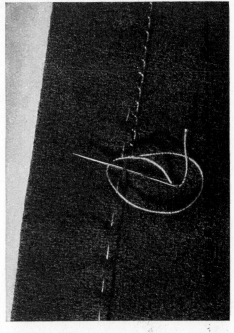

Hems

Hems are a part of almost every piece of needlework, and there are innumerable ways of making them. From the simplest slip-stitched hem, which is the one most frequently used and should be worked particularly neatly, to the most delicate rolled hem, all have their use, for different materials require different methods of treatment. The simple hem, about 2 in. wide, may be described as a dress hem which is suitable for materials of medium thickness. Thanks to its turn-in it can be used to lengthen skirts, unlike the other kinds of hem shown here. That is why the hem should always be left to the last, when the length of the garment has been finally determined.

Fell-stitches come undone easily or wear out after lengthy use; thus, in the case of garments which are worn a great deal (skirts, for instance), it is better to employ the more lasting chain-stitch,

80

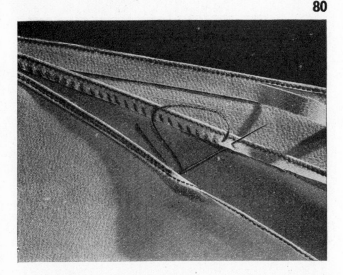

blanket-stitch, or buttonhole-stitch. The two latter stitches, however, should not be used for thin materials, as the tiny knots might show through on the right side.

Rolled hems, or hems bound with bias-binding, should be used for all thin or medium-thick materials. The binding may be narrower, but should not be wider than $\frac{1}{8}$ in. The bias-binding must not be tacked on so loosely that it forms folds, nor so tightly as to pucker the edge of the material. If the strip has been

81

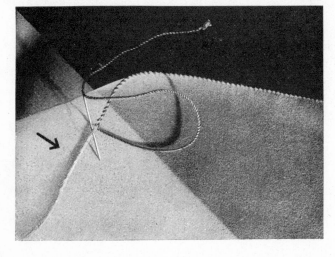

79. HEM EDGES are worked with blanket- or button-hole-stitch. This stitch is particularly hard-wearing, as the little knots prevent it from coming undone. Selvedges, too, are secured with buttonhole-stitch.

80. FOR THIN MATERIALS, where it is important that the hem edges should remain flat, work a row of stitching close along the edge. This can be neatened by a second row of stitching, trimming, or overcasting.

81. THE ROLLED HEM is used to edge dainty materials. Roll the edge between left thumb and index finger and overcast. To strengthen the hem, it may be rolled round a length of sewing thread.

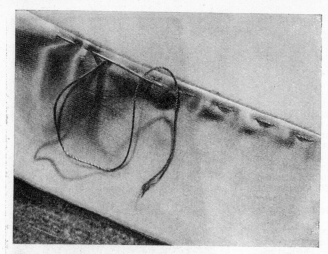

82

83

cut evenly in width all along, the bound hem too will be even. When turning and felling the strip, take up the stitches of the first row of stitching; in this way you will avoid stitching through the material accidentally, so that the stitch becomes visible on the right side.

The other hem finishes present no special difficulties in working.

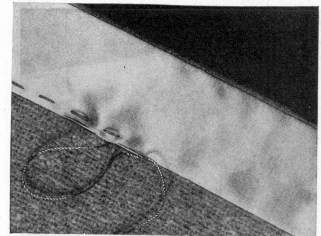

84

82. A FALSE HEM is useful if you are short of material. A strip of lining about 2 in. wide and matching in colour is sewn on to the material, right side to right side. It is then turned and tacked down on the wrong side so that the edge of material projects a little beyond the folded edge of the lining.

83. THE UPPER EDGE of the facing is turned in, tacked down, and slip-stitched. The finished seam is pressed both before and after the tacks are removed.

84. A ZIGZAG SEAM, or a machine hem-stitched edging which is then cut through, can also be used to secure the edges of thin materials, giving a picot-edge finish. Most modern sewing-machines are supplied with a zigzag attachment.

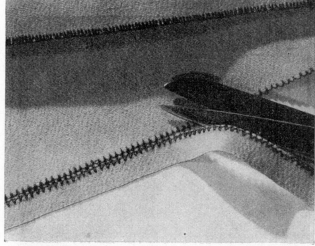

85

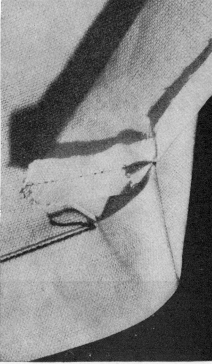

87

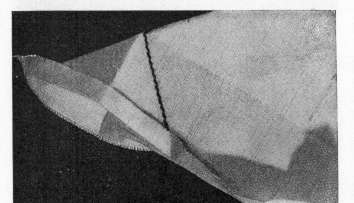

86

Hem Corners

85. HEM CORNERS. When sewing hems, great care must be taken to make clean, sharp corners. Begin by folding the hem turnings all round, then open out and fold the corner over in a right angle so that a diagonal fold line is formed.

86. For hand-sewn corners the triangle outside the diagonal fold line must be cut off. Machine-stitching will give a neater result: the material should be folded in half and the stitching carried out along the diagonal fold line from the point to the edge of the turning (this must be not stitched).

87. Trim the corner seam and smooth it out. It is then turned over. Fold in the hem line again and stitch the hem down close to the edge. If the corner does not lie flat, this is because the stitching has not been carried out exactly in the diagonal fold.

88. This is how the finished corner should look. If a false hem is to be added, then the facing must be joined on all round, breaking the thread and starting afresh in each corner: the corner seam can then be sewn in the same way.

88

Hem Facings

89

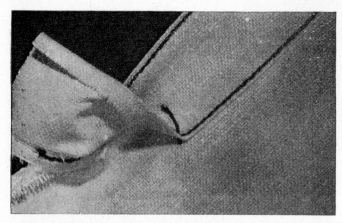

90

91

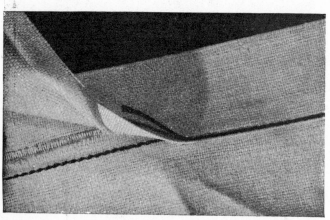

89. FACED HEM. A band of any width desired, of the same or a contrasting colour, may be stitched on to the wrong side of the material and turned over to the right side with the seam exactly in the fold; the facing serves as a false hem or for decorative purposes. The inner edge of the facing is stitched down.

90. An additional row of stitches can be worked along the outer edge, which will then be kept in the fold when the article is being laundered.

91. EXTENSION FOLD. This should be cut in double width and one side stitched on so that the cut edges lie on the right side. Smooth out the seam with the edges pointing towards the facing, fold the facing, and stitch down close to the seam.

93. BIAS-STRIPS are strips of material, the cut edge of which lies at a right angle to the line of the thread. The seams which join the single strips run diagonally—always in the same direction; the whole strip is therefore absolutely straight. The illustration shows the method of cutting.

92

93

Bias-binding

Bias-strips are narrow strips of material which have been cut on the cross, i.e. diagonally across the material. They may be used for many purposes. They are applied as a binding or facing to all edges which do not run in the same direction as the threads of the cloth, curved edges, for instance, since they are elastic and therefore adapt themselves to any shape. This is how the strips are cut : the corner of a rectangular piece of material is folded over diagonally so that the cut edge is parallel with the selvedge. The resulting fold gives the line for cutting. Take a piece of cardboard and cut into it several notches to indicate the width of the strips which are to be cut. With this gauge chalk out the remaining lines parallel to the first bias line. The corner which has been turned over can be cut off, and is shown in the illustration (92) simply for the sake of clarity. When sufficient strips have been marked out—the necessary length can be calculated beforehand by measuring the edges which are to be bound—cut them off and join them together. The length of material available will determine the length of the strips which can be cut. The joins are diagonal, and will therefore be almost invisible since the stitching will follow the line of the weave, and the strips, assuming they have all been cut in the same direction, will match in pattern, gloss, and run of thread.

Before stitching them together, the strips can be pinned with their right sides facing. It will save both time and material if all the joins are stitched with one thread, which is then cut when the last seam is done (94). 95 shows the finished strip, pressed and neatly trimmed.

Bias-piping

Piping made of a matching or contrasting material can be sewn on to seams and hems to neaten and strengthen them. To make the piping, cut bias-strips of the required length and about 1 in. wide, fold in half and press. When pressing, stretch the strips a little. The piping is then tacked between two seam edges so that it projects about ⅛ in.; be careful not to stretch the piping too much, or it will pucker the seam. If the seam is to be sewn on the wrong side, the seam edge lying on the piping should first be tacked down with slip-stitches. By this method, however, it is somewhat difficult to obtain a piping that is even in width. A simpler method is to tack on the seam edge and stitch it down on the right side close to the fold.

Corded piping is a little more troublesome to work. The cord can be obtained in various thicknesses; it is very soft and will adapt itself to any shape. The bias-strip should be creased in half lengthways, and the cord placed in the fold and sewn in with running-stitch. The piping is then tacked on to the material and, as in the case of the two methods described above, either stitched on to the wrong side, or close to the edge on the right side. If the piping cord is very thick, the adjustable corder, which is supplied with most machines, should be used. This attachment is in two parts and has, in addition to a fixed presser-foot on the left of the needle, a " bow " which can be adjusted to suit the various thicknesses of cord.

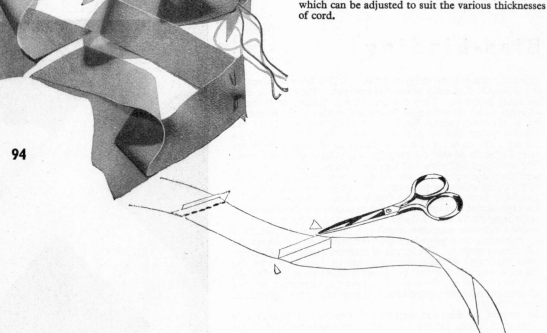

94

95

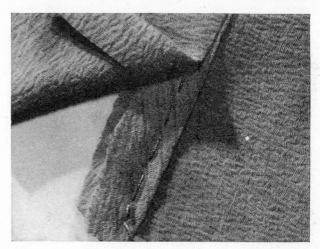

96

96. SIMPLE BIAS-PIPING consists of a bias-strip creased in half lengthways and sewn between two seam edges.

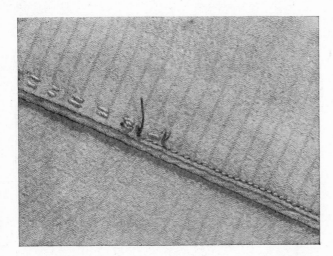

97

97. The upper seam edge should be hemmed down close to the edge after having been tacked on to the piping. The piping should project evenly.

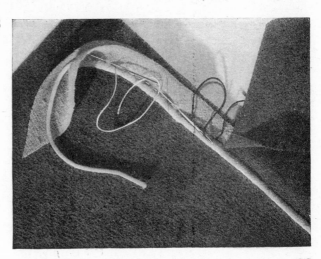

98

98. CORDED PIPING may also be set between two seam edges, or it can be applied as an edging; in this case it is stitched on to the wrong side, turned over, and felled.

B

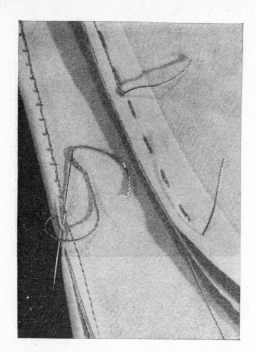

Neatening the Neckline

99. SHAPED FACING. The outline of the neckline is marked out on the facing material. The facing is then cut out in an even width, stitched on to the left side, and hemmed over on the right side.

100. TO ROLL OR BIND with bias-strip, fold the strip double lengthways, tack or stitch it on, then hem the folded edge over on the wrong side. This makes the work easier and enables you to obtain a binding that is perfectly even.

101. In the case of thicker materials the bias-binding should be used in single thickness only, as the seam edge would otherwise be too bulky. Turn in the edge which is to be felled, taking care that the turning is even and smooth.

102. BIAS-FACING. To neaten a neckline, strips ¾ in. to 1½ in. wide, cut on the bias, may be used. If the opening comes to a V-point, the ends of the strip should meet in the centre of the front.

103. The bias-facing is stitched on to the wrong side of the material. It is then folded over with the seam in the fold, the material being cut at the front point as far as the seam. Finally the edge of the facing is stitched down close to the edge of the material. The facing should lie quite flat and must not wrinkle or pucker.

99

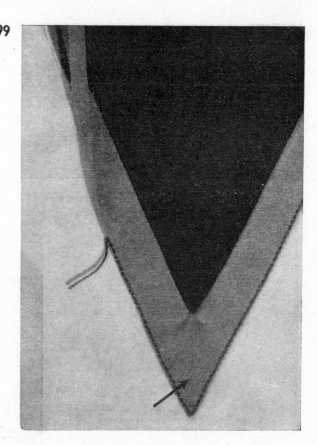

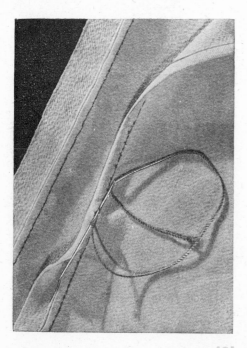

101

102

104. BIAS-BINDING. This is the name given to bias-strips which have been felled over the edge of the material and may be used to finish off neck openings. The bias-strip is stitched on to the right side, folded over, and felled to the row of stitching on the wrong side. The width of the binding must not exceed $\frac{1}{4}$ in.

105. Instead of being felled on the inside, the bias-binding may also be stitched down by machine. The stitching will have to be done on the right side, as the seam must run close beside the first row of stitching. At the front point the binding may be either folded over or mitred.

104

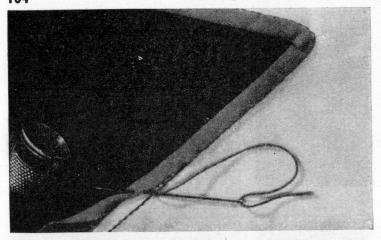

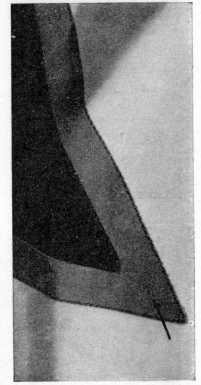

103

105

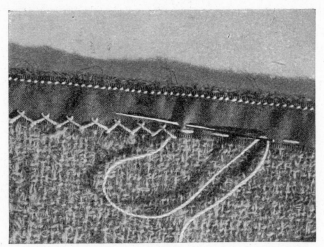

Hems

Seam-binding or binding-braid is used in various ways to neaten hems. Instead of turning the edge of the material, the binding or braid may be faced on to it. But if the material is a particularly thick woollen and it is not desired to do without the cut-hem turning, binding or braid may be stitched on to the edge of the material and then fastened down. In this way you avoid the bulky hem which would result if the material had to be turned in again. Whether herringbone- or buttonhole-stitch is used will make no difference to the wearing qualities of the hem. This method of neatening, as well as that in which lining bias-strips are used as a facing, may also be recommended for materials which fray easily; the springy threads of material which would un-ravel so easily if the hem were an ordinary

107

106. SEAM-BINDING used as a facing will produce a softly falling hem in the case of thick materials. The seam-binding is stitched close to the edge on the right side of the material and secured to the inside with herringbone-stitch.

107. BRAID, too, may be used for neatening hems. It is particularly useful for hems which are not straight, since it is elastic and will adapt itself to curves. It is stitched on the right side and blanket-stitched on the inside.

108. FOR CLOTH AND VELOURS which do not fray, the open edge of the hem-turning is notched to give a pinked edging. The hem is secured by slip-stitching below the points, these remaining loose.

109. If the hem is to be covered by a lining which will be felled on, it need only be catch-stitched to prevent it moving out of place under the lining.

109

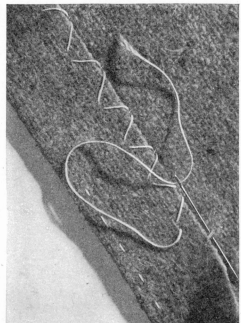

108

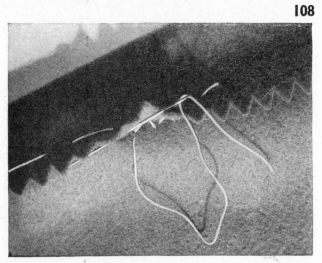

turned hem will be fully secured if a
seam- or bias-binding is applied.

110

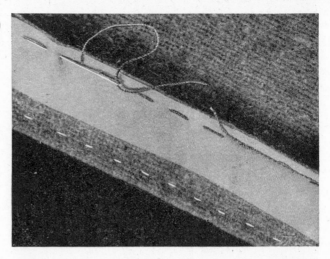

The pinked, slip-stitched hem is also intended
for thick materials, but only for such as do not
fray. Coats with a loose lining (the lower edge
of the lining should also be neatened) may, in
the case of a cloth-like material, be neatened with
a pinked hem. The cutting of the points may
be done with a special pair of pinking scissors or
simply by snipping.

Open seam edges may be stitched on either with
zigzag-stitch, or with herringbone-stitching. If
the herringbone-stitching is worked closely, a
matching thread being used, it may be treated
as a regular hem neatening even if no lining
is to be hemmed over.

Practice will teach the correct hem for any particular material.

110. THE FACINGS and hem edges of unlined coats and
jackets are bound with bias-strips. Satin and satin Duchesse
are suitable materials for this purpose. The bias-strip should
be stretched slightly while tacking it on.

111. When the bias-binding has been stitched on, it is
folded over and stitched with large back-stitches which should
be placed in the line of the first row of stitching. This second
seam is often sewn by machine to save time.

112. THE BOUND EDGE is slip-stitched on to the
material. The stitches must be placed back a little so that
the edge of the binding appears loose and is not pulled out
of shape by the seam.

113. A "CONCERTINA HEM" is made by binding
with an extra-wide bias-strip which is pressed to a pleat and
then felled on so that the binding covers the hem edge.

111

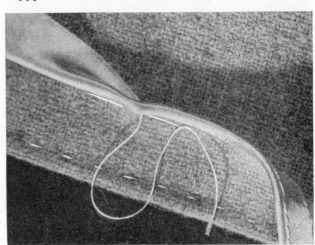

113

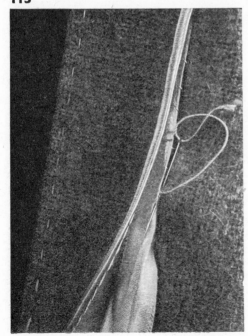

112

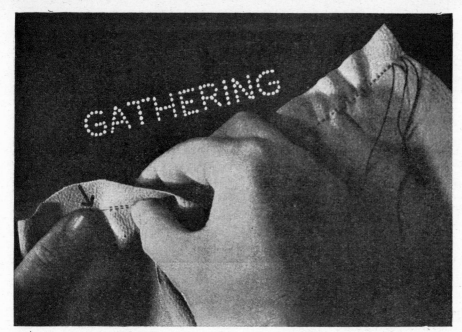

114

Gathering

It is a common belief that gathering is a simple process, which merely involves the taking up of a few running-stitches, drawing out the needle, and starting afresh. That, however, is not expert gathering : to do it properly, you should keep the needle in the material from the beginning to the end of a row of gathers, without drawing it out in between the stitches. The gathering thread must be long enough for the length of material to be gathered. The running needle should be as short as possible. Begin with a knot and a fastening back-stitch, and run the needle into the material, holding the edge between thumb and index finger of each hand. The work should be done from right to left, the right end of the material being pinned firmly to the table or to the lap so that it can be kept taut. Hold the needle with the thumb and index finger of the right hand and push it forward with the middle finger, while the left hand moves the material up and down in front of the point, which will take up a few threads every time the material passes before it. The stitches should not be more than $\frac{1}{16}$ in. long. The gathering thread will follow by itself. If the row is a very long one, the needle may be taken out once at about the middle and the thread drawn through so that it remains hanging as a loop at this point (115). In order that the fullness of the material may be distributed as evenly as possible, two rows of gathers should be made about $\frac{1}{6}$ in. to $\frac{1}{8}$ in. apart at least. The ends of the gathering threads should be secured temporarily by winding them round a pin stuck into the material. They should not be fastened until the width has been finally determined.

115. **A TURNED-IN EDGE** of material which is gathered some distance away from the edge forms a ruching, also called a heading. With this heading the gathered piece is lapped on.

118. **GATHERING.** To make the running-stitches, push the needle through the material with the thimble while the left hand moves the material up and down and so feeds it in folds on to the needle. There is no need to draw the thread through: it will follow as the needle passes through the gathers.

119. In order to obtain perfectly **REGULAR GATHERS**, push the folds together, and secure the left-hand end of the thread with a pin and the right-hand end of the material with a clamp. A needle can then be used to draw each little fold under the left thumb and press it there firmly.

120. This is how the **FINISHED GATHERS** look; they are now ready to be joined neatly and evenly to a piece of plain material. Gathering by machine is much simpler work; but see that the tension is slackened so that the stitches are bigger.

115

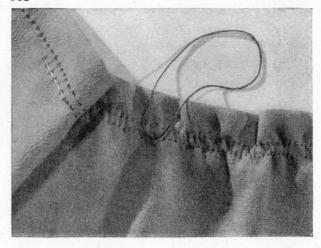

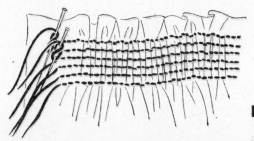

116

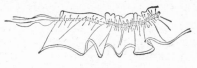

117

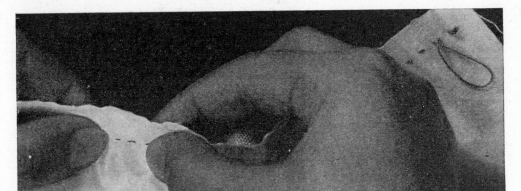

118

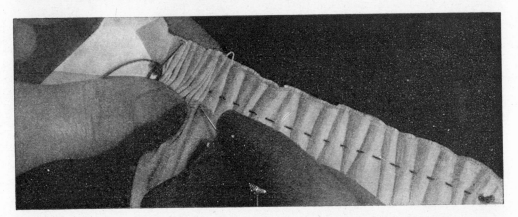

119

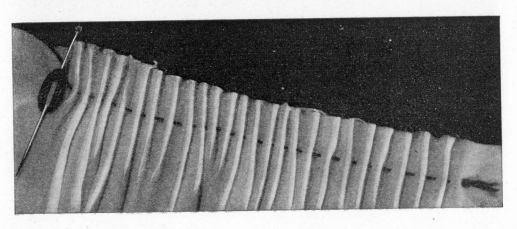

120

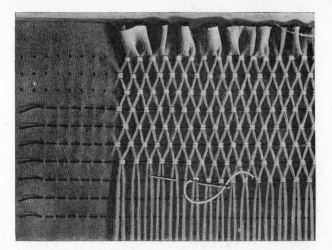

Smocking

The necessary rows of gathers for smocking must be evenly spaced and carried out with very neat and even stitches. The design should first be marked off, and this is best done with a smocking transfer, which may be ironed off on the right side in the case of a design in which every stitch will conceal every dot (e.g. a honeycomb pattern), otherwise on the wrong side. Then begin to gather, using a thread which is not too thin. The needle enters at one point and comes out between two points. Pull the gather threads from the right so as to form raised folds, but do not tighten too much, in order that the folds may be adjusted as required. The threads are knotted together or wound round a pin in pairs. The little folds are secured on the right side by means of embroidery stitches carried out in mercerised twist, mercerised embroidery thread, or washing silk. Work evenly, taking up only the upper edge of the folds, and do not pull the thread too tight, so that the work remains elastic. When all the embroidery rows have been worked, draw out the gathering threads.

The honeycomb pattern, unlike most others, is worked from right to left. For the reversed over-stitch pattern (123) work from left to right. Take up two folds, bring the needle out on the second fold a little below the point where it entered the material. The next stitch will take up the third fold at the same level, coming out a little higher up.

The zigzag pattern (124) is also formed out of over-stitches.

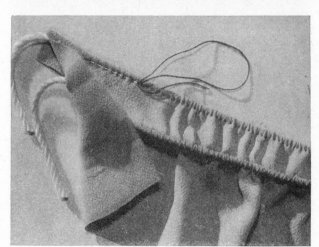

122

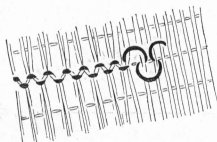

123

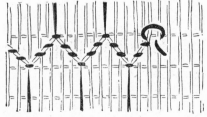

124

121. THE WAFFLE or honeycomb pattern is the simplest form of smocking. Gathering-stitches, worked from right to left on a design made up of dots form the basis.

122. Particularly thin materials are gathered over cord. Several rows, about ¼ in. to 1½ in. apart, make up a pretty trimming. A thin piping cord is used for filling.

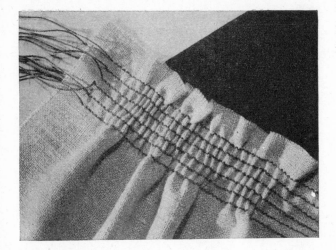

125

Curved Hems

Sometimes it is necesary to provide curved skirt edges with a hem turning, though usually they will be finished off by binding with bias-strips. In such a case there will be a super-fluous fullness at the edge of the turning which may be reduced by pressing, if the curve is slight, or otherwise by putting in tiny pleats. The pressing should be done carefully, from the edge inwards, and a damp cloth should be used. The hot steam causes the cloth to shrink, and it will then draw together smoothly and without folds. In the case of a flared skirt small pleats regularly spaced and equal in depth will have to be made. These should be pressed, and the turning tacked and hemmed, a slip-stitch being used.

125. GATHERING BY MACHINE gives a harder-wearing result than if the work is sewn by hand. The machine must be adjusted to give a longer stitch and the upper tension must be slackened. The gathers are formed by pulling the lower thread.

126. For curved hem edges, such as those on flared skirts, etc. the hem turning must remain even throughout.

127. SMALL PLEATS are made to take up the superfluous fullness. These should be pressed flat and stitched on while felling.

126

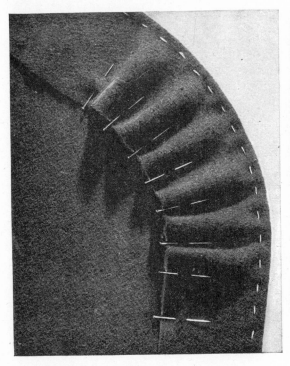

127

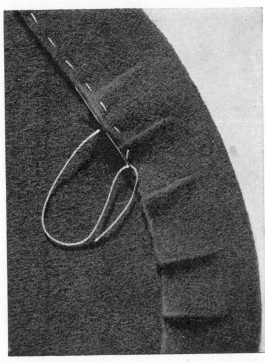

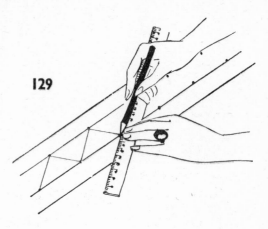

128. The saw-tooth lines should be marked out on the wrong side of the material with the help of a cardboard marker or ruler; the facing is then tacked on underneath, right side to right side.

Saw-tooth Edging

For the making of evenly spaced points, a pattern should be prepared. Take a strip of cardboard, half as wide again as the height of the points required, and on it draw two parallel lines, the distance between the lines being equal to the height of the points. On the upper line mark off the points to the required spacing. The lower line is similarly marked, the points here, however, falling exactly half-way between the points on the upper line. Join up the dots by diagonal lines from top to bottom and cut out along these to form the pattern (129).

The marking is done with tailor's chalk on the wrong side of the material. A strip of facing or doubling material is placed on, right side to right side, and tacked so as to project beyond the points. A row of tacking should also be worked along the line of the points. For thin weaves the same material can be used for facing ; in the case of thicker materials apply a lining to match.

If the double thickness of material is too bulky, it will be necessary to place a stitch across each point, outer and inner. Only in this way is it possible to shape the points neatly (130). The seam edges are trimmed off across at the outer points, and slashed at the inner points (131). When turning the facing, the outer points should be drawn out with a needle and the edges tacked through. Press well. The edge of the facing remains loose and is hemmed or stitched separately.

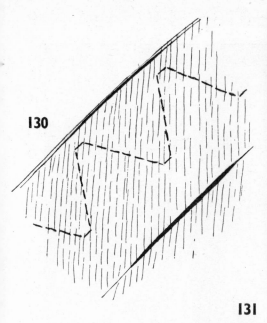

130

131

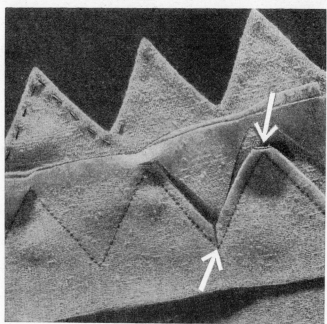

132

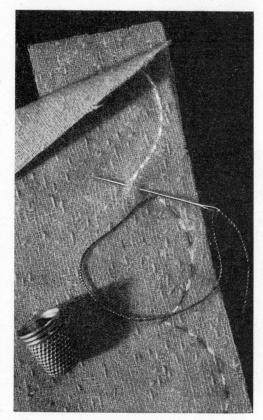

131. When the stitching has been done, the points are cut. The illustration also shows a turned saw-tooth edging. The slashes and points must be worked very carefully.

132. **SCALLOPS** are marked out with the help of a cardboard pattern and the facing is then tacked on with small stitches.

Scallop Edging

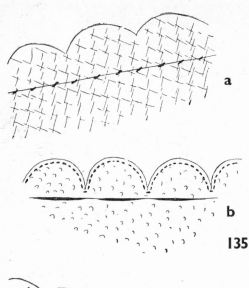

a

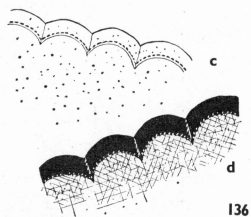

b

135

133

c

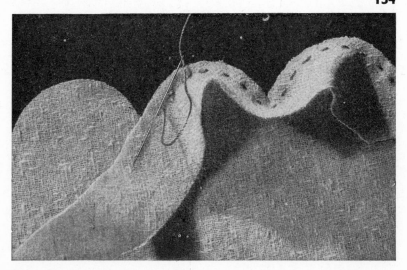

d

136

134

133. Having stitched on the facing, cut the seam edges close along the stitching. A snip into the points will make it easier to do the turning.

44

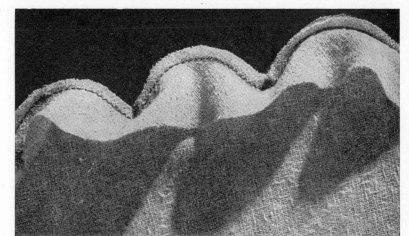

137. THE BIAS-BINDING Is stitched on, right sides facing, and is then turned over to the wrong side. For this purpose the edges at the scallop points will have to be slashed.

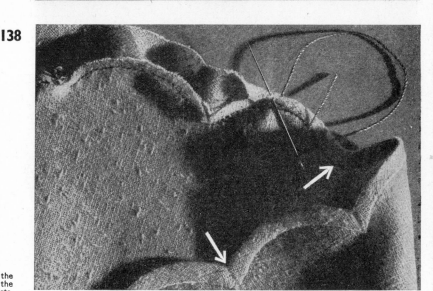

138. THE BIAS-STRIP is hemmed to the seam and is then pressed and fitted into the points by hemming it over into dart pleats.

Scallop Edging

As in the case of saw-tooth edging, a cardboard pattern of the scallops should be prepared. The semi-circles or arcs can be drawn with the help of coins, cups, or reels. Draw a few scallops and cut out. For the facing of the scallop edges (colour, thickness, etc.), the same remarks apply as in the case of saw-tooth edging. When the facing has been turned, the scallops should be well smoothed out, tacked, and pressed, and, after the tacking threads have been removed, pressed again to remove the marks left by the threads (see 133). The inner edge of the facing may be turned in and slip-stitched on to the material; this is particularly necessary where the scallops are very shallow (135 a). If the scallops are fairly deep, the facing may be cut away close behind the points of the scallops, then turned in and hemmed separately, so that the edges remain loose (135 b). In this way no stitches will be visible on the right side; the scallop edges can be stitched through. If the stitching cannot be brought to a point, join the ends of the scallops with a cross-stitch.

The edges of the scallops may also be finished off by rolling, i.e. binding with bias-strips. Bias-binding of the same or a contrasting material is tacked on with small stitches; this may be done either before or after the scallops have been cut out. The binding should be eased only a very little at the points, as the fullness will otherwise be troublesome when the strip is being rolled. The points should be stitched very neatly and accurately.

When the bias-binding has been stitched on, right side to right side, it is hemmed on the wrong side with small stitches worked along the first line of stitching. When doing this it will be impossible to avoid rounding the points
(cont. on p. 47)

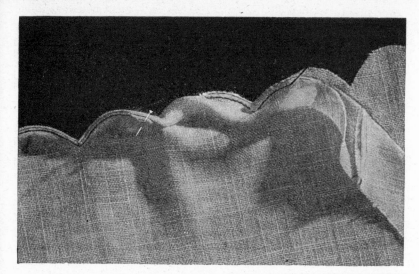

139

140

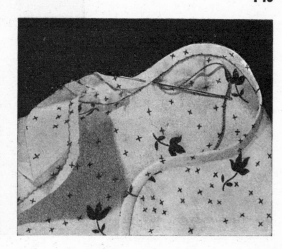

141

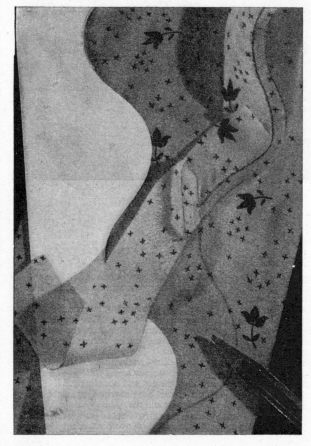

140. SHALLOW CURVES are best neatened with bias-binding which will shape itself smoothly to the curves. The illustration shows how the strip, which has been sewn on, is turned and felled.

141. The shape of the scallop is sketched with pencil or chalk and cardboard cut to shape. The bias-binding, which may first be tacked into place, is then stitched on before the scallops are cut out.

142. To obtain an evenly rolled hem more easily, the bias-binding is hemmed on folded double. The fold lies outside the edge of the material and it is then a simple task to turn and fell it.

143. DEEPER SCALLOPS with sharp points are neatened with facing material. When hemming, put a stitch across the point of each scallop : this will make it easier to turn the facing.

144. When the scallops have been turned and well smoothed out, turn in the inner edge of the facing and hem it down. For delicate lingerie it may be felled by hand.

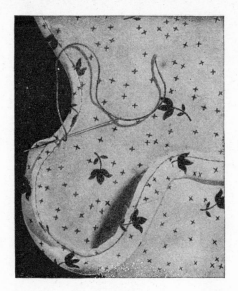

142

143

144

of the scallops. They can be made sharp subsequently by
creasing each point. 138 shows two finished points and one
which has not yet been creased.
The binding with bias-strip may also be done by another
method. Instead of hemming the strip over as a visible
edging, it is turned in as a facing. For this purpose it must not
be stitched on evenly, but must be creased into a little pleat at
the points of the scallops. These pleats must remain open to
begin with, and therefore the seam-fastening on the bias-strip
must be begun afresh for each scallop; this is a somewhat
tedious piece of work which must be executed very carefully.
The binding is turned over with the seam in the fold, the little
pleats are hemmed in (see 136 c), and the strip is then hemmed
down. In the same way a binding which has been stitched
on to the wrong side may be turned over to the right side and
stitched down as a trimming (136 d). In this case the pleats
are better done by machine.
For piped scallops a bias-strip folded double must be stitched
on to the right side of the material with the open edges outwards (see 137). The strip is turned to form a narrow piped
edge. The scallops are stitched through close along the first
seam, the bias-strip being secured at the same time. The
folded edge of the binding remains loose.
Braid may also be used for the binding, facing, or piping of
scallops.

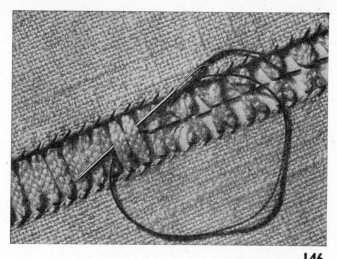

146

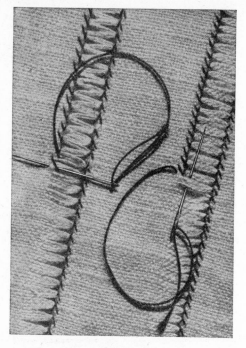

145

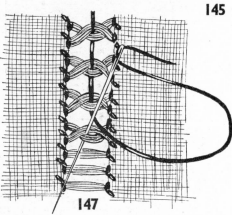

147

148

145. The upper row of hem-stitching shows even bundling, the lower row alternate bundling, this latter producing a zigzag pattern. In thicker weaves the number of threads which go to each bar should be counted.

146. **AN X-PATTERN** is obtained by taking up the bars in pairs exactly in the centre and winding them round tightly with a back-stitch.

148. **A HEM TURNING** may be neatened by hem-stitching. The stitches take up the double thickness of the material and the bars. It is not absolutely essential to carry out the inner row of hem-stitching.

Hem-stitching or Drawn-thread Work

Hem-stitching can only be worked along a straight thread, and the curved edges of a section cannot therefore be finished off by hand hem-stitch. Machine hem-stitching can be worked in any direction of the weave, as it is not necessary to draw out the threads.

The width of the hem-stitching in a hand-worked drawn-thread hem is usually from ⅛ in. to ¼ in. It may be narrower in a fine material, or even wider in a coarse stuff. Once the first thread is removed, the others can be drawn out easily ; if the row is a long one the threads should be removed piecemeal. Drawn-thread work is impracticable in materials where the warp and the weft threads are not of the same thickness, and particularly in all fancy weaves.

The long threads (warp) and the cross-threads (weft) must be of the same thickness so that the bundles of threads both down and across are equal in thickness.

The illustrations show linen drawn-thread work for the working of which pearl thread or other embroidery thread is suitable. Incidentally, unless special effects are desired, the thread or sewing silk used should always match the material. By gathering two or more bundles of threads together it is possible to obtain a great variety of patterns. Fig. 147, for instance, shows bars twisted together in pairs by passing a thread through. More complicated work is not often used on lingerie, but offers many possibilities as dress trimming.

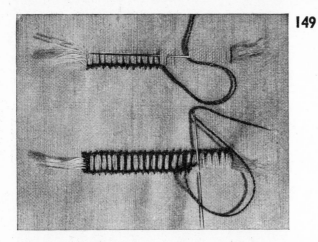 **149** **150** 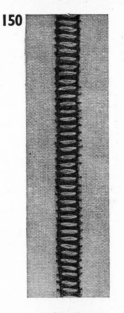 **152**

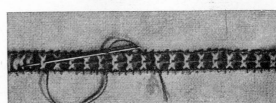

151 **153**

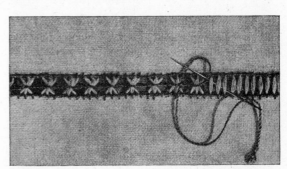

154

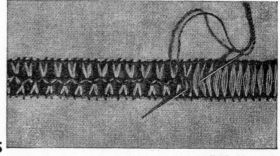

155

149. SIMPLE HEM-STITCH. The hem edges are secured by working a single line of hem-stitching. The ends of the 8–12 drawn threads are turned in when corners are being formed and fastened with blanket-stitch. The work is carried out on the wrong side.

150. DOUBLE HEM-STITCH. The little bundles of 4–5 threads should form an even row. The hem-stitch shown in 149 is much more durable than the simplified one so often used.

151. THE CORNERS in hem-stitching are neatened and made secure by so-called spiders. A thread is stretched from the inner to the outer corner. This is overcast, working back to the middle. The second and third " spider feet " are then worked, the centre is secured with a few satin-stitches, and finally the last " spider foot " is overcast.

152. SIMPLE DIAGONAL HEM-STITCH. The little bundles of threads formed in the first row of stitching are divided in the second row.

153. HEM-STITCHING WITH TWISTED BARS. The bars of a finished hem-stitched seam are crossed or twisted in pairs by means of a centre thread which is passed straight through without any knotting.

154. HEM-STITCHING WITH BARS BUNDLED INTO GROUPS. For this, too, the hem-stitching is carried out on the wrong side of the material. The bars, five at a time, are bound together by a chain-stitch on the right side.

155. ZIGZAG PATTERN. The hem-stitching must be worked with the bars fairly wide apart. The bars are then chain-stitched together in pairs, each bar of a pair being in addition caught up with the next pair.

156

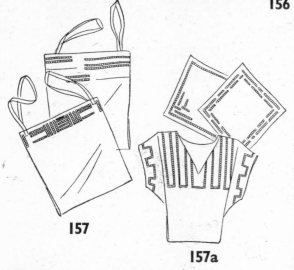

157

157a

158

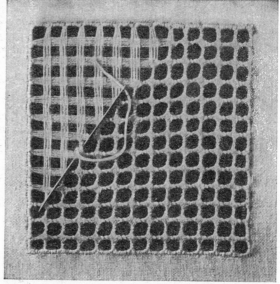

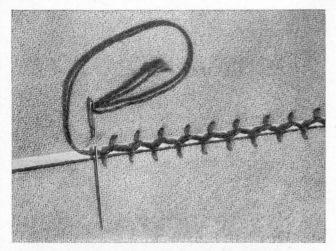

156. TRELLIS OR LATTICE OPEN-WORK. The same number of threads down and across are drawn out as are left in. The edges of the pattern are secured by close satin-stitch. The threads are oversewn in steps, two stitches to each step.

158. This stitch, evenly spaced, may be used to join two folded edges, selvedges, or edges neatened by turning in and tacking. The stitch must pass through a double thickness of material.

159. This hard-wearing stitch is also frequently used to join on single piping of any width, tubular piping, braid, or ribbon. A paper pattern should be tacked on to the material before the stitching is begun.

Faggoting and Bar-faggoting

In addition to drawn-thread hem-stitching there is also bar-faggoting, which consists of various kinds of twisted bars, or of a joining stitch which closely resembles the herringbone-stitch. With this kind of stitch all kinds of materials and shapes can be ornamented, and it is as pretty when used to join diagonal or curved seams as when applied to a straight edge.

For all the methods shown here the parts which are to be joined together must have a folded edge, or their edges must be turned in, hemmed, or stitched down to neaten them. The faggoting-stitches will wear well only if passed through a double thickness of material.

To facilitate the work a strip of paper on which guide lines have been pencilled to ensure even spacing is tacked on to the parts which are to be joined. Now, following the directions, work either the simple bars shown in 160, or else the twisted bars; for the latter several threads are

159

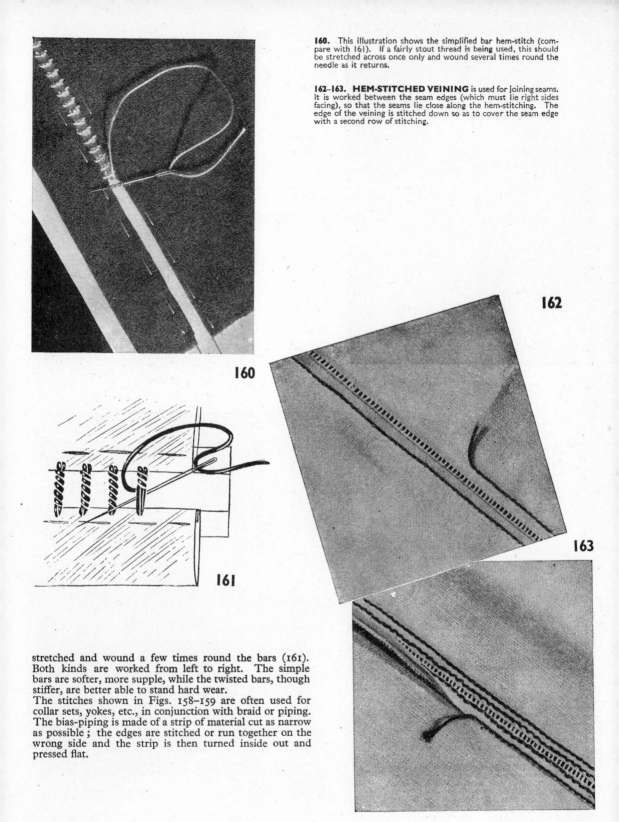

160. This illustration shows the simplified bar hem-stitch (compare with 161). If a fairly stout thread is being used, this should be stretched across once only and wound several times round the needle as it returns.

162–163. HEM-STITCHED VEINING is used for joining seams. It is worked between the seam edges (which must lie right sides facing), so that the seams lie close along the hem-stitching. The edge of the veining is stitched down so as to cover the seam edge with a second row of stitching.

160

162

161

163

stretched and wound a few times round the bars (161). Both kinds are worked from left to right. The simple bars are softer, more supple, while the twisted bars, though stiffer, are better able to stand hard wear.

The stitches shown in Figs. 158–159 are often used for collar sets, yokes, etc., in conjunction with braid or piping. The bias-piping is made of a strip of material cut as narrow as possible; the edges are stitched or run together on the wrong side and the strip is then turned inside out and pressed flat.

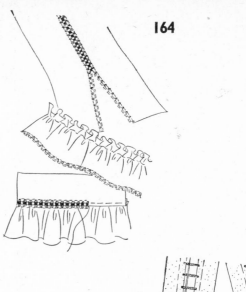

164

165

166

167

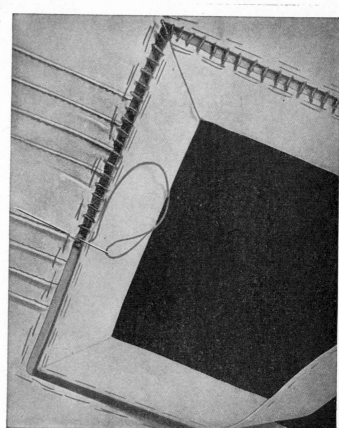

165. NECKLINE BORDER, joined on by bar-faggoting. For a square neckline a straight border is sewn to shape. Allowance must be made for an open space about $\frac{1}{8}$ in. to $\frac{1}{6}$ in. wide between the border and the edge of the garment. The mitred corner seams are trimmed narrow and smoothed out, and the edges turned in and tacked together.

166. A strip of paper on which guide lines have been traced is tacked on to the border and edge of the garment. When inserting the needle take up the double edge of the border and the turned-in edge of the garment. In going from one stitch to the next, the needle should pass along inside the folded edge of the material. The double or treble stitch must be wound round closely.

MACHINE HEM-STITCHING is used to join two pieces of material or can serve as a neatening if it is cut through (167). If machine hem-stitching is used to neaten the edge of frills, the material is cut to twice the width of the frills. The hem-stitching is then machined along the centre and when cut produces two frills.

52

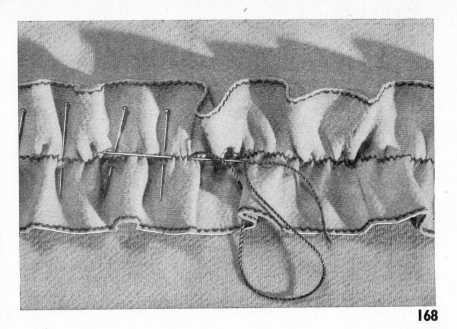

168

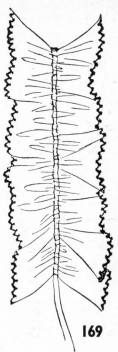

169

170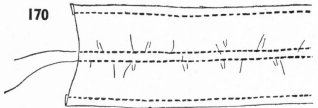

171

Ruches and Ruffles

Ruches may be set on or used as an edging. The easiest to make are ruches of ribbon, as their edges need not be neatened. If some other material is to be employed, cut it into straight strips (bias-strips may also be used), taking care not to cut them so wide that the ruche, when made, has a tendency to droop. The edges can be neatened by hemming, machine hemming, zigzag edging, or picot edging (see 169). The gathering may be done by hand, in the case of delicate materials, or by machine, in which case the thread tension should be slackened (see 170). Two rows of gathering will make it easier to mount the ruche, which may be sewn on by hand or by machine, according to the material. If the sewing is done by hand, a running-stitch and a back-stitch should be employed alternately.

Ruches and frills require about double their finished length of material, less if cut on the bias. The ruche shown in 171 is made of a straight strip, the lower edge being machine hemmed and the upper edge gathered with a narrow heading. The heading is machined or hand-sewn on to the material, the edge of which will have to be neatened separately.

Gathered frills may also be stitched on reversed, pressed over, and the seam edges neatened from the inside by overcasting or by turning them in against each other.

Double bias-cut frills (174) are used only if the part to be trimmed can bear the extra weight. The bias-strip is cut to double the width of the frill and is then folded in half. Great care must be taken not to crease the material in any way, as this would prevent a good fall. The fold is

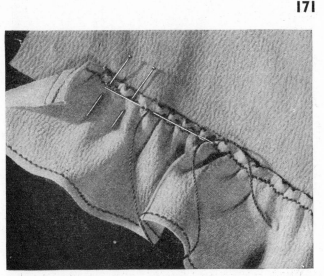

171. **RUCHES** may be made of strips of material cut on a straight thread or on the bias. The strips, neatened by hemming or by picot edging cut through, may be gathered by hand or by machine.

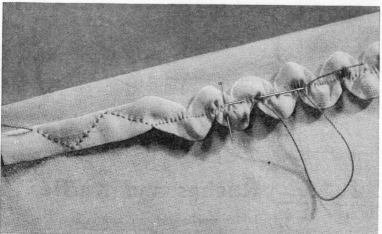

pressed only lightly at first, and the cut edges are then run together and slightly eased on the thread. Cross-frills do not have "gathers." The easing merely causes the frill edges to flare a little. The frill is attached to the edge of the material by a reversed seam.

Flare frills are cut in rings or half-rings and joined together. 172 shows the shape of the frill when laid flat and when joined together. The bigger the diameter of the inner circle, the less flared the frill. Several small rings will give deeper flares. The outer edge may be neatened by picot edging, zigzag edging, or by stitching down a single turning.

Shell ruching (173) is made by gathering a narrow strip of material in a zigzag line. The thread is then drawn to a straight line. This produces a pretty shell ruche which is used as a trimming on coat or cloak lining, lining pockets, and often on furs.

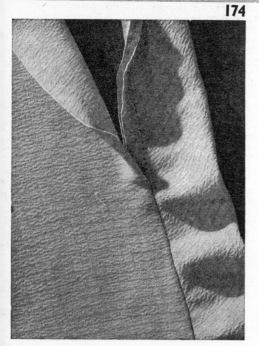

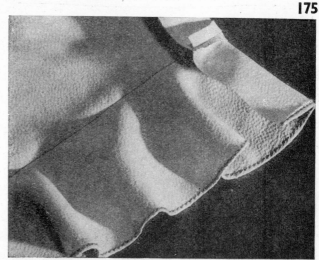

174. A wide strip cut on the bias is folded in half and stitched on to the material by running a thread through the double thickness, the cut edges being slightly eased as the stitching proceeds. Such a frill has a particularly good fall, and at the same time makes the edge of the material heavier.

175. This frill, consisting of several rings joined together (see 172), may be turned in at the upper edge and stitched on to the material close to the fold. It may also be stitched on reversed and the seam pressed open.

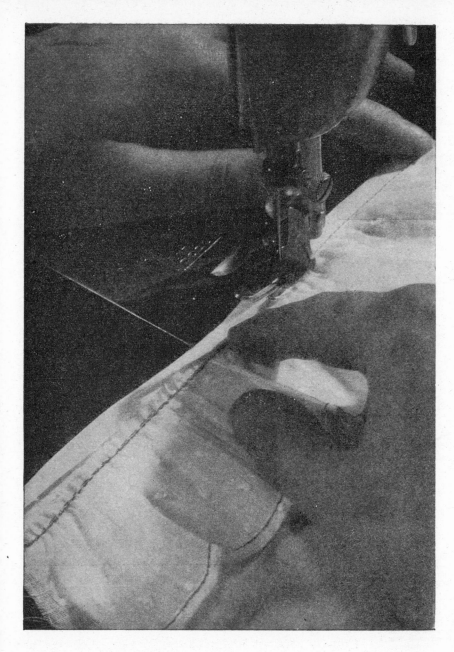

176

176. FRILL EDGING. The strip of material intended for the frill is neatened at the outer edge. The gathered inner edge is sewn on to the material, right side to right side. The edge of the material should project far enough over the edge of the frill to enable it to be stitched down as a raised seam.

177

179

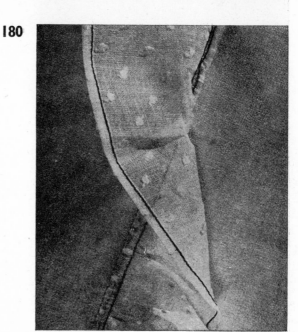

180

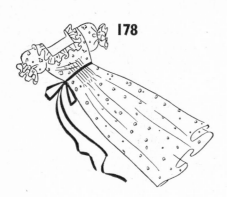

178

177. DIFFERENT METHOD. Frilled edging may be joined on to straight-edged material with a binding. Frill and facing are together stitched on to the material on the wrong side. The binding is turned over and stitched down close along the edge.

179. CURVED EDGES, necklines or instance, have the frill joined on by means of bias-binding. The bias-strip, slightly stretched, is stitched with the gathered frill edge on to the right side of the material. The binding is then rolled over to the wrong side and hemmed on with slip-stitches.

180. FRILLED TRIMMING may be stitched on to the wrong side, turned, and secured with a second row of stitching. The frill edge is best gathered twice by machine, with a space of ¼ in. in between, so that the stitching down can be done in the second row of gathering.

181

56

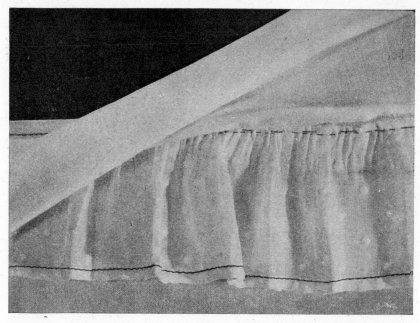

183

Cushions and Pillow Cases

183. FRILL TRIMMING, placed between a tuck sewn on the wrong side. The frill may be made of the same material, or a lighter fabric, such as mull; it is gathered and tacked on to the right side of the material. Corners cannot be made by this method, as the material would pucker when the tuck is being made. The tuck should be about $\frac{1}{4}$ in. wide.

184. A narrow strip of material or galon stitched on to cover the top of a frill will make this wear better and is at the same time a further trimming. The gathered edge of the frill is tacked on to the material and is then covered with a strip of facing about $\frac{1}{2}$ in. wide. The edges are turned in narrowly and stitched down.

184

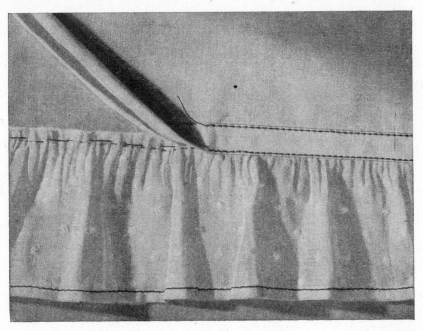

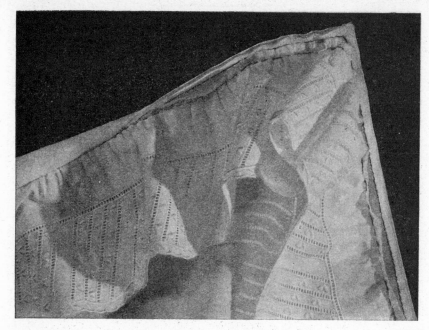

185

186

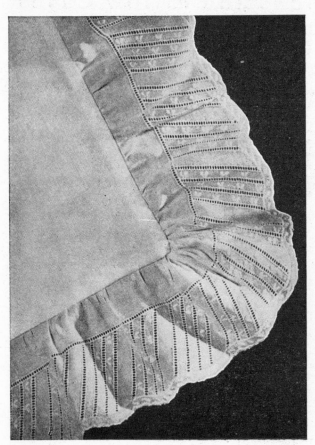

185. FRILL EDGING for pillow cases and eiderdown covers. The gathered frill is tacked on to the right side of the upper part of the cover, the gathers being pushed together very closely at the corners. The edge of the cover should project so as to allow for a seam turning and is stitched on to the lower part of the cover.

186. THE COVER is then turned inside-out and the second seam along the edge, which encloses the edge of the frill, is sewn. The cover is turned back again and is now as shown in the illustration. An edge binding may be stitched on in the same manner. As an alternative the cover may be finished off with a wide hem.

187. If the edges of a pleated ruche have not been neatened before pleating, they must be turned in and stitched afterwards. This stretches the edge and gives it a particularly soft and rich hang. The ruche is stitched on in the direction of the pleats.

188. THE PLEATING of narrow ruffles is simplified by marking out several strips on a large piece of material, picoting along the guide lines, pleating the whole piece and then dividing the strips in the picot seam. The strips can then be joined end to end.

189. A PLEATED FRILL which is to be used as an edging should be set on to the material, right side to right side, and the seam edges pressed over inwards and neatened by blanket-stitching.

190. In the case of very thin materials in which an overcast seam would show through on the right side, the edge of the material should be allowed to project beyond the pleated edge; it can then be turned over and hemmed on to the stitching.

191. BOX-PLEATED RUCHES are made of straight-cut strips of material. Three times the finished length of the frill will be required. The box-pleats may be ¾ in. to 1½ in. wide and are stitched through as they are being laid.

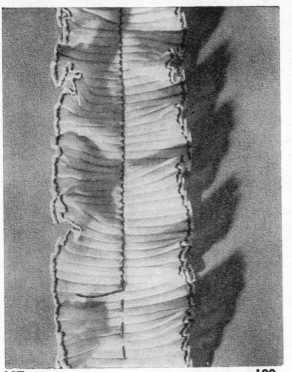

187

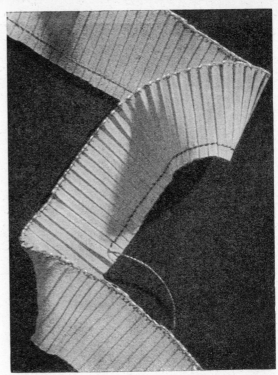

188→

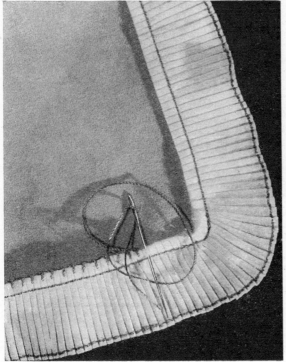

189

Pleated Frills, Box-pleated Ruches, and Rose Ruffles

For the frills shown (187–190), the narrowest pleating that can be made should be used. These frills are particularly suitable for thin materials. Three times the finished length of material is required.

The hem edge should be as flat and thin as possible for narrow pleats; picot edging or the ornamental zigzag hem are therefore the most suitable finishes.

If a short frill has to be neatened, the picot edging is machined along the edge and the narrow-edge strip is then cut off. If several strips are required, take a piece of material large enough to produce the necessary number and mark off the width of the thread with coloured silk tacking. The picot edging should be machined along alternate marking threads, as each row of stitching, when cut through, neatens two edges, and the inner edges of the frill do not require neatening since they will be sewn on to the material. When the pleating has been done, cut the strips apart and stitch them together in such a way that the ends are concealed in the inner fold of a pleat. If the frill edges are to be finished by stitching, a single turning will be sufficient, provided the material does not fray easily. The stitching of the frill at the edge may be done before the pleating. If it is left till afterwards, the edge will become slightly stretched and the ruche will have a somewhat "frizzy" appearance. This method, however, takes away some of the stiffness of the pleating; often, indeed, the edge of the pleating will be ironed out on purpose, so as to give it a soft fall.

Box-pleats are laid by hand; straight-cut or bias-cut strips of material may be used for the purpose. The

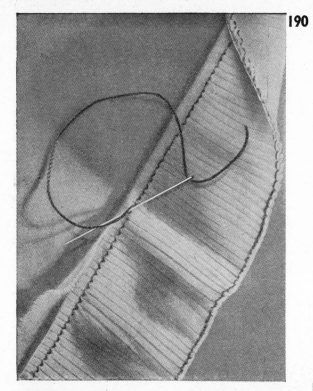

190

191

192

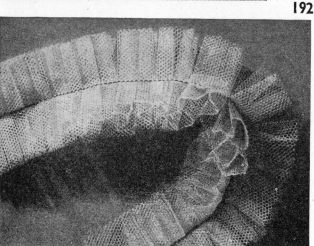

193

box-pleats may be ¾ in. to 1½ in. wide. They are laid with the help of a cardboard gauge or tape measure, and held in place with small running-stitches. If lingerie material is being used, the pleats should be stitched through by machine, a large stitch being employed ; the pleats are laid as they are being stitched. The ruches must stand up and should therefore not be ironed. In use, however, they come to lie flat after a time ; they should therefore be undone occasionally, the strip ironed out, and the pleats laid anew.

To make the so-called rose ruche, the pleats should be caught together in the centre, just below the edge (see 191). 193 shows a particularly charming example of this type of ruche. Rose ruches are sewn on by hand, before the folds are caught together.

192. FOR NET RUFFLES either a double or three-fold strip should be used, or the pleats can be folded double, so as to ensure a very full ruffle edge. The length of strip required depends on the method adopted.

193. ROSE RUCHES are made of taffeta bias-strips, frayed out at the edges. The upper double pleats should be stitched together in the centre, a very full ruche being thus produced.

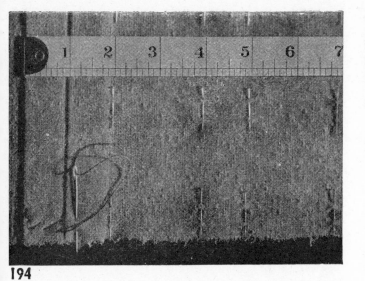

194

195

How to lay and press Pleats—The Pleated Hem—The Arrowhead

If a length of material is to be laid into pleats of equal depth, touching each other, the amount of material required will be three times the finished length desired. A pleated section 10 in. long would therefore require 30 in. of material. The cloth is spread out and the pleats marked with pins, a tape measure being used; mark out alternately the width of the pleats and their depth, which should be twice their width. The pleats may now be tacked with long stitches, or pinned on to the table or ironing board and pressed lightly so as to mark the pleat folds. The tacks or pins are then removed and the pleats are pressed thoroughly, using a damp cloth, the degree of dampness depending upon the nature of the material. A dry cloth may be placed underneath the damp one to avoid damaging the material. When pressing pleats, care must be

194. To obtain regular folds, the width and depth of every fold must be measured off with the tape or a cardboard marker and marked out with pins. The pleats can either be tacked or pressed immediately.

196. Pleated sections often consist of several lengths of material. The necessary seams must be placed inside the folds. The pleat which is to cover the seam is tacked on, and not till then is the seam sewn.

196

197

198. PLEATS IN NARROW SECTIONS should be pinned on an ironing board. The width and the depth of the pleats are marked out with chalk, and the pleats are then laid in position by stretching and pinning the material. The pressing should be done lightly at first, and then thoroughly when the pins have been removed.

202. THE ARROWHEAD serves many useful purposes. It is used to secure the ends of a seam above inverted pleats, and may be applied to the ends of plackets or pocket openings. The arrowhead is embroidered with buttonhole twist or embroidery thread.

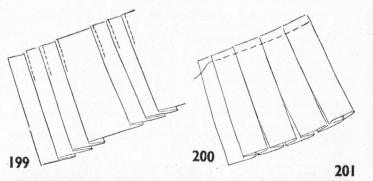

199   200   201

taken that the pleat folds leave no marks in the material, underneath or on top, as they would be visible when the pleats open out. It may be necessary to place strips of stout paper under the fold edges of the pleats. The pressing should be done lightly on the right side, and then thoroughly on the wrong side. The row of pleats is tacked through at the top. The pleats may be secured a few inches down either side by edge stitching or by sewing them on the inside (199–200).

When joining several pleated sections the seams should be placed in the inside fold of the pleats at the ends. The seam edges are either turned in and hand-run together, or neatened by oversewing both edges together. At the lower edge of the pleated section, the hem should be sewn first and then the seam which passes through. The end of the seam should be cut away a little, slantwise, when the seam is being neatened (see 197).

It is very useful, particularly in the case of narrow, knife-like pleats, to stretch and press the folds in narrow-pleated sections (198). Care should be taken that the pleat folds follow a straight thread, since the pleats would otherwise not hang straight and would "draw" easily.

To make an "arrowhead," mark out an elongated triangle about $\frac{1}{2}$ in. to $\frac{3}{4}$ in. high with chalk or tacking at the top of the pleat. If the material has not been laid in several folds, a piece of lining or linen should be placed underneath on the wrong side.

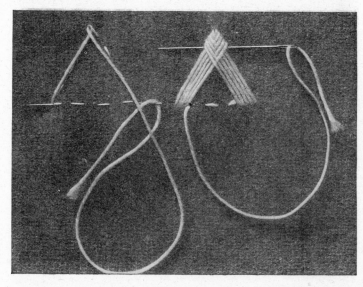

Pleated Panels

Pleated panels require far less material than do sections pleated throughout. Since in any event the upper third, or even more, of the pleats in a section pleated throughout is usually sewn up, pleated panels are sufficient to widen a skirt or dress.

Whether the panel will have to be formed of two pleats or a row of pleats will depend upon the extra width required. For the set-on panel with one pleat on each side, all that is needed is a slash a little shorter than the panel in the material underneath. The slash should begin at the same level as the pleats which open out just below the stitching. The pleats are pressed so that the cut edges meet on the inside. The upper edge of the panel is turned in (the turning can be either straight or mitred), tacked, and then tacked on to the material. The cut edges of the panel and the slashed edges of the material beneath will now meet and should be stitched together on the inside. The panel is stitched on to the right side, close to the edge.

Inset pleated panels require a cross-cut for the pleat turnings, in addition to the slash in the material which is to be widened (see 205-209). The deeper these cross-cuts are, the deeper will be the pleats. Here it is most important to secure the corners. When the outside material has been sewn on, and the inner pleat seam stitched, the upper pleat edges should be either caught lightly on to the material, or else cut away on a slant so that the corners cannot bend over. The pleat edges are best overcast; other methods of finishing should not be used, as it is most important that the seam edges remain flat and thin.

If groups of pleats are to be made, long cross-cuts will again be

203. THE PLEATED PANEL, used to give increased width, must be a little longer than the slash in the material underneath. The pleats are pressed before the panel is set on, either with a straight or a mitred line.

204. The pleated panel is stitched on to the right side and joined to the slash edges by seams sewn on the wrong side. Over-casting or blanket-stitch is used to neaten the seam edges.

205. The width of the pleat panel depends on the cross-cuts which determine the distance between and the turnings of the pleats. Neaten the cross-cut corners before turning in and tacking.

203

204

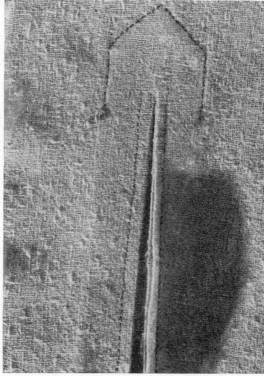

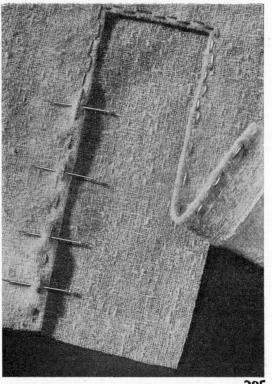

205

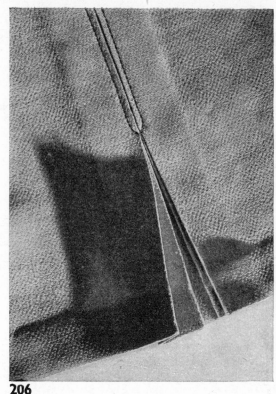

206

207

required, both for set-on and for inset panels. More difficult to work and suitable only for woollen fabrics is the inset slot pleat shown in 209. The panel is stitched right side to right side, on to the long slash edges in the material, bringing the seams together to a point at the end of the slash. These seams form the pleat fold when the panel is turned. The reason why this panel is suitable only for woollens is that puckers will inevitably form at the end of the slash, and these must be well pressed out, a thing that is only possible in the case of woollen fabrics. 208 shows the inside, 209 the outside of the pleat, which is held up by a row of stitching across the top.

Double Inverted Pleats

206. DOUBLE INVERTED PLEATS are produced by placing two or more pleats one on top of the other. They may be arranged singly or in groups. The illustration shows double inverted pleats laid throughout the length. Pleat panels may also be set into seams which are left open, or into slashes, in which case the joining seams must be placed in the outer fold.

207. PLEAT EDGES and slash edges must be stitched on. The seam must lie in the inner pleat fold. In the case of thick materials the upper pleat edge should be lightly caught on the inside.

208

209

Knife Pleating : Accordion Pleating

Knife pleating is the term used to describe narrow, close pleats which are produced by machine, or pressed by hand. 210 shows the commonest form of knife pleating. Fashion offers us the choice of a number of variations, such as group pleating, honeycomb pleating, accordion pleating, and sun-ray pleating. The material required is three times the finished length. Pleated sections should be cut along a straight thread; if the section is to consist of several parts, these should be cut along the same thread (warp or weft).

The upper edge of the pleated section may be secured by stitching it through with a fairly long stitch, allowing the pleats to pass under the presser-foot in a forward direction. Alternatively the edge may be tacked through with slanting stitches (see 210), which take up each pleat, or it may simply be tacked through with running-stitches so that the pleats may be moved along on the thread.

If the pleats are not to open out the whole length, they may be held in by rows of stitching across, or in a zigzag or curved pattern, or by sewing a tape on the wrong side with blanket-stitch (see 210).

For cartridge pleats the upper edge of the part which is to be set on should first be neatened. Thin and very soft fabrics are not suitable for this type of pleating.

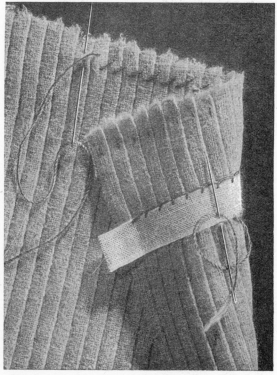

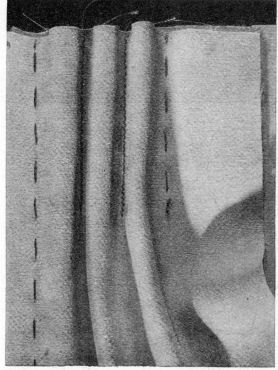

210. **PLEATED SECTIONS** are tacked through at the upper edge before being worked up, so that the pleats remain in place. A seam tape secured on the inside by blanket-stitch will prevent stretching.

211. If the upper of two pieces of material placed on top of each other is pushed together evenly, tacked, and stitched for a few inches, cartridge pleats are produced.

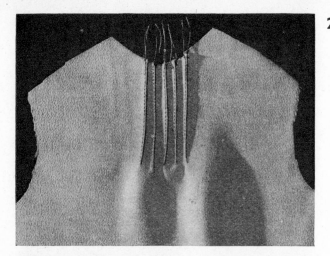

Dart Pleats for Rounded Backs

An uncomfortable badly fitting back-piece on a garment hinders movement and, above all, tears very easily. It is chiefly in the case of bad carriage (216) or a rounded back (214) that a little width will have to be added at the centre of the back-piece. The pattern will have to be moved in, about $\frac{1}{2}$ in. to $\frac{3}{4}$ in. away from the material fold (215). When cutting out, ample allowance should be made at the material folds for turnings on the neckline, especially those at the centre back. The extra width thus obtained is taken up by making several darts or small pleats which reduce the neckline to the proper size. This extra width also increases the width of the back-piece at the waistline, and here, too, it will have to be taken up by darts or gathering.

Divided patterns consisting of centre- and side-pieces are fitted to the body by means of curved seams, and therefore do not require this extra width to be added. In the case of patterns with undivided parts which cannot be made to fit and where not even darts will give the right shape, it is possible with careful fitting to put in the dividing seams oneself. These seams should be placed about the centre of the shoulder; in front they pass over the bust to the waistline, while at the back they are curved inwards towards the waistline.

213

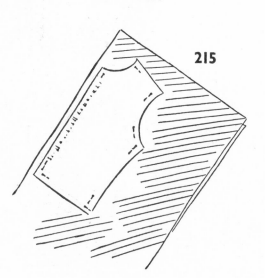

214

215

216

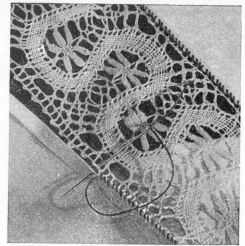

217

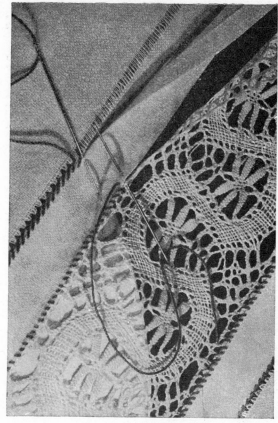

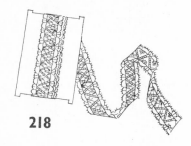

218

219

Lace and Lace Insertions

212. A GROUP OF DART PLEATS will reduce the added width of the back portion of the neckline. The pleats should be even in depth and about 3 in. long.

213. " PIN " DARTS are used in the case of a rounded back. They are placed on the inside on either side of the middle of the back and are stitched so as to end in a point.

217. LACE INSERTIONS are set in by oversewing. The edges of the materials are turned in once to be trimmed off later, and the insertion is sewn on with short close stitches.

219. SIMPLIFIED HEM-STITCHING is used to secure the edges of the material, the turning here being made a little wider. This method serves at the same time to neaten the joint between lace and material.

220. WHIPPING may also be used. The edge of the lace is whipped on to the edge of the material which has been rolled between the left thumb and index finger. The seam should be smoothed out.

220

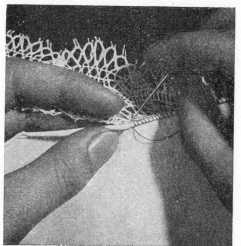

221-222. Lace may also be sewn on by a double seam. It is first sewn on to the right side of the material and then stitched over on the wrong side.

223. Lace motifs are tacked on to the material, the edges are closely oversewn with satin-stitch and the material cut away on the wrong side close to the stitching.

224. Narrow lace set on in several rows forms a pretty trimming. The lace is gathered by pulling a draw-thread woven in along the edge, and is stitched on with back-stitch, widely spaced.

221-222

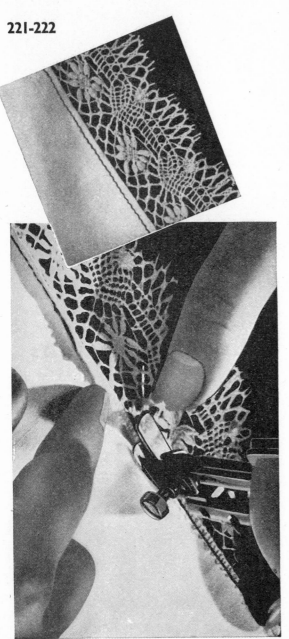

223

224

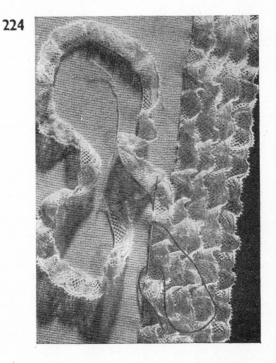

225

Lace Trimmings and Edgings

Gathered (shirred) Valenciennes lace may be used as an edging or as a trimming. If several rows of lace are to be sewn on, the lace should not be wider than $\frac{1}{8}$ in. to $\frac{3}{4}$ in. One strip should always cover the beginning of the next one. Valenciennes lace is used almost exclusively in conjunction with very dainty fabrics and is therefore often sewn on by hand. The gathering of the lace is done by pulling a thread which is woven in for the purpose on the straight edge. In delicate lace this thread is very thin and must be pulled very carefully, or it will break.

The lace should be stitched on close to the edge, and as it is not gathered very closely this stitching should present no difficulty.

On delicate materials the lace is whipped on; lace and material are placed together, right side to right side, and both are overcast together. The edge of the material may at the same time be rolled in as for a rolled hem, if it has not been hemmed beforehand. Lace insertions are used to join two hemmed parts or may be applied as an inset. For this purpose the insertion is tacked and stitched close to the edge and the material underneath is cut away, leaving only a narrow margin for a turning, which is rolled in to the row of stitching and overcast (226–227). With each stitch the needle takes up a stitch of the first row.

Working with Lace

There are all-over laces having so close and strong a texture that their cut edges do not require any neatening. More delicate laces with much net foundation, on the other hand, would soon roll up if their edges were not secured. Thin silk to match the lace in colour is the most suitable for neatening. Narrow bias-strips—the finished binding must not be more than $\frac{1}{8}$ in. wide—are cut and stitched on, right side to right side. The delicate material is often drawn together in the machining and tissue paper should therefore be laid under before the stitching is begun; this can afterwards be pulled away carefully. The bias-strip is rolled in and hemmed on to the row of stitching on the wrong side (see 229).

Another method of finishing is shown in 228. Narrow rick-rack braid stitched against the lace on the wrong side and folded over and stitched down on the right side gives a neatening which resembles a woven edge.

A zigzag hem or machine hem-stitching may be used to neaten a cut edge or to join parts together.

Extension seams which are to remain invisible may be hidden by cutting out one edge and matching it on to the other edge. Such a seam may be curved as required by the pattern (230). The joining stitches should be set very closely so as to take up each mesh of the net foundation.

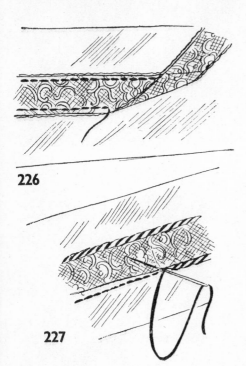

226

227

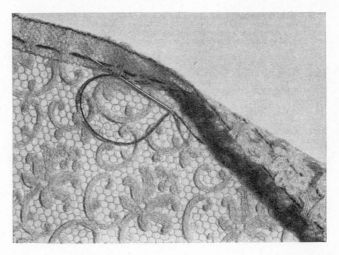

228

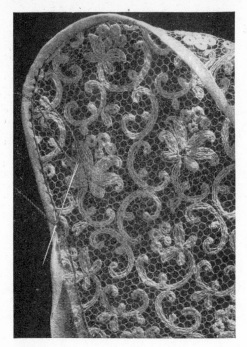

229

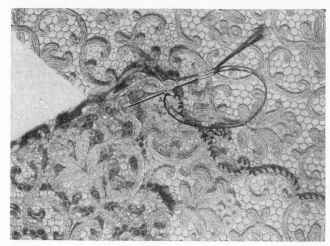

230

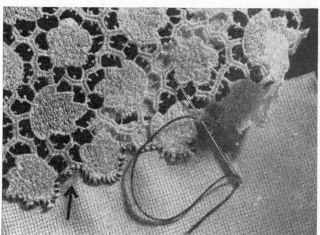

231

225. LACE EDGING can be stitched on to a hem, or whipped on to the edge of the material. Lace and material are placed together, right sides facing, and are oversewn together.

226. The cut edges of lace material can be neatened in various ways. For instance, a strip of net may be stitched on to the right side, turned over and hemmed, giving an almost invisible finish and at the same time strengthening the edge.

229. ALL-OVER LACE may be rolled in with bias-binding of georgette of the same shade as the lace. The strip, which should be about ⅜ in. wide, is stitched on right side to right side, rolled in closely and hemmed on to the wrong side.

230. By skilful piecing together even the smallest cuttings of lace may be used up. A section of lace is cut out, the pattern being followed and stitched on with close overcasting stitches.

231. LACE AND MATERIAL are joined together in the same way. The lace is cut out and oversewn on to the material, which is afterwards trimmed off along the seam. Alternatively, it may be stitched on by a machine zigzag seam.

232. STRAIGHT LACE may be curved as required by means of darts, which must follow the motif exactly and should be oversewn together with close stitches. In this way straight lace can be used in the place of round woven lace.

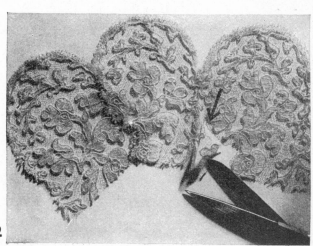

232

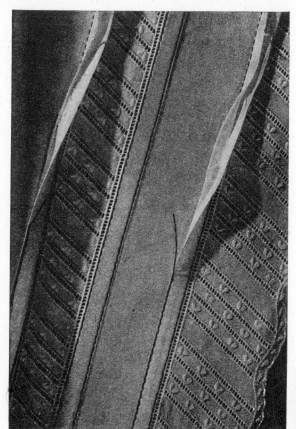

233

Embroidery Insertions and Trimmings

233-234. A simple seam directed to the wrong side is used to join material and embroidery. The edge of the embroidery is turned in and stitched down close along the fold.

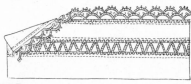

235

235 and **236** show how bobbin lace and insertions are stitched on, the edges of the material being stitched down afterwards on the wrong side.

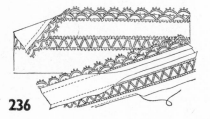

236

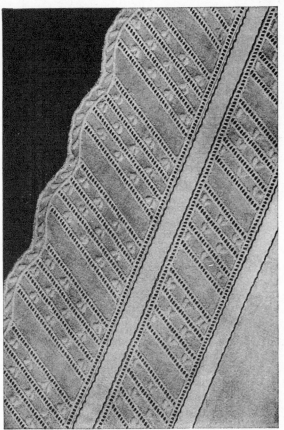

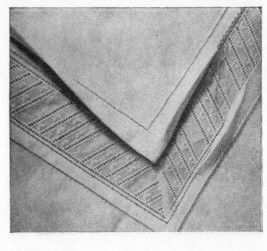

238

237

237. RAISED SEAM. The nsertion is stitched in with the seam edges to the wrong side; the plain edge of the insertion is turned in and stitched over the first seam.

238-239. Embroidery set into corners. The plain edge of the insertion (about ⅛ in. in width) is turned in for the purpose of tacking the insertion to the material from the inside. The corners are mitred and their narrow edges closely oversewn. When the insertion edge has been stitched down on the wrong side, the material is cut away on the right side so as to leave a narrow turning which is stitched down.

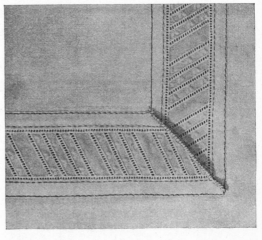

239

To be Well Dressed Means—

To know oneself—to be mercilessly critical before the mirror—to note every fault and blemish of the figure, no matter how trifling. This is the only way in which one can attain that " personal style " which is so necessary if one is to be regarded as well dressed. If it happens that your face is a trifle severe, your figure angular rather than attractively curved—then it means that you will have to do without those too graceful frills and furbelows, those ruches and flowers, and, even in the case of afternoon and evening dresses, to choose things that are simple in style, that tend almost to the " sporty." Fashion fortunately allows a woman to choose at any time one style or another without making herself conspicuous or appearing to be old-fashioned. The only thing that matters is to observe the general line of fashion and to make use of new fabrics and novel colour combinations. Details on collar, sleeves, hips, and skirt should be adopted only in so far as they suit and help the figure. Admittedly there are women who may permit themselves the luxury of dressing to-day in a boyish sports costume, to-morrow in a daintily romantic dress, but they are the few, the lucky ones who can wear " anything." For all the others, reticence must be the rule, and the careful discernment which knows and can choose between what is fashionable and what is suitable.

For the " tall and slim," and the " short and stout," clothing may be chosen according to well-established principles. The woman who is taller than the average must not accentuate this by selecting tight-fitting clothes, seams which run the whole length, rows of buttons, or vertically striped materials. That a somewhat fuller cut, wide puff sleeves, jabot, tunic, will work miracles is shown in the two sketches at 241, which are based on the same figure. The belt division, and the use of different colours for jacket and skirt as well as the extra width, will prevent the excessive tallness and slimness from becoming noticeable. Large patterns and shoulder-capes are also useful " shorteners," and cannot therefore be recommended to the other group, who are short and stout. For them, the very opposite is right. For them the vertical stripes, the beltless styles, long narrow sleeves, light fabrics used only for small embellishments, otherwise mainly dark, plain materials, or dark materials with an unobtrusive self-pattern. Hats should have swaying, wide brims only if their wearer is very tall. Even the style of hairdressing makes a difference to a person's height, as is shown in the sketches.

We have explained who may wear checks and large floral designs, who need not fear stripes, and who should confine herself to small-patterned materials. By way of consolation we may mention that small, fine, polka dots will suit anyone, and that only the colour combination need be considered ; large dots, of course, are confined to the slim ones.

When planning an outfit it is very important to choose one colour as the basic motif and to repeat this in every detail of dress. For instance, if brown is decided upon, coat, hat, shoes, gloves, and handbag should have brown as the main colour ; variety can be introduced by a dress colour which will harmonise with brown, such as beige, copper, yellow, or green. Often a trimming of another colour will suffice. Blouses, too, offer scope for variety. Patterned materials which repeat the colour scheme in the design or in the chief colour are very suitable for the completion of an ensemble. With the classic black and with navy blue excellent colour combinations may be carried out. When once you have discovered the advantages of dressing so that all the details are in harmony, you will never be satisfied with anything else, for it is the combination of suitable cut, colour scheme, and, above all, faultless fit achieved by first-class work, which forms the basis of a perfect turn-out.

240

241

242

243

Good Tools are Important

Successful work depends a great deal on the right tools, always well looked after. It is not advisable to economise when buying your equipment. A good pair of scissors is most important. A small pair is used when sewing, while large cutting-out scissors with double-sided handles and sharp cutting edges will cut through material cleanly and evenly. The big handle of the scissors should rest upon the cutting-out surface while the work is being done. Scissors should not be dropped or thrown about, as this loosens the rivet and so impairs their efficiency. If the scissors stick or squeak, oiling is urgently required. Frequent sharpening is a matter of course, for one should work only with sharp scissors.

The thimble should have a pitted surface, so that the needle will not slip when the thimble is used to push it through the material. Remove the thimble from time to time so that your finger, which will get rather hot while working, may cool.

Needles are classified by numbers according to their thickness. In addition, there are medium-long and long needles. The smaller the number, the thicker the needle. For ordinary use one should buy packets of assorted needles from 3 to 8; 8 is the thickness most commonly used. Use a longer needle for tacking than for hemming. If you find after a little use that the needle no longer glides easily through the material, push it a few times through a piece of emery paper, or smooth it by drawing it across a strip of leather, the sole of your shoe, for instance.

Pins should be of steel, as they must neither rust nor bend easily, and must have very sharp points or they will damage the material by leaving small holes.

The tape measure should be firm and made of a stout material or it will stretch with use, so that it is no longer accurate. It should not be folded or rolled up, but must always remain flat and legible. Tailor's chalk is also important. It is used for transferring patterns or marking lines for cutting. Chalk marks are easily removed and are often of great help during the work. The chalk should always be well sharpened so that clean lines can be drawn. The sharpening is done simply by scraping the chalk with a pen-knife. Keep the shavings; they are useful for removing oil stains, which may easily occur if the machine has been oiled a little too well. The shavings are finely powdered and scattered over the stain. They can be left till the oil has been absorbed, and then brushed or shaken off.

A few words must be said about the various threads, cottons, and sewing silks.

Tacking thread should not be too hard, otherwise it may damage the material when the tacks are removed. For this reason ordinary sewing cotton or thread should never be used for tacking, but only the proper tacking thread, which is sold in large reels. Delicate fabrics are tacked with sewing silk of a light shade.

Machine cottons are supplied in two qualities. The best is six-ply, which is used on the top reel. It is stronger and shiny, whereas the cotton used in the bobbin is soft and dull-looking.

For making dresses, sewing silk is usually used, as it is obtainable in all shades and is more supple than cotton. Cotton frocks are better sewn with a fine cotton. Buttonhole twist is used for buttonholes, arrowheads, and fancy stitching.

Keep a Permanent Record of Your Measurements

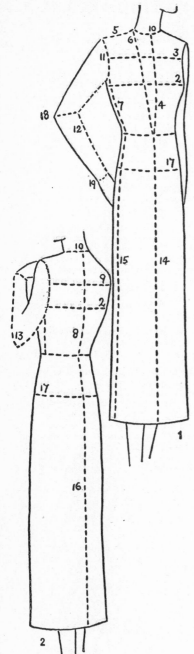

It is most important that the home dressmaker should know thoroughly and accurately her own measurements as well as the measurements for those for whom she is dressmaking. The chart at the left is a complete guide for the taking of measurements and is a very real help.

1. Tie a tape rather tightly round the natural waist; this is a guide for other measurements which are taken to or from the waist. ....

2. Round the bust. Measure loosely. ....

3. Across the chest between the armholes, 4 in. below the throat. ....

4. Length of front (from the two little bones at the base of the throat to the waist). ....

5. Length of shoulders. ....

6. From waist to back waist, right over the shoulders. ....

7. Under-arm, from well up in the armpit to the waist. ....

8. Back, from the nape of the neck to the waist. ....

9. Width across the shoulder-blades, at the widest part of the back. ....

10. Round the throat. ....

11. Round the armhole. ....

12. Front seam of sleeve, taken with arm extended, from the front of the armpit to the wrist. ....

13. Outer sleeve measure. Measure this with bent arm, as in Fig. 2, from the top of armhole to elbow, and then to wrist. ....

14. Skirt—front length from the waist to the bottom of skirt. ....

15. Skirt—side length between the same two points. ....

16. Skirt—back length between the same two points. ....

17. Hips, taken loosely round 9 or 10 in. below the waist. ....

18. Width round the elbow with the arm bent. ....

19. Round wrist. ....

Paper Pattern Adjustment

Few women are stock sizes in all their measurements, so while a paper pattern is obtainable in a variety of sizes, it sometimes happens that the pattern needs one or two slight alterations to fit the individual figure. Always try a pattern, by pinning it together and measuring on the figure, before cutting out the material.

To enlarge a portion of a pattern, cut it through in the correct places, indicated in the diagrams, separate the pieces the necessary amount and paste them this distance apart on a strip of paper placed underneath them.

To reduce a pattern piece, make folds or pleats of the depth required in the correct positions on the paper, and pin or paste these folds in place.

Bodice or blouse alterations are shown in **244** (reducing back and front) and **245** (enlarging back and front).

To make a two-piece sleeve pattern shorter, pin across the width of both upper and under parts a very small pleat above the elbow and another about half-way between elbow and wrist. Then straighten the edges of the pattern where the making of the pleats has thrown it out (see **246**).

To make a two-piece sleeve pattern longer, cut the sleeve pattern across, above and below the elbow, and insert strips of paper of the required width. Trim the pattern edges if required (**247**).

One-piece sleeve patterns are altered in the same way, except that there is only one piece instead of two to pleat or slash (see **248** and **249**).

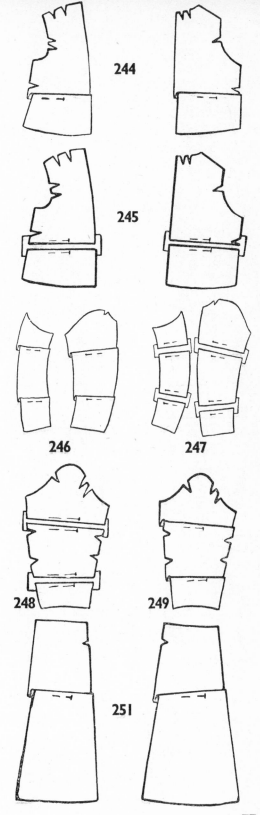

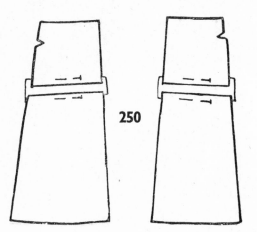

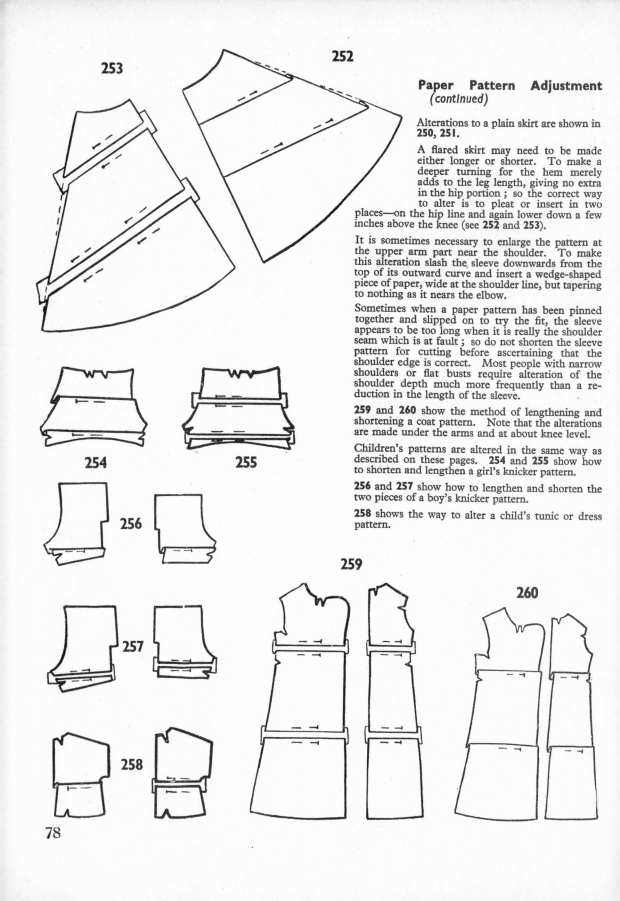

Paper Pattern Adjustment
(continued)

Alterations to a plain skirt are shown in **250, 251**.

A flared skirt may need to be made either longer or shorter. To make a deeper turning for the hem merely adds to the leg length, giving no extra in the hip portion; so the correct way to alter is to pleat or insert in two places—on the hip line and again lower down a few inches above the knee (see **252** and **253**).

It is sometimes necessary to enlarge the pattern at the upper arm part near the shoulder. To make this alteration slash the sleeve downwards from the top of its outward curve and insert a wedge-shaped piece of paper, wide at the shoulder line, but tapering to nothing as it nears the elbow.

Sometimes when a paper pattern has been pinned together and slipped on to try the fit, the sleeve appears to be too long when it is really the shoulder seam which is at fault; so do not shorten the sleeve pattern for cutting before ascertaining that the shoulder edge is correct. Most people with narrow shoulders or flat busts require alteration of the shoulder depth much more frequently than a reduction in the length of the sleeve.

259 and **260** show the method of lengthening and shortening a coat pattern. Note that the alterations are made under the arms and at about knee level.

Children's patterns are altered in the same way as described on these pages. **254** and **255** show how to shorten and lengthen a girl's knicker pattern.

256 and **257** show how to lengthen and shorten the two pieces of a boy's knicker pattern.

258 shows the way to alter a child's tunic or dress pattern.

Cutting Out and Pattern-marking

The correct grain of the material should be especially noted

When the paper pattern has been altered to fit the individual measurements, the material is prepared for the cutting out. Smooth out any creases in it with a warm iron, and lay it out according to the plan, with the selvedges towards the cutter.

Careful cutting out makes so much difference to the look of a finished garment that this first process should never be hurried. Allow plenty of time for cutting out, and, as far as is possible, arrange to be undisturbed. A good light, a large, steady table, and a plentiful supply of good pins are essentials. Pin abundantly, placing the pins within an inch of the edge of the pattern, and at intervals of about 3 in.

All parts of the pattern must be arranged on the material, exactly as shown in the diagram, *before* any cutting out is done. This is much more important than it seems, for the cutting diagram is very carefully planned to save both material and time, and any rearrangement of the pattern pieces will spoil the hang of the finished garment. The perforations which indicate the correct grain of the material should be especially noted, as grain plays an important part in successful dress cutting.

When, as sometimes happens, parts of the garment are cut singly in order to save any waste of material, it is advisable to cut these parts of the pattern again in paper, so that *all* the pattern pieces are pinned into position on the material, before the cutting out is started. **262** shows the sleeve and bodice parts of a dress pattern cut singly.

When *all* the pattern pieces are securely pinned into position, the cutting may begin. Long, smooth cuts with sharp scissors should be taken; a professional cutter uses the middle of the blades and not the tips of the scissors. (And here the dressmaker is strongly advised to use the best possible cutting-out shears. I-XL Chromium-plated scissors are thoroughly recommended. They are made in Sheffield and combine the advantage of stainless steel with a sharp cutting edge.) Avoid raising the material during the cutting out by lightly resting the left hand on the material. **263** shows the correct position of the hand during the cutting out. Never cut the notches, but mark them with pins, or chalk, as they are a valuable guide to the assembling of the various parts.

When the cutting-out process is completed, the material pieces should be pattern-marked. Use a tracing wheel (see **264**) if the material is thin, and tailor's chalk or tailor's tacks for heavier materials. Every notch, pleat, and perforation, as well as positions for draperies, trimmings, and pockets, should be clearly marked on the material. A little extra time

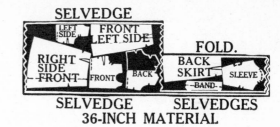

SELVEDGE
LEFT SIDE · FRONT LEFT SIDE
FOLD.
RIGHT SIDE FRONT · FRONT · BACK · BACK SKIRT · SLEEVE
BAND
SELVEDGE · SELVEDGES
36-INCH MATERIAL

261

261. When using a material with a definite surface, such as velvet or face cloth, all pattern pieces must be placed on the material in one direction.

SELVEDGE
RIGHT SIDE FRONT LEFT SIDE · RIGHT SIDE BACK LEFT SIDE · SLEEVE · COLLAR · FOLD. FRONT
BACK
SELVEDGE
36-INCH MATERIAL

262

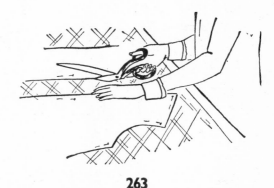

263

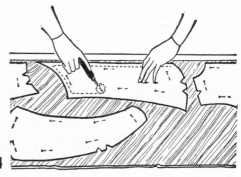

264

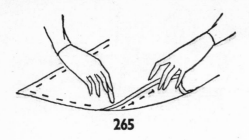

265

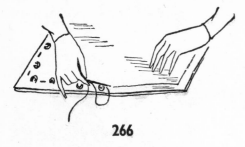

266

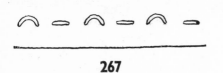

267

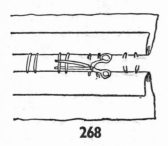

268

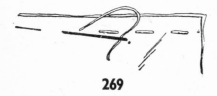

269

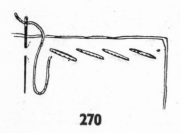

270

Cutting Out *(continued)*

Every pattern piece must be marked with tailor's chalk or tacks

and patience spent in pattern-marking will save hours of troublesome fitting and fixing later on. Any easing should be marked with chalk and then a temporary gathering thread to draw up when fixing.

TAILOR'S TACKING OR MARK-STITCH is used as a guide in the assembling of the various parts of a garment. It is done immediately after the cutting-out process. Pin material on pattern, placing extra pins in the fitting line of pattern, 1½ in. apart on the smaller parts and round curves, but 3 in. apart on straight edges. It is essential that these be exactly in fitting line, which, on most edges, is ⅛ in. from the edge, but special care must be taken that the exact trimmings are allowed on all edges ; they may vary according to the design.

Turn over material, so that the back of the pin line is facing you, and with tailor's chalk mark carefully over every pin (see **265**). Then join up the chalk line between the pins and mark every notch. Now remove both the pins and the pattern and proceed to tailor tack on the chalk line (see **266**).

Use cheap basting or machine cotton, No. 40. Have long double strands. Pick up two stitches ¼ in. long and draw the needle through. Now leave a space of ¼ in. Take up two more stitches ¼ in. long and draw needle through, leaving a loop large enough to get the first two fingers into ; continue doing this on all the chalk marks (see Diags. **266, 267**). Then carefully pull the material apart, keeping it flat on the table, and, lifting the top material as far as loops will allow, snip the threads with small, sharp scissors, as shown in **268**. (Do not cut the threads until all the tack loops have been drawn down.) Keep the material flat on the table, without opening it out, and smooth a warm iron over the tacking threads. This presses them down and so prevents them from working out.

In the assembling of a garment, these tailor's tacks serve as a reliable guide in matching one part with another—as well as indicating the fitting line.

Tacking is used for holding the various parts of a garment together while the fitting is being done. At later stages of the making, it holds pieces, seams, etc., securely in place while the permanent stitching is being done.

Begin tacking securely with a knot and double stitch, and tack exactly on fitting line (see **269**). Tacking-stitches and spaces should both be about ¼ in. in length. Fasten off securely with a double stitch.

BASTING is used to secure two pieces (as distinct from edges) of material together, to keep pleats in place or elsewhere where there is no strain. **270** shows just how it is worked.

80

How to get Accurate Fit

As soon as the material is cut out and pattern-marked, the various parts are pinned and tacked together for fitting. Here are some tips that will help the home dressmaker to get a professional fitting to the coat or dress that she is making at home.

If the back of the bodice and skirt hang in wrinkles as shown in **271**, it is because the shoulders of the wearer are rounder than the average. Let down the shoulder seams at the front as much as possible, then unpin the side seams and lift up the back of the garment, at the same time dropping the front. Re-pin and cut away a little of the material from under the arms at the back. The front of the bodice will now be a little longer than the back (see **272**) and this extra length is trimmed away until it is level with the back. **273** shows the alterations in detail.

Should the garment hang in wrinkles as shown in **274**, unpin the bodice seams, lift up at the shoulders, make a dart at each underarm of the bodice front and re-pin (see **275**). The back of the bodice will now be a little longer than the front and the lower edge is cut away until it is level with the front. **276** shows the alterations in detail.

When the bodice of a garment wrinkles under the arms as shown in **277–278**, unpin the bodice seams and smooth the wrinkles upwards from under the armhole at both the back and the front. Lift the shoulder seams, at the shoulder ends, and gradually slope them up at the neck end. Arrange a lower armhole as shown by the pins in **279–280**, cut away the superfluous material and re-fit and you will find that the wrinkles have disappeared.

If the waist of a skirt is too big, the sides of the skirt will drop and any pleat or flare is thrown out of line and looks like **281**. To remedy this, lift up the sides of the skirt at the seams and make two short darts about 3 or 4 in. long. Trim off the top edge until it is level (see **282**) and you will find that the skirt and the pleats now hang correctly.

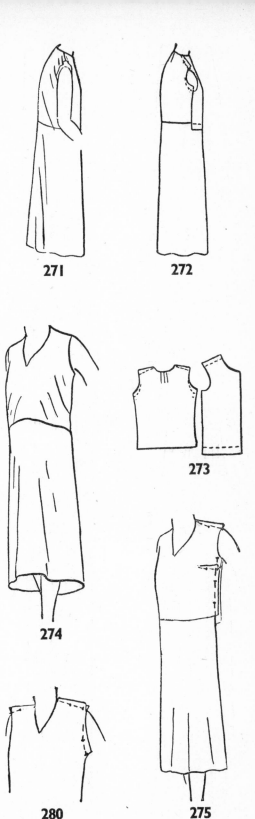

271   272

273

274

275

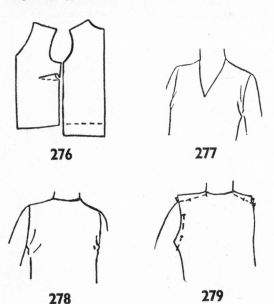

276   277

278   279   280

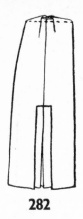

281

282

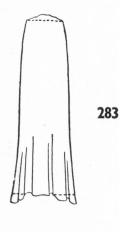

283

287

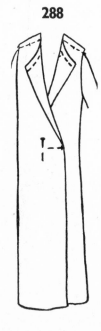

288

Accurate Fit *(continued)*

A flared or circular skirt always drops a little—and it is better to arrange that this happens before the bottom edge is fixed. So, as soon as the side seams are joined, hang the skirt (or dress) on a hanger and leave for a night, or longer, if you have the time to spare, so that the flare can drop. Then the bottom is levelled up as suggested in **283** and the top is lifted at the centre back and front as indicated by the dotted lines in the diagram.

SLEEVES. Before fitting sleeves, the seams are pinned or tacked. Then the sleeve is pinned into the armhole, with the sleeve notches placed to the corresponding notches in the armhole itself. If the sleeve length has to be altered, the alteration must be made at armhole or wrist, the elbow easing to be kept in its correct position. Bend the arm whilst fitting a sleeve, to make sure that there is ample room to bend the elbow comfortably. If the sleeve hangs in wrinkles in front, as suggested by **284**, the back of the sleeve has been set too far to the front and needs re-setting more towards the back. If the sleeve hangs in wrinkles at the back, as in **285**, then it has been set too far towards the front and needs to be readjusted. **286** shows the correct position of the sleeve in the armhole—the straight of the material (i.e. grain of the material) must be in a straight line from the shoulder to elbow.

COATS. If the coat fronts fall away, as suggested by **287**, lift them up from the bottom, and pin the fronts into the position half-way up the coat—as the pins suggest in **288**. Then unpin the shoulder seams and lift the coat fronts until they hang correctly. Re-pin the shoulder seams, which will now be a little deeper at the neck end, and cut away the superfluous turnings. Then cut off from the top of the rever almost the same amount of material that has been lifted at the shoulders—as suggested by the dotted lines in **288**. Re-pin and fit, and you will find that the coat now hangs splendidly.

284

285

286

Tailor Tacks and Tacking

Tailor tacks, as well as trace wheeling, tacking, or chalking, are used to mark the lines and signs of the pattern on to the under portion of the material which is lying folded double for cutting out. In the case of sections with uneven sides, which are cut out singly, tailor tacks are not required. The loops must be placed close along the outline of the pattern, which must first be pinned to the material, or on the chalk line if the pattern has been marked out in chalk. Along straight edges the loops can be spaced more widely, but along curves or sawtooth lines they should be very close together. The loops must not be longer than $\frac{3}{5}$ in. Pull the two parts apart as far as the loops will allow and cut the long threads, which will now be in between the two sections, through the middle. Cut the threads along the outer edges first, then very carefully those towards the centre, shoulder pleats, waist darts, etc., without pulling out the tailor tacks. The important signs which indicate how the various sections fit together are marked with a few loops across, if these signs are on the outside. Be careful when cutting the threads. Signs towards the centre of the pattern which are intended to show a joint are transferred with a single stitch.

(Cont. on p. 85)

289

289. FOR TAILOR TACKS use a long double thread. Begin without a knot and draw out the needle after each stitch.

290. The two cut edges are pulled apart as far as the loops will permit. This produces long stitches which must be cut in the middle, so that cut-thread ends remain in each section.

291. The length of the tacking-stitches will depend upon their purpose. Make them $\frac{1}{2}$ in. to $\frac{3}{4}$ in. long for straight single seams, $\frac{1}{4}$ in. to $\frac{1}{2}$ in. long for curved edges, edge stitching, or for trimming or drapery lines.

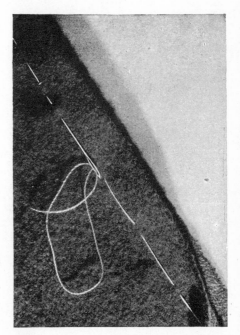

291

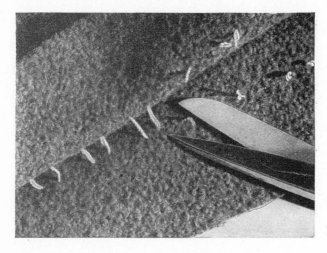

290

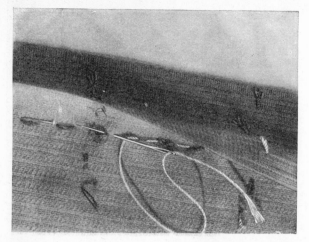

292

293

292. Following the tailor tacks, the sections are pinned together from the inside and tacked exactly in the line of the tailor tacks.

294

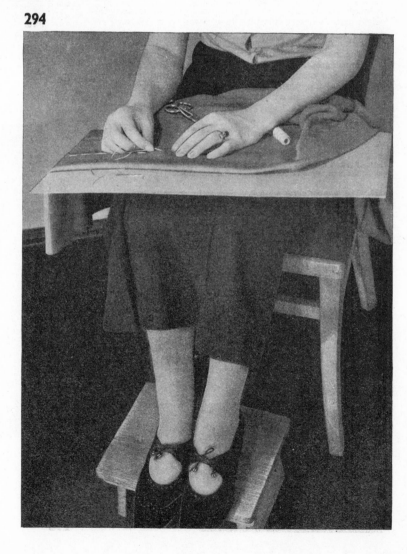

Seams which have been tacked on the wrong side with ordinary tack-stitches, or which have been slip-stitched on the right side, may be lightly pressed open or flat before the first fitting. This will give an excellent idea of the complete garment. The turned-in and tacked edges of onsets, however, must be pressed before they are tacked to the material which will come underneath (see 295).

Large sections may be tacked together sitting down, but it is better to do it standing up in front of a large table upon which the sections have been spread out flat. As a general rule all tacking should be done on a firm surface upon which the hands can rest. Don't work in the air! The material is bound to be pulled awry. If small sections or hems are to be tacked, a knee-board may be used as shown in 294.

If you are working upon your lap, keep your feet close together on a footstool. Never cross your legs or draw up your knees, and above all, sit straight! Then even long hours with the needle will not make your back ache.

296. SLIP TACKING carried out on the right side is used to join up two sections exactly in accordance with shape, grain, or pattern. The needle takes up a few threads in the turned-in edge of the upper part and a few in the part underneath.

297. About 2 in. should be allowed for skirt hem turnings. They are tacked through from the right side. If the length of the skirt has been determined, the hem is tacked or pinned up. The edge is not turned in.

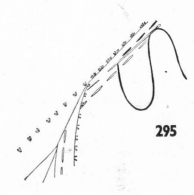

295

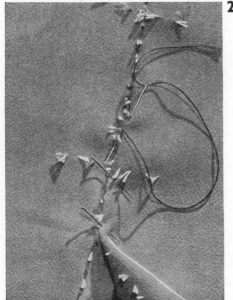

296

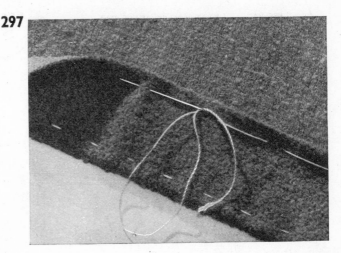

297

The First Fitting

Alterations which will frequently have to be made

1. Looseness in the shoulder seam and along the edges of the armhole, folds, puckering, etc., are caused by sloping, rounded shoulders. To remedy this, the shoulder parts will have to be lifted; that is to say, after the tacking threads have been removed, the edges of the shoulder parts are taken up as much as may be necessary to enable the front and back sections to lie flat. The shoulder seam is now pinned so as to come to a point at the neckline. It may also be necessary to alter the front dart by deepening it towards the shoulder seam. These alterations can only be made if sufficient allowance has been made for turnings at the armhole.

2. If the bust is large, the front dart will have to be very carefully worked. If it has not been laid deep or long enough, cross-puckering will occur at the sides. There is no remedy unless sufficient turning has been allowed at the armhole and side seams. Unpick the shoulder seams, darts, and side seams. The darts must be fitted and pinned first; then the shoulder seams are tacked again, the side seams adjusted, and the armholes dealt with last of all.

3. Where the shoulders are exceptionally straight, the shoulder seams must be lifted at the neckline. The neck-opening is thus reduced in size and will have to be cut out afresh.
Generally speaking, the shoulder edges of back and front sections must be lifted by the same amount. If the back is round, however, the shoulder edges of the front section will have to be lifted rather more than those of the back sections, and vice versa where the bust measurement is considerable.

298

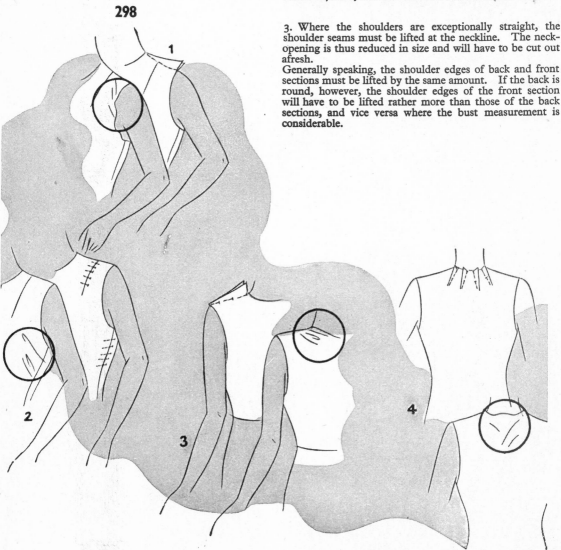

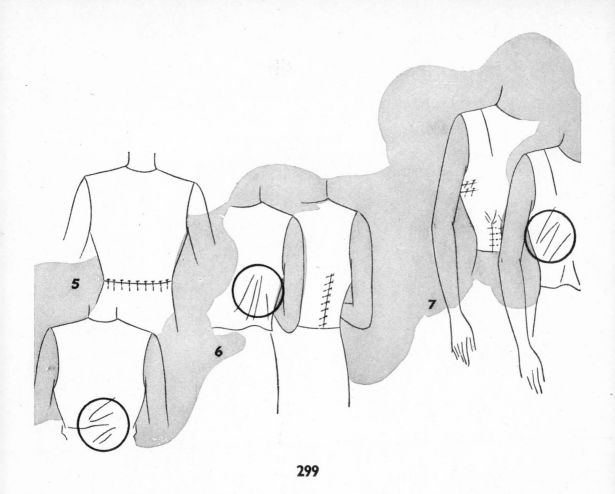

299

4. A round back requires back pleats or darts. The same means will remedy a neckline which does not lie closely enough. Begin by pinning a single deep pleat, and then distribute its width among four or five small pleats.
If the neckline has been cut out too deeply, it can only be altered by lifting the shoulder edges of front and back sections an equal amount. Ample turnings, particularly at the lower bodice edge, are required for this alteration.

5. Cross-folds at the waistline of the back section have a tendency to form on the so-called "hollow back." In a one-piece princess shape they may be removed by putting in a dart at the waistline coming to a point fairly near the side seam. Alternatively the seam which joins skirt to bodice must be placed a little higher up.
If a dress cut in a princess shape has a tendency to "drop" a little at the sides, the necessary adjustment can be effected by placing cross-darts at the height of the waistline. These should come to a point about 4 in. to the front and the same distance to the back of the side seams.

6. The insertion of darts will result in a snug-fitting back section. The darts are placed about $3\frac{1}{2}$ in. to 4 in. to each side of the back centre and are carried about half-way up the back. In princess-shaped frocks or in joined-on skirts they may be continued below the waistline. These darts, as

well as the similar ones often inserted in the front, are suitable only for slim figures. In the case of fuller figures the bodice should be "bloused" slightly; this is done by gathering the bodice a little at the waistline, or by putting in a few short pointed pleats.

7. Where the bust measurements are very considerable, deep bust darts alone will not achieve a faultless fit. Cross-darts under the arms, however, will lift the front sections far enough at the side seams to remove all cross-wrinkles and folds. The width at the waistline is taken up by two pleats which should open out below the bust. In this way an excellent shape can be obtained without making the bust too prominent. A well-fitting dress hides the shape better than a loosely-fitting one would.

8. Skirts will often drop a little at the back, and shortening the hem will not remedy this. The skirt must be lifted sufficiently to straighten out the lower edge, so that the back section hangs perfectly and without folds. This lifting will also improve a skirt which reveals the shape of the wearer too candidly. It is hardly necessary to mention that a skirt will not fit well unless there is ample width at the back, which is taken in at the waist by darts. If you find on fitting that there is not this sufficient width, then you will have to let out the side seams.

The Order of Work
when Finishing Off the Garment

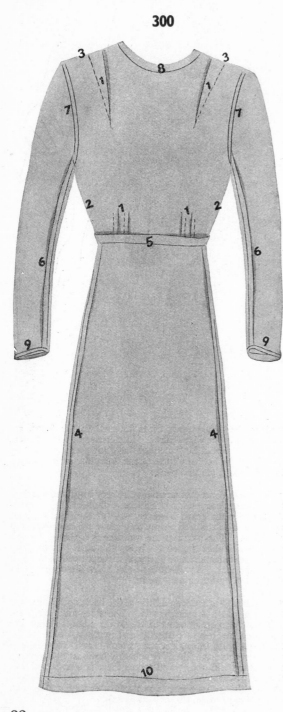

300

A correct sequence in carrying out the work is important if the work is to be satisfactory. Every pattern tells you where to begin with the sewing and how to finish the work. Press frequently as you go : that rule is as important in needlework as in dressmaking.

1. Stitch darts and pleats in the front and back sections and at the waistline of the skirt. Remove tacks and press.

2. Stitch side seams, remove tack threads, and press. Bind the seam edges or turn them in. Overcasting may be left until the final neatening is being carried out.

3. Stitch shoulder seams and remove tack threads. In very thin materials, close the seams with the edges turned in and stitch or run them together. Press in the direction of the back section. In thicker materials, press open the shoulder seams and finish off as above.

4. Stitch skirt seams, remove tack threads, press, and finish off the seams as above.

5. Stitch skirt to bodice and remove tack threads.

6. Stitch sleeve seams and darts, remove tack threads, and finish as above.

7. Set in sleeves and bias-strips and fell over.

8. Finish the neckline, and

9. Finish sleeves at wrist. In both cases bias-strips are stitched on right side to right side and hemmed over on the inside.

10. Hem skirt, press seams and hem, attach the trimmings, and last of all, press the whole garment.

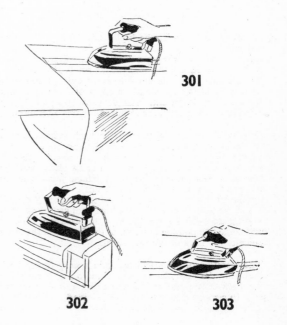

301

302   **303**

Shoulder Darts

There are many possible ways of taking in at the front shoulder edge the fullness required for the bust, and it is always necessary to choose the correct one according to material and figure. Usually the pattern will only indicate " dart," but this may be altered to suit the case. For light, soft-falling materials, short pleats, opening out at the lower end, will generally be preferred to a severe, closely moulding dart. If the figure is tall and very slender, then a close-fitting model should also be avoided—a graceful fullness, such as is produced by pleats or gathers that open out, will make the figure appear more rounded, and if the figure is an outsize one, then it is better to conceal its shape beneath a loosely hanging dress than to make it more obvious by moulding the garment closely. It is only in the case of dresses, coats, and jackets made of heavy woollen materials that the simple dart is always right.

Darts and pleats must, if looked at from the inside, always lie turned towards the front, and this should be borne in mind when tacking the shoulder seams together. The pleats or darts should not be caught in the tacking of the shoulder seams, so that there will be no difficulty in stitching them along their whole length after the fitting. If, however, they should get caught inadvertently in the tacking of the shoulder seams, the tacking threads will have to be removed later on when stitching wherever necessary. This can be avoided by a little care at the beginning.

308 shows pleats and shoulder seams after pressing. The simple dart may be pressed in three different ways, as shown in the illustration; firstly, towards the front, when the seam appears to be pressed over to the right side and remains

304

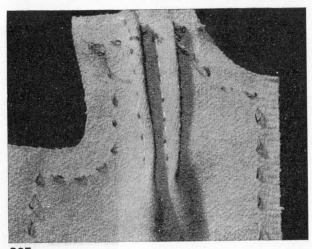

305

306

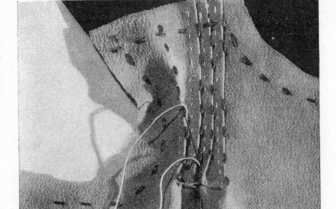

304. The point of the dart must be worked with particular care. It should be reduced gradually to nothing, so that it merges almost unnoticeably into the smooth portion of the material.

305. A considerable degree of fullness at the front shoulder edge is better and more evenly distributed in two pleats. The pleats open out half-way down; the seams must be absolutely parallel.

306. In very thin materials four to five narrow tucks equal in width should be used to distribute the fullness; they serve at the same time as a very pretty trimming. The little tucks must be carefully executed and should be stitched on the inside.

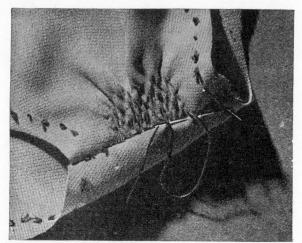

307

visible. The second, which results in a flatter and less visible seam, is to press it straight down, so that the seam remains in the middle of the dart (309). This is the best method for medium heavy woollens. In the case of heavy materials the third method is used ; the dart is cut open and pressed flat.

When pinning shoulder seams and side seams together on a tailor's dummy, the turnings of the back sections are always pinned over the turnings of the front sections and are tacked on with slip-stitching. But if a well-fitting pattern is used, the sections may be tacked together on the wrong side following the indications on the pattern.

307. THE SHOULDER EDGES may be taken in by shirring or gathering, either over the whole width or only in the middle, as desired. The ends of the gathering threads must be well secured on the inside.

308

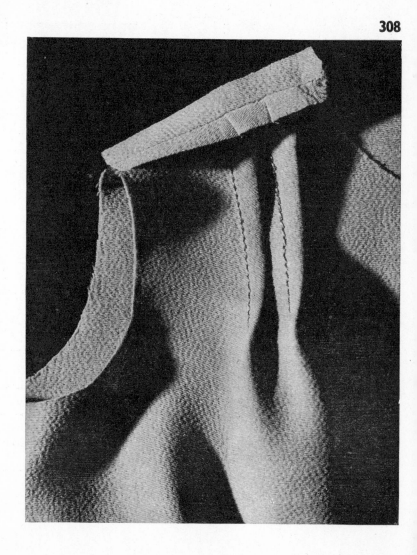

309

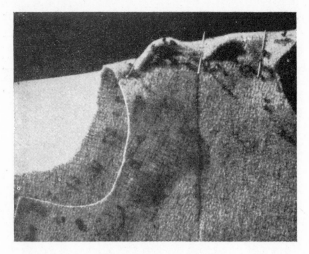

310. Here the still-remaining fullness of the back shoulder edge has been evenly distributed by pinning, so that no folds are formed when tacking together.

311. IN THICK MATERIALS, coats, and jackets, the dart must be cut open and pressed out so that it does not bulge too much. The point remains uncut and must be pressed down flat.

311

Well-fitting Sleeves are achieved by Correct Preliminary Work

A cross tacked into the cloth to mark the run of thread is a help later on when setting in the sleeves. Beginning at the highest point of the sleeve top, tack a thread downwards in a straight line and another across the middle. The sleeve will later have to be set in in such a manner that the down thread runs in exactly the same direction as the

312

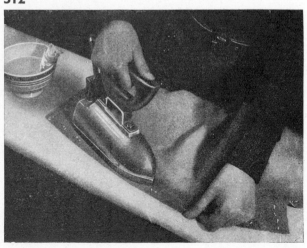

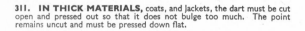

313

312. THE INNER SLEEVE EDGE must be stretched at the place marked on the pattern. The material should be well dampened with a rag before pressing.

313. THE OUTER SLEEVE EDGE must be eased. It is pinned over the inner edge and tacked with slip-stitch. The sleeve seam must show a slight curve.

shoulder seam. Directions for stretching on the front edge, and for easing on the back edge of the sleeve top are always marked on patterns showing one seam and two seam sleeves, and must be followed (314 a). The front edge is dampened in the middle—just where it will " give " least—and is stretched by continuous pressing until it becomes rounded. The dampening must be done on the wrong side of the material. A short gathering thread is run into the back edge where it is to be eased and the fullness removed by pressing, or alternatively two or three darts may be put in to reduce the fullness. The turnings must be snipped where they are too tight (314 b, c, d) so that the seam can be well pressed out. This makes the material give and the seam lie flat, otherwise it would be drawn in and become too tight. To finish the sleeve seams the notches could be overcast closely and neatly to prevent the material fraying. If all the seams are to be bias bound, the notches should first be overcast.

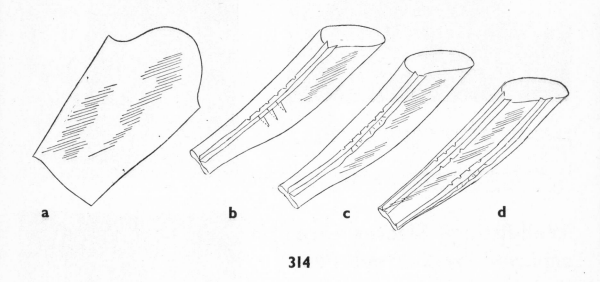

a   b   c   d

314

The Sleeve is Tacked in and Tried on

If the work is being done with the help of a pattern, the sleeves should be set in in accordance with the directions. For single-seam sleeves it is of the greatest importance that the sleeve seam meets the side seam with absolute exactness. Note the front curve at the top of the sleeve : this enables you to distinguish between right and left sleeve, a thing that is often difficult in the case of a straight, plain pattern. To discover which is which, place the sleeve on the table folded in such a way that the seam forms the centre line of the sleeve. The front edge of the sleeve will then be that on which the top line shows the greater curve.

The sleeve will sit perfectly if it is pinned in on the dummy, since it is then easier to distribute the fullness (which has been allowed for the curve of the sleeve top) than when the pinning is done on the table.

The front and back edges of the sleeve are pinned on the dummy at about the upper third of the sleeve length (315 a). The top of the sleeve is then turned back suffi-ciently so that the lower edge of the sleeve can be pinned from the inside to the lower part of the armhole. The top edge must now be pinned on with the turning folded in. The extra fullness will cause little puckers to form between the pins (315 b) and this can be distributed evenly by means of the gathering thread which has been run round the top edge. The lower part of the sleeve is tacked in on the armhole, the upper part on the sleeve (315 c). When trying on, see to it that there is sufficient freedom of move-ment ; the arm should be lifted and bent (315 d), and if necessary a little width should be let out from the back section and the sleeve.

If the upper part of the sleeve has a tendency to form diagonal folds, the sleeve must be turned round a little to the back and lifted at the front seam (315 e). If the sleeve is tight at the top edge and forms cross folds, extra width must be provided, if necessary, by letting out the sleeve seam (315 f).

92

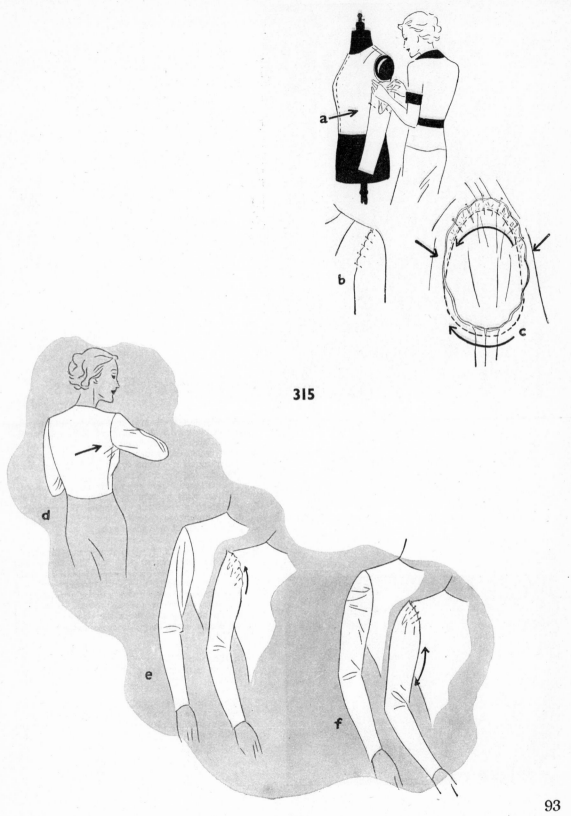

a

b

c

315

d

e

f

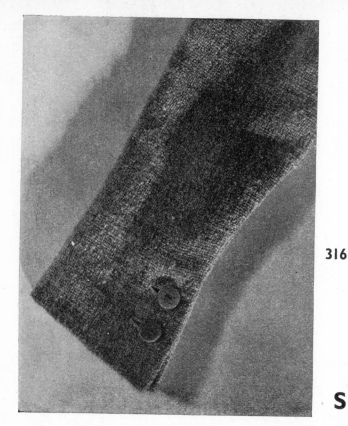

316

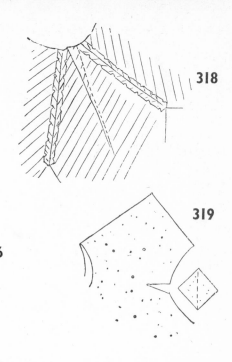

318

319

317

320. THE PUFF SLEEVE must be gathered in at least two rows at the upper edge and the lower edge to take in the width.

320

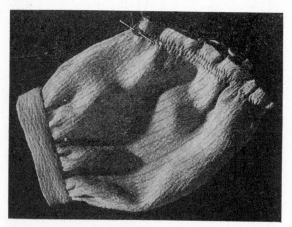

Sleeve Styles

321–323 show the usual sleeve styles apart from the simple blouse sleeve. The puff sleeve approaches the blouse sleeve in shape, but is often cut more than twice the width. The gathers must be closer together in the upper half of the sleeve than in the lower part, near the sleeve seam. The gathered sleeve edge is stitched in between the two rows of running gathers so that these cannot be pushed out of place. The gathering of the lower sleeve edge is held by binding or it can be finished off with elastic.

The shoulders of raglan sleeves may be shaped by a centre seam or a dart. The sleeve and bodice edges are then joined together in the shoulder seams (318). If the turnings are to be pressed open, small snips will be required; if the seam is to be pressed over, the turnings should be pressed towards the sleeve (317), and the sleeve seam and side seam then joined together.

In the case of a kimono sleeve the gusset (319) with its turnings must be 1 in. longer than the slash.

The coat sleeve (316) used for tailor-made costumes has a piece of canvas about 4 in. wide and a cut facing placed at the lower edge and the opening edges.

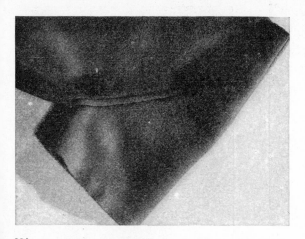

321. THE RAGLAN SLEEVE is set between front and back section before the sleeve seam and the side seam are stitched. The seams may be stitched down.

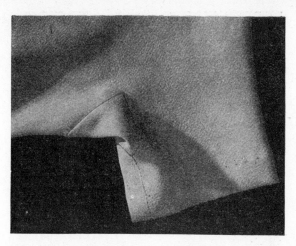

322. IN A KIMONO SLEEVE a square-shaped gusset is set into the lower part of the armhole after stitching the side seam.

323. When stitching in a sleeve, a bias-strip should be sewn on with the same seam and then hemmed over the seam.

How to Stitch in and Neaten Sleeves

The sleeves must be stitched in on the sleeve edge, beginning at the side seam. Care must be taken that the fullness along the upper edge does not cause little folds to form.

The best way to finish off sleeve-seam edges is to bind them with bias-strips (cut from the same material if it is thin, otherwise from silk lining). These bias-strips are stitched on together with the sleeve and may be tacked beforehand on to the armhole. The ends of the strip meet at the side seams. They are joined by a diagonal seam on a straight thread.

After a little practice in sewing it will be found that the strip need no longer be tacked on, but can be laid under when the sleeve is being stitched. The short join in this case will be done last.

The seam edges are trimmed down to $\frac{1}{8}$ in. and the bias-strip is turned in and felled along on the line of stitching. The binding is pressed flat with the point of the iron (see 324). The sleeve seam must be carefully pressed on the wrong side on a cushion, and only round the top edge (the seam should be turned towards the sleeve), the lower half remaining unpressed.

324

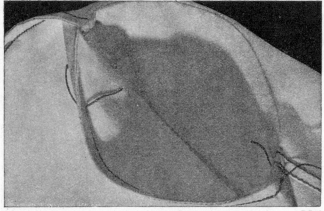

325

326a

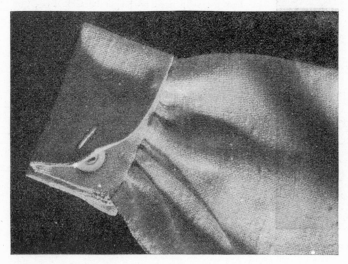

326b

326

325. Having smoothed out the first seam and folded it with the stitching in the fold, the second seam is stitched so as to enclose the cut edges. Blouse sleeves, too, may be set in in this manner.

326. A SLEEVE-SEAM BINDING consists of a strip of material folded double and is stitched on from the inside to the gathered sleeve edge. The upper part of the binding is turned and felled on.

326a. A WRISTBAND is made of material folded double and is stitched to the gathered sleeve edge from the wrong side. The outer edge of the band is stitched over close to the edge.

326b. The lower edges of blouse sleeves are gathered in by a band or double cuff.

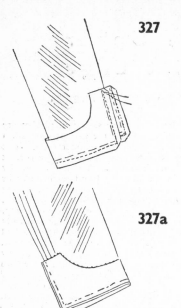

327a

The fullness at the wrist of a straight blouse sleeve must be confined by a band. For this purpose the sleeve edge must be gathered twice, ⅛ in. being left between the two rows of gathers. If the band fits closely round the wrist, then a slit at the back seam will make it easier to pass the hand through the opening (the slit is neatened by facing it with bias-binding or a simple narrow band).

The width of band or cuff may be as desired. Often a double facing ⅜ in. wide, the ends of which are fastened by a button or press-stud, will be sufficient. The cuff, 5 in. wide, is cut out of double material (326a) and is tacked on to the sleeve edge right side to right side. The seam must be stitched upon the cuff. The loose cuff edge is hemmed over. Press the seam flat and the turnover down. Four buttonholes may now be worked in, facing each other in pairs. They are fastened with double buttons.

A close-fitting, darted sleeve is fastened with a button or press-stud in the lower half of the dart, which should be left open. If the dart does not provide sufficient material for the laps, the facing strips must be joined on. A sleeve edge and lap may be finished in one operation by stitching the facing to the sleeve edge, turning it over and felling (327, 327a).

328. THE CLOSE-FITTING SLEEVE with dart may have open edges that meet and are fastened with loops and buttons.

329. Alternatively the fastening may be concealed. If the dart is deep enough it will provide the lap.

330. FOR A PRESS-STUD FASTENING, the studs are sewn on spaced out to 1 in.

328

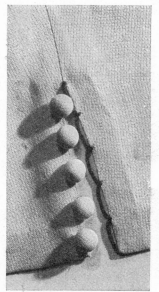

329

330

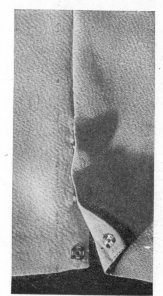

D

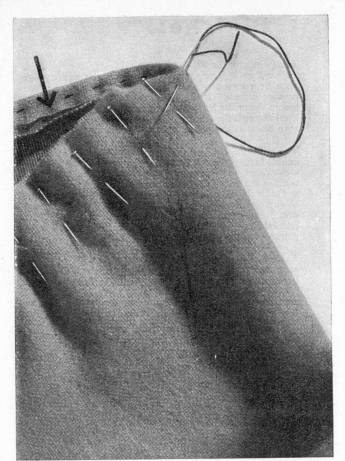

The Upper Skirt Edge

How to secure Pleats

When all seams of the skirt and placket are completed, but before the hem is finished, a waistband is put into the upper edge. The fit of the skirt depends largely on the correct putting on of the waistband. Begin by turning in the waistband and sewing two or three hooks and eyes on to its ends, paying due attention to the waist measurement. Neaten with binding tape or a strip of lining. If the length of the upper skirt edge is already fixed by the pattern or by fitting, the finished waistband may be pinned and tacked on to it, but it is better to put the waistband on, draw over the skirt, and pin it on in accordance with the requirements of the figure. The upper edge is reduced by darts at the back, or it must be taken in at the side. By lifting the skirt, a faulty fit can easily be adjusted. Underlap and waistband finish together at the side-fastening, but on the overlap the waistband must only reach as far as the facing edge.

The method of neatening the skirt edge with single and with double waistband is shown in 331–334.

SKIRT BUTTONED ON TO BODICE. In addition to these various methods of finishing off the upper skirt edge, the stitched-on waistband must also be mentioned. This is tacked on to the skirt edge in such a way that it covers the edge and can be turned in. If the skirt is to be worn with a belt, the upper edge may be topstitched on the right side. Darts in the skirt edge may either be stitched so as to end in a point, or else simply tacked and pressed. The tacking thread must then be removed so that the dart gives to each movement (335).

331. THE SKIRT EDGE is pinned on to the waistband and can then be caught between the double edge of the waistband or neatened by a facing which is felled over.

335. A waistband with woven-in elastic will keep the blouse neatly under the skirt edge. The waistband may be stitched on inside and the skirt edge stitched through from the right side, close along the edge.

336. The inner edges of pleats which do not reach up to the upper skirt edge may be lightly sewn down or held up by binding tapes which join the pleat edge to the upper skirt edge.

333

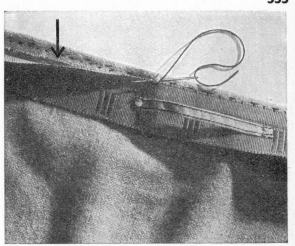

334

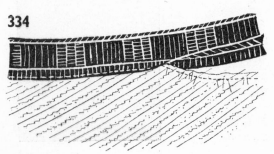

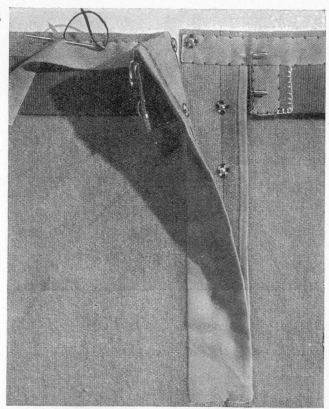

332

Pleats which are open at their upper edge may be fastened with strips of lining or with binding tape (336). By this method there will be no need to turn back the pleat edges, and the pleats will not stick out at the lower hem edge. If strips of lining are being used, these should be cut the same width as the pleat, their long edges hemmed, and the cross-edges sewn to the pleat edge and the upper skirt edge.

A skirt bodice may be sewn on or buttoned on, and may be made of lingerie material or of lining. As bodice skirts are made only for children, or for figures for which close-fitting skirts are not suitable, it is necessary to allow for a comfortable fit by making the skirt edge and the bodice edge a little wider than the waist measurement.

335

336

337

338. The slit, about 6 in. long, may be stitched over with a pleat in order to conceal the placket edges.

338

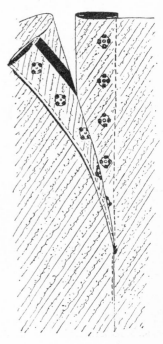

339

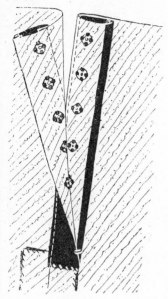

341. For this type of placket the seam must be pressed open and, rather like a slot seam, must be furnished with a strip of material for the under-lap.

The Placket

The side seam is left open to form a placket which is fastened with press-studs. At least ¾-in. turnings are required to provide sufficient width for the underlap and the facing of the upper edge. 339 shows the fastening with the seam pressed open. The facing of the upper edge is bound with a strip of lining which forms at the same time an interlining for the fold edge. By this method the press-studs may be sewn on to double material without catching the outside material. By stitching through the front edge the fastening is given a firmer hold. A strip of lining is set against the underlap. 340 shows how the seam is pressed open and snipped across for the underlap; the underlap reaches beyond the end of the opening. A bar worked across the end of the placket will prevent the latter from tearing.

For the sake of clearness all the plackets illustrated in 338–341 are shown with press-studs. When the placket edges of the skirt have been neatened, the waistband must be put on before the press-studs can be sewn.

344

345

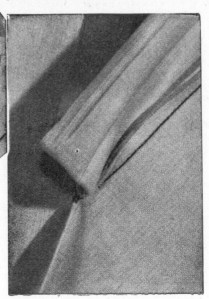

345. SLIT NEATENING. Continuous placket. Apart from binding with bias-strips, this is the simplest and neatest method of finishing slit edges. No stitches will be visible on the right side. Cut a strip of material about 1¾ in. to 2 in. wide and twice the length of the slit. This is stitched all round the slit on the wrong side.

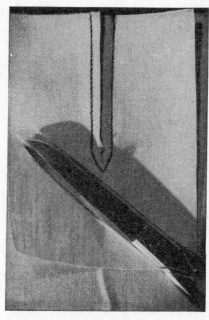

343

343-344. SIMPLE SLIT FACING. Begin by marking the slit with a tack thread. A facing-strip is tacked over which should project at least 1¼ in. to 2 in. on each side and at the bottom end. A row of stitching, about the width of the presser-foot away from the edge of the slit, is worked all round, ending in a mitre at the bottom. The slit is then cut open. The facing is turned and stitched down on the inside or slip-stitched.

342. A slit is secured by facing it with two single strips of material for the overlap and the underlap. The strips are cut about 2 in. wide and a little longer than the slit. They are set on from the wrong side by a single seam, and are stitched over to the right side in such a way as to cover each other exactly. A row of stitching across will secure the end of the slit.

Openings

346

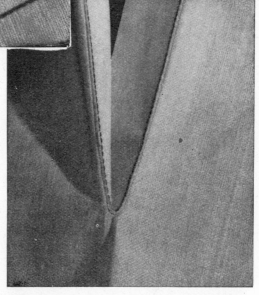

347

347. Make a few small cuts into the seam edge at the end of the slit and turn over. Fold the strip in half lengthways and stitch the turned-in edge over the first seam. The slit edges now overlap and may be held together at the end by a crossbar.

348

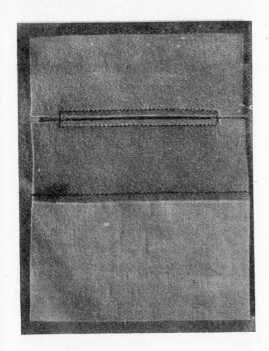

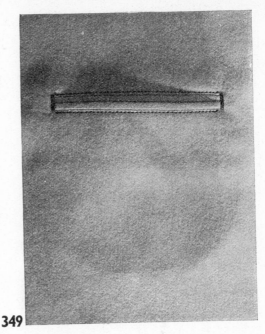

349

350

348. THE BOUND OR PIPED POCKET (also called slot pocket) is made like a bound buttonhole, by setting against it two narrow or one wide bias-strips.

349. After the strips have been turned, the lower pocket edge is edge-stitched. When stitching the upper edge, do not forget to catch on the other half of the pocket.

350. A PATCH POCKET may be finished off plain, or it may have a flap or facing.

Slot or Piped Pockets. Patch Pockets

For a slot pocket the slit is marked and a strip of lining or canvas tacked under ; one wide or two narrow bias-strips are tacked on top, right side to right side. The stitching all round the slit may be brought to a point at the ends or may be worked straight across. The inner binding is lengthened with a piece of lining for the pocket. Cut the slit open, snipping at the ends, and pull the bias-strips through this opening ; these are now like wide pipings. The lower pocket edge is now stitched close along the first seam ; next, the second pocket part, which also consists of material and lining joined together, is tacked under the upper pocket edge and stitched on the right side. Bars are worked to secure the ends of the slit. 348–349 show the outside and the inside of the pocket.

351

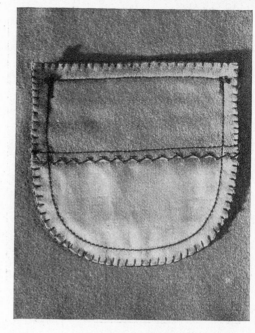

352

352. THE POCKET SECTIONS are rounded at the corners and stitched together. The seam edges are neatened with buttonhole-stitch or bound with bias-strip.

Patch pockets are often lined (351). The turning must be deeper at the top than at the sides or bottom, so that the lining, which is felled on lower down, does not become visible from the outside. On the other sides, too, the lining is not taken up to the edge. In heavy materials the pocket is edge-stitched separately, tacked on, and then sewn by hand from the wrong side with close back-stitches.

353

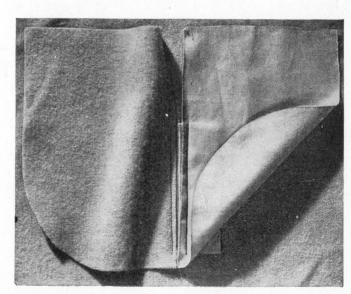

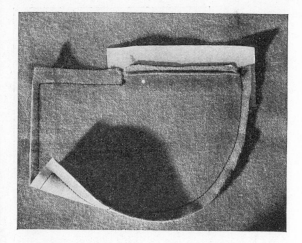

355

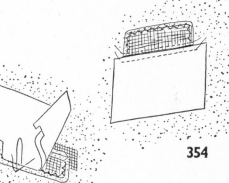

355. The inner part of the pocket section is made of the material if the garment is to be unlined, otherwise of lining faced with a strip of material at the edge of the pocket.

354

356. The cross edges of the welt are fastened invisibly on the right side with slip-stitching, or else secured from the wrong side with small back-stitches.

356

Welted Pockets

The vertical welted pocket requires a special pocket bag. Lining is applied under the opening, and the welt, cut of double material interlined with canvas, is then tacked to its front edge. The pocket sections, made up half of material and half of lining joined together, are tacked on to the right side and stitched on. A slit is now cut between the two rows of stitching and the pocket sections are pulled through it to the wrong side; this causes the welt to lie over the slit. The pocket bag is closed up by a seam. The welt is slip-stitched down at both ends and secured with worked bars.

For a breast pocket on a costume coat the welt is placed horizontally, slightly sloping down towards the front. To give the work a "professional" appearance, the foundation for the welt should be cut of canvas and covered with material, the turnings being catch-stitched down.

The welt is stitched to the lower pocket edge, and one edge of the pocket bag to the upper edge, as shown in the sketches (354). The welt is turned to the wrong side and the facing (this should have been cut on the lower pocket section) is felled on to it. The welt is then turned back to the right side and the side edges are fastened down with long stitches or slip-stitching.

D*

Flap Pockets

The flap, like the welt, must be worked over lining or canvas. If the flap is to be pointed, the material must be turned in carefully at the corners and neatly felled (358). The welt is lined and tacked on to the lined upper edge of the pocket opening. The pocket section, which consists of a bias-strip of material with a set-on of lining, is tacked on to the lower pocket edge. Stitch and cut the slit open, with snips at the ends to form triangles. Turn the pocket section and fold the flap down. Edge-stitch the lower pocket edge. The second pocket section is fastened by stitching it invisibly into the flap seam (see arrow in 361) and joining the sections (see 359).

Patch pockets, too, may have flaps. The flap may be slip-stitched on, stitched on by machine, or stitched on reversed and pushed through a slit. The pleated pocket (362) has the pleat folds sewn fast. The flap is set in; the resulting second slit edge below the flap is fastened to the flap lining with back-stitch.

The ends of every pocket opening must be secured and strengthened by worked bars.

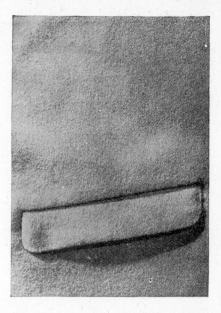

357. The horizontal welted pocket is used chiefly for jackets. Often the edge of the welt and the seam are slip-stitched narrowly.

358

359

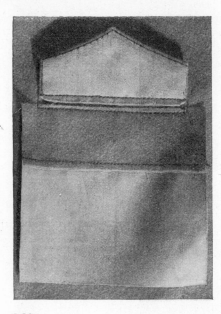

360

360. After the pocket section and the flap have been stitched on, the slit is cut open and slashed in a right angle or cross-snipped at the ends.

361. The line of stitching which secures the pocket section is worked in the seam of the flap and remains invisible. The flap pocket may be closed with a button.

362. This pocket has a box pleat and two inverted pleats. The outer edges remain loose, the fold edges, half an inch deep, are held down with slip-stitches on the inside.

361

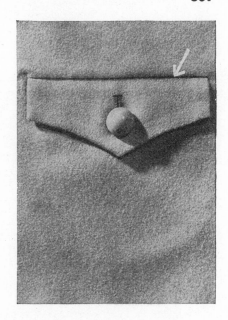

362

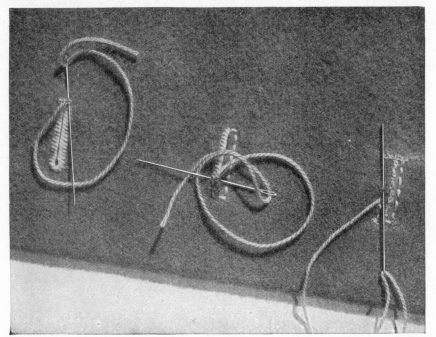

365. Braid in a contrasting or matching colour can be used as a binding for buttonholes to provide a pretty trimming.

363

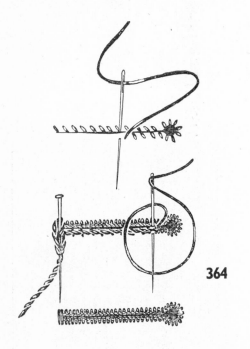

364

365

108

Worked and Bound Buttonholes

There are two kinds of worked buttonholes, the simple and the tailor-made.

The buttonholes are marked out with chalk; they must be evenly spaced and at an even distance from the edge, depending upon the size of the buttons. If the edge is straight they should be so arranged that the button, when fastened, is placed at a distance of half its diameter away from the edge of the garment. In accordance with this rule, the button is placed on the material and its centre (marked with a pin) then gives the end of the buttonhole. The length of the buttonhole, measured from that point inwards, will depend on the diameter of the button.

The buttonholes should always be worked in double material interlined with calico or canvas.

The simple worked buttonhole must be stitched

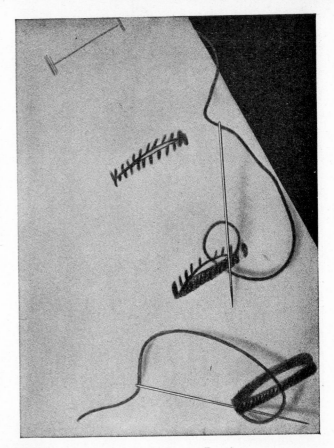

366. BUTTONHOLES are lightly marked out and cut in with buttonhole scissors. The cut edges are overcast and worked. The bars at the ends are made as the work proceeds.

367. BUTTON-FASTENING. Pillow-cases and eiderdown-covers have the fastening at the back. A hem-turning 1½ in. wide must be allowed for when cutting out. The hems are laid one upon the other and stitched together for a distance of about 4 in. from each end. The material is then folded in such a manner that the hems are about 3 in. to 4 in. away from the lower fold edge, and the side seams are stitched. The buttonholes are worked in lengthways in the upper edge, crossways in the lower edge.

366

367

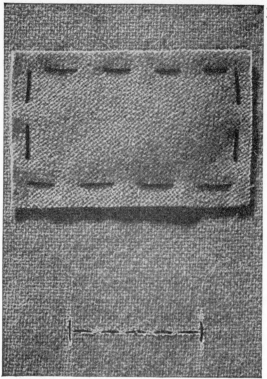

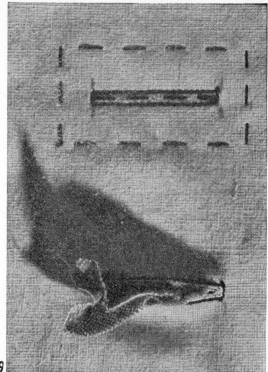

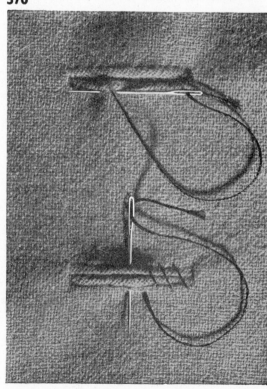

all round to hold together the double or treble material. This stitching must be done by running or by machine; if the slit has already been cut, its edges are overcast. The buttonhole-stitches are worked from left to right; in front, the buttonhole is worked round, and by drawing on the thread more tightly, more space is afforded for the button. The ends of the buttonhole are secured by worked bars.

The stranded or tailor-made buttonhole is first of all cut in. The round hole in front is shaped out with a stiletto or hole pincers, or by cutting it carefully with scissors. The cut edges are overcast together with the " strand," that is, a double strand of linen thread twisted together and drawn through beeswax which is laid round the buttonhole; this makes the buttonhole-stitches very full. The little knots of the stitches must lie on top. The strand should be secured at the barred ends of the buttonhole.

368. A line is chalked to show where the buttonhole should be cut and tacked through to mark it on the wrong side (i.e. on the interlining). The bias-strip for the binding is tacked on to the right side.

369. The buttonhole is machine-stitched about $\frac{1}{12}$ in. away from the tack thread. The tacking is then removed and the buttonhole cut open, the ends being slashed in a right angle, and the bias-strip is then pulled through to the inside.

370. THE BINDING, which is like a narrow edging or piping, is stitched through with tiny back-stitches on the right side in the first seam. Before pressing, the buttonhole should be tacked together by overcasting.

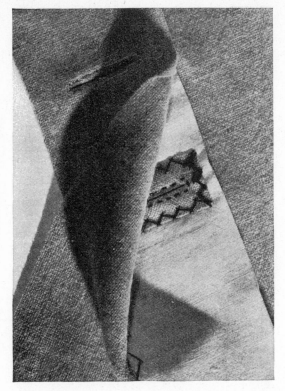

371

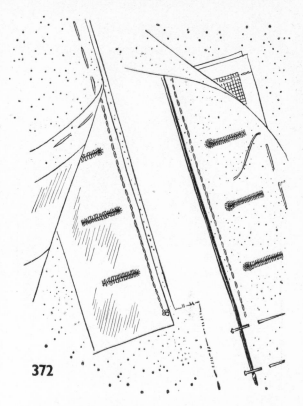

372

374

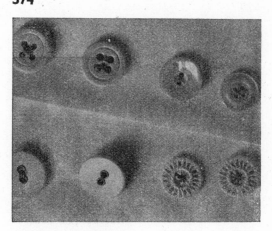

Concealed Fastening.
How to Sew on Buttons

371 shows the last stage in the making of a bound buttonhole. Three points must always be borne in mind : (1) Bound buttonholes always require material, interlining, and a facing. For a single buttonhole a piece of lining should be tacked under. (2) The binding must be cut on the cross. (3) When the facing is being turned, the seam edges must be turned round at the same time ; they should not lie in the edging.

For a concealed fastening, the buttonhole may be either worked or bound. The outer material and facing remain open for the length of the fastening, and each must be supplied with an interlining and a facing. The buttonholes must lie on the upper side of the facing and not on the lining. Lining and interlining are stitched through from the inside 1¼ in. above the top and below the last buttonhole, or, in the case of sportswear, the fastening is stitched through from the right side behind each buttonhole.

Buttons must always be sewn on to double material and must be provided with a stem (373).

371. The edges of the bias-strip are caught on to the interlining. So that the facing may be cut correctly, the buttonholes are marked through from the right side with pins. The facing is felled round each buttonhole.

374. BUTTONS should be held a little away from the material when sewing them on, and the stitches between button and material wound round closely with thread, so that a stem is formed which will leave room for the edge of the garment that is buttoned. The stitches used depend upon the type of button.

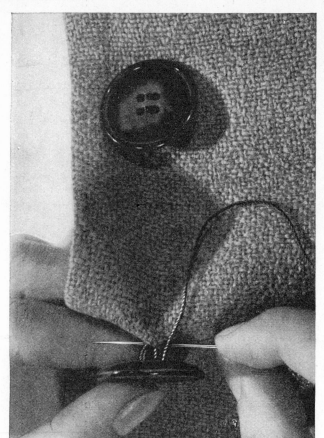

How to Sew on Buttons

The " stem " or " neck," consisting of several long strands closely wound round, which is used to sew on four-hole buttons may, in the case of buttons having only two large holes, be replaced by a strip of material or tape. In 375 such a button is shown fastened with a narrow tubing of material. The tubing (ribbon, braid, cord, or leather may be used instead) must not be larger than the holes in the button. It is threaded through the button, and a hole is pierced through the material at the point where this is to be sewn on ; the ends of the tubing are pushed through this hole, and stitched on flat on the inside (see 377). As in the case of the wound stem, a space must be left between button and material, so that the button will lie flat on the top of the button-hole without pulling it out of shape.

Buttons with a tape or ribbon strap may be caught between a seam (see 378, top).

If the buttons are to be sewn on to single material, another small button or a little piece of material or ribbon should be sewn on the other side of the material under the button (see 378, bottom). This should be done even in the case of purely ornamental buttons.

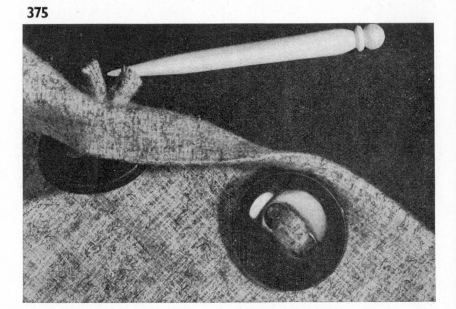

375

376

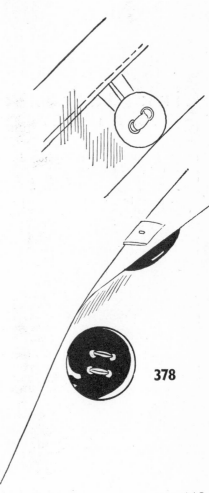

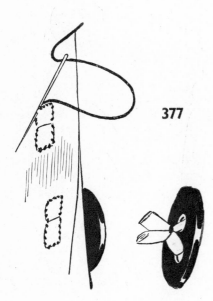

377

378

Link Buttons: Covered Buttons

Link or double buttons are held together by a strip or tube of material, or may be sewn together with a few long stitches closely worked over with buttonhole-stitch (379). If using the latter method, the end of the thread should be knotted on the " wrong " side of the button.

When covering wooden or cardboard buttons, the sections of material should be cut with ample allowance for turnings. In the case of thin materials, the edge is turned in and run through. Thicker material is overcast. The cover is placed round the button and the running thread drawn tight, so that the covering closes up ; the end of the thread can then be secured. The button should be sewn on with a stem or a set-on ribbon neck.

380 shows interchangeable buttons held by a tape passed through the shanks. 381 shows ornamental buttons sewn on with a contrasting thread, and shank buttons which are sewn on without a stem.

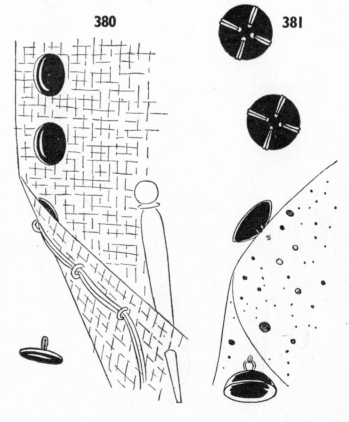

380

381

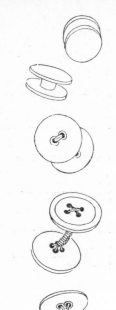

382

383

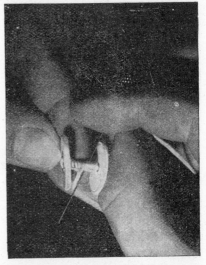

384

384. LINK BUTTONS, which are also used for buttoning bed linen, consist of two buttons joined by stitches about ⅜ in. long. The link is held over the left index finger and sewn over closely with buttonhole-stitches.

385. BUTTON-BANDS to fasten pillow-cases and cushions are made of bed-ticking or linen cut to the required width and length. The adjustable button-band is useful: two tapes are held together by movable tape-loops which are secured in the centre by buttons.

386. ADJUSTABLE BUTTON-BANDS can be purchased in complete sets in various styles.

385

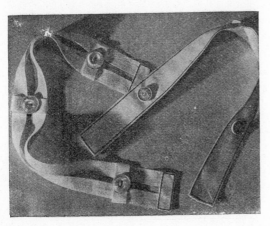

386

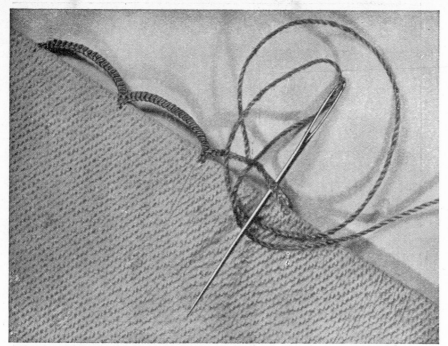

387

387. WORKED LOOPS of sewing silk or buttonhole twist are very frequently used in conjunction with small buttons (on sleeves and slits, for instance).

389. BIAS-STRIPS of thick material are made singly by hand. If the loop is to be sewn on to a coat edge, the ends of the loop are pushed into the seam with a stiletto.

390. In the case of thin materials a bias-strip may be sewn together in one piece, turned inside out, and sewn in loops to the edge of the garment.

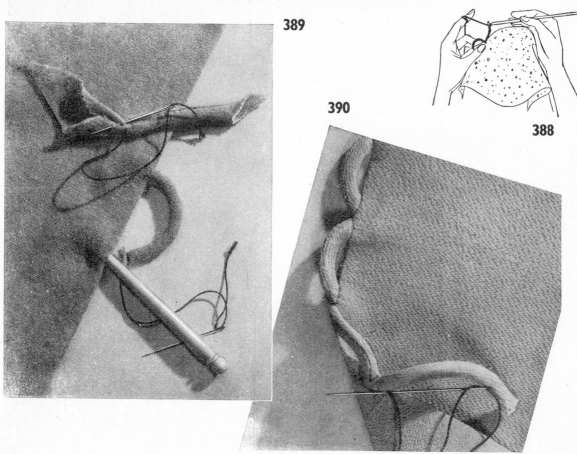

389

390

388

Loops for Button Fastening

If the front edges of the garment overlap, they are held together by buttonhole fastening ; if they meet, loops are used to hold the buttons.

Worked loops of sewing silk or buttonhole twist are set on closely together. Bigger buttons require stronger loops than the small flat buttons, and the number of threads used will accordingly be greater or smaller. The threads are stretched and worked over closely with buttonhole-stitch to render the loop hard-wearing. When stretching the threads it is important that every stitch should sit sufficiently deeply in the material so as to lessen the risk of the loop being torn out.

Crocheted loops will also wear well ; the chain meshes can be strengthened by crocheting them over with very tight meshes. Loops made of bias-strip can be sewn by hand or by machine. Single loops for coats or jackets are usually worked by hand. A bias-strip about ¾ in. wide is turned in as narrowly as possible, the turning forming the filling. The little roll is sewn together by slip-stitching, a double thread being used so that the stitches may be pulled tight. The ends of the roll are secured by winding them round with thread, and are then pushed into the seam edges with the help of a stiletto. If the facing is still open, on the inside of a coat edge, for instance, the loops may be stitched fast on the inside ; otherwise they will have to be stitched on from the wrong side. The size of the loop is tried out with the button. The loop must be flat rather than bulky so that the edge of the opening will lie close to the button when fastened. If a bias-strip is folded in half lengthways and stitched ⅛ in. to ⅕ in. away from the fold, according to the thickness of the material (391), and is then turned inside out, a stitched loop is obtained. The strips must not be made too long or it will be impossible to turn them ; if the material is not very suitable, then each loop should be made separately and stitched on with its ends close together.

392 shows how the loops are stitched on to the outer material and covered by facing.

392

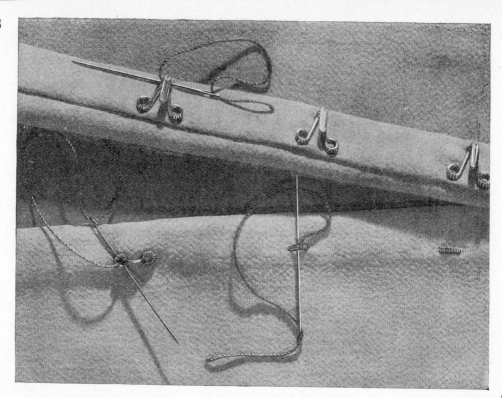

394

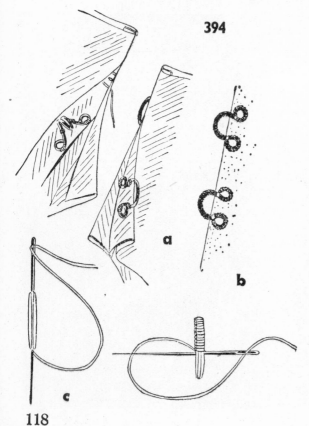

a

b

c

Hooks and Eyes

Hooks are nearly always made in the same shape. Eyes, on the other hand, may be obtained either deep or shallow; in addition, their place is often taken by loops (394 c). 393 shows worked loops and a shallow eye.

The edges of the opening—like all opening edges —must be made of two thicknesses of material. The hooks are sewn on to the overlapping edge, the eyes or loops on to the underlap. The fastening will hold more firmly if the hooks and eyes are placed on each side alternately (see 395). Before they are sewn on, the hooks and eyes should be opened a little. The hooks should be secured not only at the little rings, but also at the front part, just behind the bend, with close overcasting stitches. Hooks and eyes, particularly the latter, should be concealed by covering them with a strip of material (394 a), or they may be worked over and stitched on with buttonhole-stitch (394 b). Both the shallow eyes and the loops are placed on the underlap in such a way as to enable the edges of the opening to overlap properly, whereas the deep eyes must be sewn underneath the edge of the material; in the latter case the hooks should be set back a little so that a close join results when they are fastened.

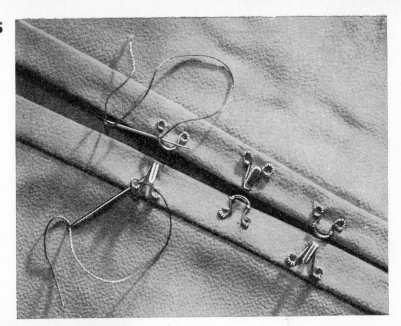

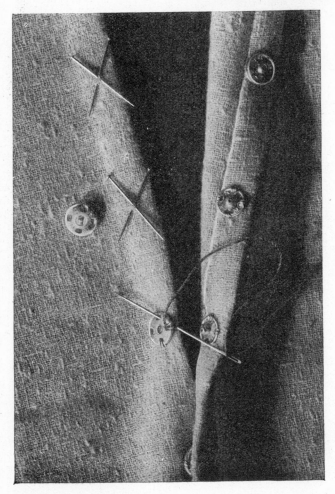

Press-studs

Press-studs, too, may only be sewn on to a double thickness of material. If the lower part of the press-stud has to be sewn on to single material, a piece of tape, lining, or material must be stitched underneath on the wrong side. In order to strengthen the edges of the opening, binding tape may be inserted throughout the length (397). This provides a double-thickness foundation for the press-studs, and there will be no risk of catching the outside material, a thing that may easily happen otherwise in the case of thin fabrics.

The upper part of the press-stud is sewn on first, and the studs should be evenly spaced. It is of the utmost importance that the lower part of the press-studs should be correctly placed ; in order to make certain of this the opening edges are laid the one above the other so that the head of the upper part of the studs touches the material underneath ; two pins are inserted crosswise to mark this point, and when the lower part is sewn on the head must be placed upon it. Another way to ensure exactness is to rub chalk on the heads of the upper part and press them on to the underlap ; quite often pressing alone, without any use of chalk, will be sufficient.

A bar (399) consisting of two or three threads stretched loosely and worked over closely with buttonhole-stitch will strengthen the end of the opening and prevent it from tearing (398).

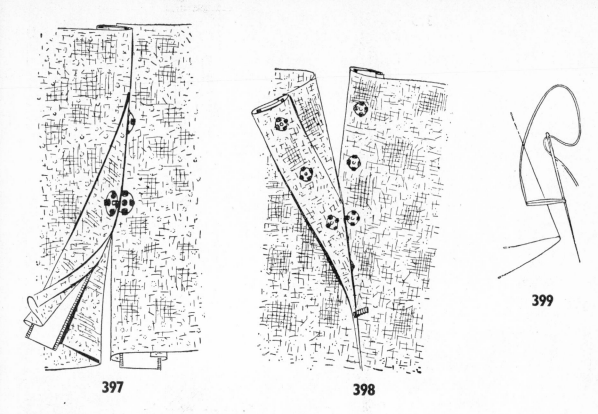

397   398   399

400. LINGERIE HOLDERS may be made of ribbon or material. They hold the shoulder straps together and prevent their annoying tendency to slip down.

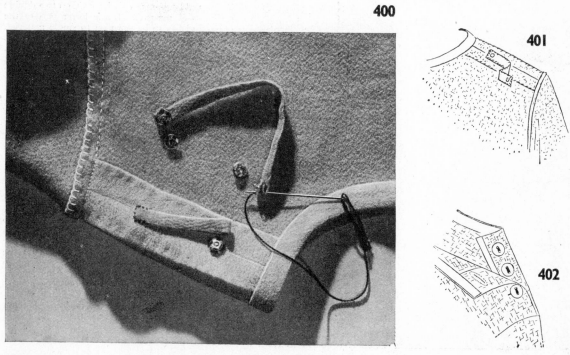

400   401   402

403

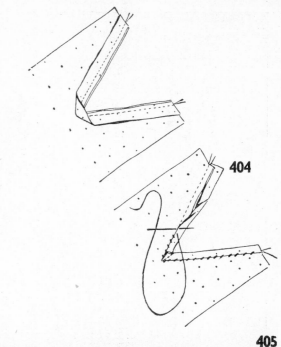

404

405

403. THE SHOULDER FASTENING is placed on the left side—more seldom on both sides. It will take up from $\frac{1}{4}$ to $\frac{3}{8}$ of the shoulder seam, according to the size of the neck opening, and may be fastened in various ways.

405. SHOULDER STRAPS for lingerie are made of ribbon or lingerie material. The strap is made of a strip about $\frac{4}{5}$ in. wide, with its seam in the fold or in the centre. Its finished length must be about 14 in., but to obtain this it will have to be cut about 18 in. long.

Holders for Lingerie Straps; Shoulder Fastening

Every dress and every blouse should be provided with holders for lingerie straps. Those bought ready-made consist of ribbon folded double, the lower part of which is sewn on to the shoulder seam on the inside (401). If you wish to make such holders yourself, use dress material or lining. A strip $2\frac{1}{2}$ in. long is creased in two lengthways and stitched together about $\frac{1}{8}$ in. to $\frac{1}{4}$ in. away from the fold. With the help of a double thread fastened to the turning and a needle it is then turned inside out and pressed. This strip will be sufficient for two holders. The upper parts of two tiny press-studs are sewn on to the neatened ends and the strip is cut in

(Cont. on p. 124.)

406

407. The strap is not sewn on the embroidery, but set on the edge of the material from the wrong side with a reversed seam. It is then folded upwards and stitched once again from the right side, following the outline of the embroidery. The side edges may be sewn on lightly if desired.

408. In dainty lingerie, made of georgette, for instance, the straps should be sewn on at the bottom of the hem. The stitches must not pass right through, but must be placed only in the turning. For greater security the straps can be fastened at the upper edge as well with feather-stitch.

407

408

Shoulder Straps

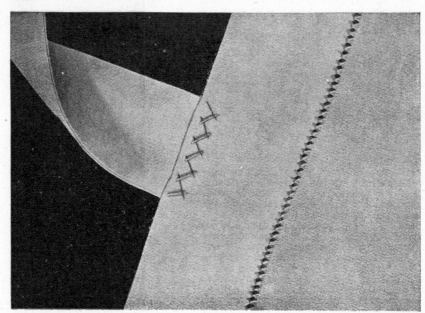

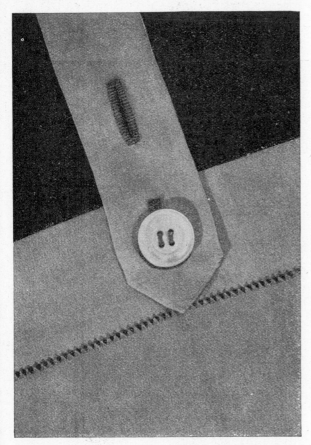

411

Slots for Tape and Elastic

409. The adjustable shoulder strap may button on in front, or if it is to be interchangeable on underslip or brassière, it may be made to button on at both ends. The distance between shoulder straps is usually 8 in. in front and 7 in. at the back.

410-411. If lingerie, a nightdress, for instance, is to have a slot for ribbon, two eyelets must first be worked in the middle of the front at the waistline so that the ribbon can be passed through. Next a strip of material, ⅛ in. to ¼ in. wide, is stitched on to the inside in such a manner that only the two rows of stitching are visible on the right side. The ribbon which is to be passed through must be longer than the slot, so that the ends can be tied into a bow.

409   410

412

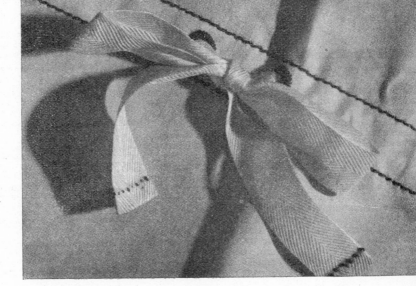

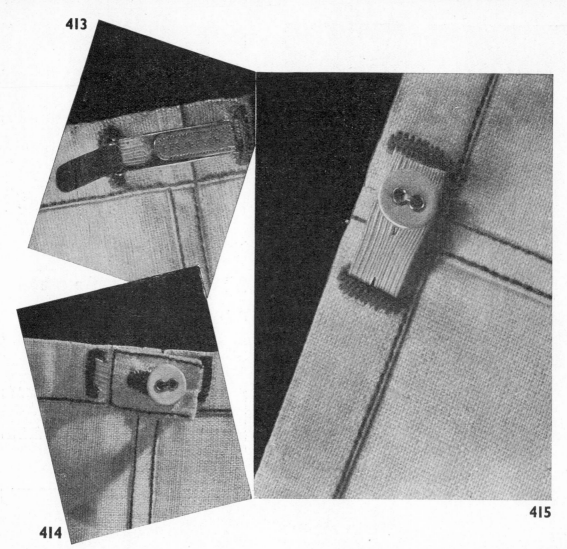

415

414

Holders for Lingerie Straps ; Shoulder Fastening (continued)

half. The cut end of the holder is felled to the middle of the shoulder seam, with the press-stud up towards the neckline (400). Holder and press-stud should be sewn on the turnings.

Dresses and blouses with a high neckline may be fastened on the left shoulder with buttonholes, or loops, and buttons, or simply with press-studs. If the first method is adopted ¼ in. of material will have to be added to the shoulder edge of the back section for the underlap, and to the front shoulder edge for the facing. If press-studs are being used, ½ in. will be quite sufficient, while for a loop fastening only, the underlap for the buttons will be required on the shoulder edge of the back section.

The shoulder seam is stitched up for a distance of about 1 in. from the sleeve line. The open shoulder edges should be prepared for the fastening before the neckline (for inside view see 404) is finished off. The underlap of the back section is faced with a strip of the same material

or lining to match. The seam may form the fold of the facing, which must be pressed down, or—in the case of thick materials—it may cover the edge as a binding. An interlining must be placed into the front shoulder edge for the buttonholes.

413. ELASTIC. If it is not possible to leave open the seam edges so that the elastic can be drawn through, buttonholes must be worked into the hem turning at the side of the seam through which the elastic is passed. A metal clip, which serves at the same time for threading the elastic, is very useful for securing the ends of the tape, particularly in the case of washing blouses.

414. A BUTTONHOLE TAB of material provides another practical fastening for securing the ends of the elastic tape. One end is stitched between a double piece of material into which a buttonhole has been worked. The other end is hemmed and a button sewn on. When the elastic has become slack, it is shortened and the button shifted.

415. Elastic with woven-in buttonholes makes it possible to adjust it to the required size at any time. The buttonholes are woven in about 1 in. apart. Thanks to their elasticity they will stretch to accommodate almost any size of button. Elastic tapes can be drawn in with the help of a bodkin or safety pin.

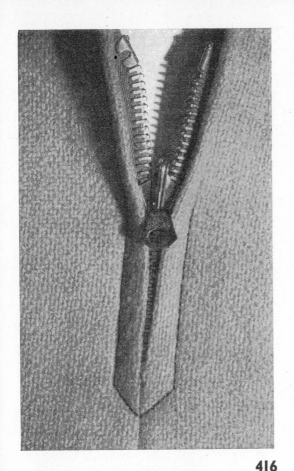

Zip Fasteners

Zip fasteners are obtainable in various lengths, made of metal or coloured celluloid. They may be concealed or remain visible. 417 shows how the teeth of the fastener edges grip and become interlocked as the slide is pushed up. A concealed slide fastener may be stitched under a seam left open for the purpose, or it may be placed under a stitched pleat.

418

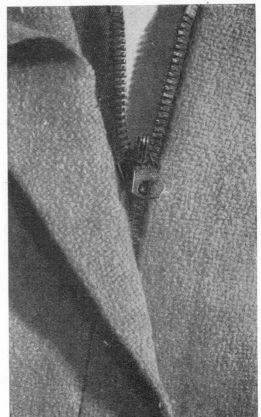

416

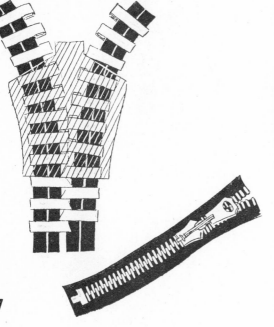

417

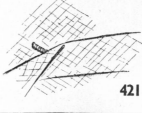

Belt Carriers, Belt Buckles, Belt Loops

Put on the belt to discover exactly where the carriers should be placed. If bodice and skirt are joined together, the belt must cover the seam and the carriers should therefore be fastened above and below the seam. The carriers may be made of buttonhole twist to match the colour of the belt; two or three threads should be stretched and worked over with close buttonhole-stitching.

If material is to be used for the carriers the strips should be cut about $\frac{1}{8}$ in. wide and fairly long, because their ends must be turned in and over when sewing them on (420).

Leather belts may be shortened by moving the buckle and cutting away the leather as required. This leather may be cut into two narrow strips and used as carriers.

To attach belt buckles, the pin is run through about 1 in. behind the end of the belt, the end is folded over to the inside and stitched down (422). A few eyelets are worked into the other end of the buckle, so that the belt can be adjusted as necessary (423).

The belt may also be attached to the dress by French tacks, i.e. worked bars; in which case no carriers will be required.

419. WORKED LOOPS or narrow strips of material stitched together and turned, which are used to keep the belt in place, serve as belt carriers. They should be as long as the belt is wide and must be placed on the side seam.

420

422

421

423

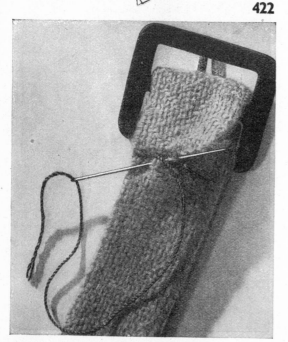

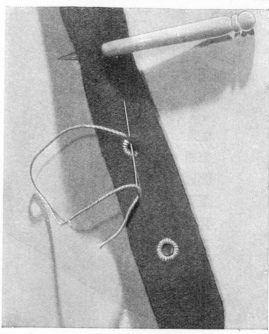

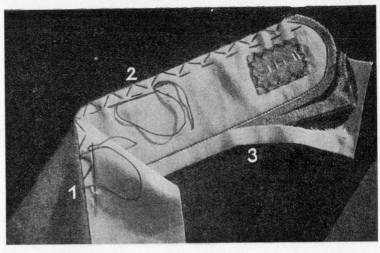

424. Three stages in the making of a cloth belt : (1) the interlining is tacked on along the fold line; (2) the fold edge is tacked through; (3) the seam is stitched, the edges trimmed, and the belt is then turned.

426. Instead of a buckle, a button may be used to fasten the belt. The buttonhole is placed on the right side, the button on the left. Bound buttonholes should be made before, worked buttonholes after, the belt seam is stitched.

Belt with Interlining

Belts may be made of double strips of material stitched together right side to right side and turned inside out. If the material is fairly thick, no interlining of lining or canvas will be required, except in the case of particularly wide belts which need some stiffening. If the material is thin, an interlining will have to be inserted to prevent the belt from folding over or becoming wrinkled while in use. As shown in the illustrations and sketches herewith, a light interlining of muslin, half the width of the belt strip, may be tacked on to the fold line before the belt is stitched together. This keeps the upper edge of the interlining in place, the lower edge being held by the seam. The edge of the interlining must be trimmed away close to the seam, but the turnings of the material, about ⅛ in. wide, remain. The belt is then turned inside out and must be pressed flat with the seam in the fold (425). Incidentally, in all belts the seam should lie in the fold, whether or not any interlining is being used. If the belt is to be made very stiff, tailor-linen or horsehair-cloth should be used instead of the muslin. The outer material may be tacked over the interlining, its edges catch-stitched, and the inner material then tacked on with its edges set back slightly. The inner material is stitched on with slip-stitch and the belt pressed flat. It can be stitched through or left plain.

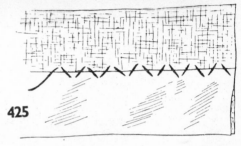

425

426

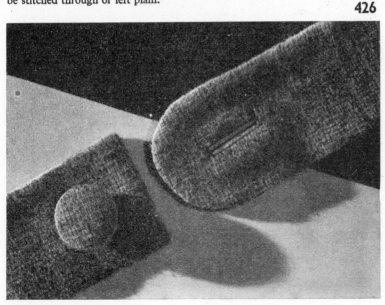

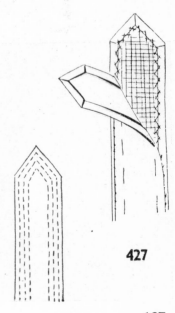

427

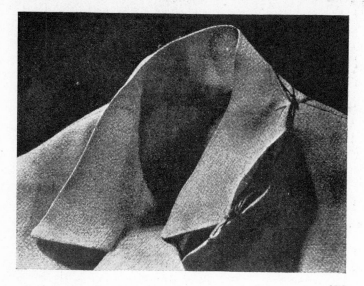

428. COAT COLLARS are stitched on to the neckline from the inside reversed, and felled over on the outside with small slip-stitches.

429. A FLAT COLLAR is stitched on to the neckline from the outside, a bias-strip being applied at the same time.

429

Set-on and Detachable Collars

Collars which are made of the dress material are sewn on fast, while contrasting collars made of light trimming material are usually only tacked in lightly, for easier removal for laundering.

A turn-down collar is made of double material cut straight. The inner edge of the upper portion is pinned and tacked to the neckline from the inside (430). The centre of the collar and the centre of the neckline at the back are marked by pins or vertical tack-stitches, and the collar is placed on the neckline so that these marks meet exactly. The overlapping front edges have to be snipped on the upper cross-edge in accordance with the width of the collar seam; they are then turned in and slip-stitched together. When the collar has been stitched on, the inner portion is turned in and felled over the seam (428). As there are six thicknesses of material at this seam it will have to be pressed very firmly over a damp cloth.

The seam of a stand-up collar must be sewn very neatly from the outside, since there will be nothing to cover it, and felled over on the inside.

When sewing on a flat collar, apply a cross-strip at the same time and fell this over towards the inside.

In the case of a detachable collar, the collar edge and the neckline are neatened with bias-strips.

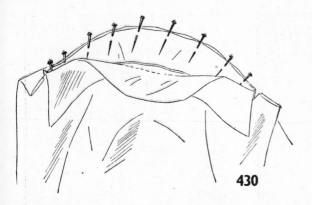

430

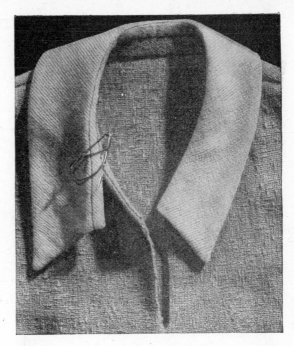

431. In the case of light ornamental collars, collar and neckline are finished off separately. The collar is tacked in for easy changing.

432. FOR PAD-STITCHING, the lapel is covered with interlining and held so that it arches outwards.

431

432

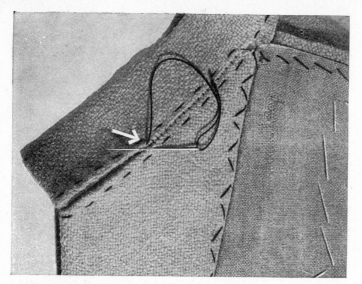

434. **A STRAIGHT COLLAR** may be set on reversed and joined to the lapel facing by slip-stitching.

435

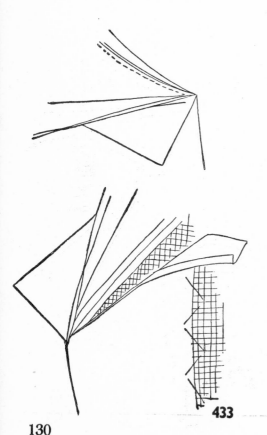

433

Padding-stitch

Jackets and coats are strengthened and shaped by means of interlining which, depending upon the thickness of the dress material, may consist of muslin, canvas, tailor-linen, or horsehair-linen. Just as the material must be " shrunk," so, too, the interlining must be well dampened and pressed to prevent it from shrinking later on if the garment should become damp. Horsehair-linen is the best for preserving the shape of the coat ; when putting it in, take care that the horse hairs which are woven in run across, as in this way they give better support to the material and prevent the formation of folds lengthways. The cut edges of horsehair-linen may be secured with strips of lining tacked over to prevent the hairs from piercing the material.

For pad-stitching, the material and interlining must not be tacked together within the width of the lapel. Hold the lapel in the left hand and draw the material with the index finger towards the hand, at the same time pushing the interlining with the thumb away from the hand. Thus, if the material is held " short," the lapel will " roll " over by itself. The pad-stitching is begun a little way behind the crease-line of the lapel, which is always marked in the pattern. Stitch straight down through the interlining, taking up just the inner surface of the material, so that only tiny dents are visible on the outside of the material.

To prevent the outside edge and the crease-line of the lapel from stretching, a stay-line $\frac{1}{8}$ in. wide is sewn along these edges and over the crease-line before the facing material is set on.

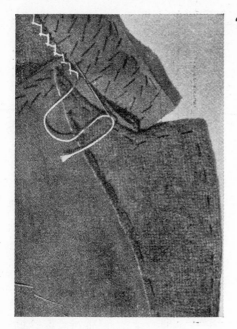

436

437

433 and 434 show the simple straight collar. The under portion of the collar is set on reversed and the upper portion joined to the edge of the facing by closely slip-stitching the fold edges together.

The shaped collar consists of under portion and interlining (both cut on the bias and with the seam in the middle), and a straight seamless upper portion. Under portion and interlining are basted together and pad-stitched. The direction of the stitches is determined by the division of the original collar shape into a standing-up portion (from inner edge to fold) and a fall-over portion (see 438). With the stitches across the stand-up portion, the collar may be held in a little and will therefore fit more snugly round the neck; the outside edge of the fall-over portion, on the other hand, must be stretched if it is to lie well. The turning of the inner edge of the under collar is tacked over and sewn with slip-stitch from the outside to the neckline and the edge of the facing (435). On the inside the seam edges are sewn with catch-stitch to the interlining. The under collar is bent over in the fold and the outer collar tacked on following the bend. Collar and facing are joined by slip-stitch. The seam edges of the back section, with that part of the collar which is joined to it, are covered by the lining which is felled over. The outside turnings of the upper collar are turned and the open edges sewn on with feather- or herringbone-stitch (437). By this method the collar will lie perfectly flat after pressing without the seam edges marking through.

Tailored Coat-collar

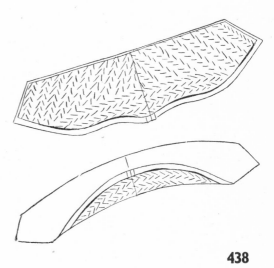

438

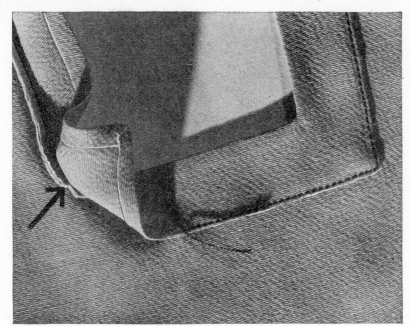

439. SQUARE NECKLINES may be finished with shaped facings or with bias-strips. They are either set inside as a binding, or on the outside to be top-stitched.

441. A V-NECK must be bound or faced with a bias-strip, the ends of which are joined by a diagonal seam in the point of the neckline.

441

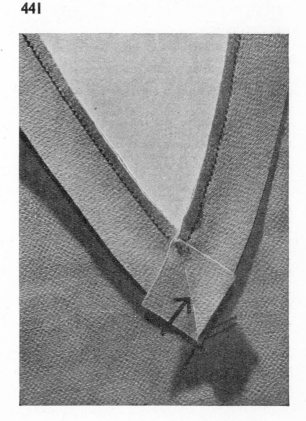

Neckline Finishes

Bias-strips are suitable for neatening all necklines. They are set on reversed, and, in the case of a square neckline, mitred at the corner, and after turning hemmed on with slip-stitch (440). In the case of round, and also of square necklines, shaped facings may be used. They are cut to shape with the help of the paper or a transferred pattern and should be about $1\frac{1}{4}$ in. to $1\frac{3}{4}$ in. wide; the same turnings must be allowed as on the neckline. The shaped facings for front and back sections are joined by shoulder seams. If the facing is to be top-stitched, it is set on reversed on the wrong side and turned to the right; if intended to be invisible, it is set on on the right side and turned to the wrong side. Before a shaped facing is turned it must be slashed; in the case of a square facing, at the corners, or in the case of a round neckline, where the curve is deepest. In the case of V-necks, the most important thing is a faultless execution of the front point (441–442).

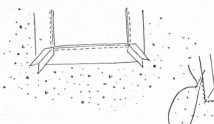

440

442. When turning over the bias-strip, the seam must lie in the fold so that the binding is not visible on the right side. It is hemmed on with fine, invisible slip-stitches.

443. SLIT OR SLASH OPENINGS are neatened by facing them. The edges of the facing remain loose, the corners only being caught on lightly.

443

442

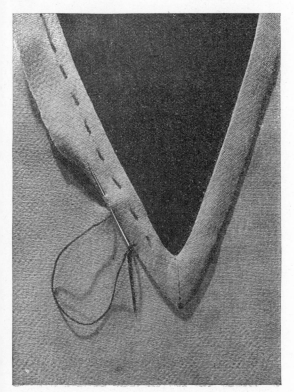

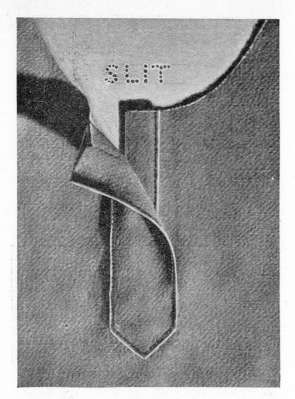

444

444. SLIT EDGES may also be furnished with a covered fastening. Straight strips of material are set either against or on the edges of the slit, depending on whether they are to be top-stitched or hemmed over.

Slit Facing: Covered Slit

443 shows a slit facing which was set on to the edges of the opening by a reversed seam, seen from the inside. If a piece of material sufficiently wide for the whole facing is not available, two pieces may be joined together by a short middle seam, which need only be as long as the projection of the facing below the slit. The width and length of the facing must always be sufficient to allow the material at the sides to reach over the neckline to the shoulder seam, where it can then be fastened. The edges of the facing are neatened by a simple hem, or just by stitching them over.

If the slit edges are to be neatened merely by binding, a bias-strip is stitched on from the right side ; this should be held in a little at the end of the slit. The hemming over must be done with the greatest care at this point.

For a covered slit (444) a narrow strip is stitched on for the underlap, another strip somewhat wider and longer for the overlap (445). To facilitate the turning of the set-on strips, a short cross slash should be cut in at the end of the slit.

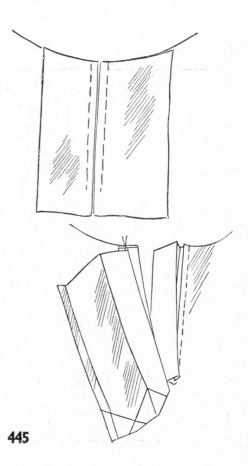

445

134

448

446

Bands. Bows

Narrow strips of material cut on the bias, straight, or to shape, and which may consist of single or double material, are called bands. They may be sewn on by hand or by machine, and are used for ornamental purposes, generally as an edge finish. Bands may be cut of the same or a different material, in a matching or a contrasting colour. Belts may be plaited with narrow bands about ½ in. wide (446). Four or more of these bands are crossed at one end and stitched together, then pinned to a firm surface. One-third to one-half of the length of the bands is lost in the process of plaiting.

In addition to the tied bow, there is a large variety of ornamental bows which are sewn. Large stiff bows, such as the one shown in 447, are often worn. To make this, double material, or material and lining, and in addition an interlining of gauze, canvas, or horse-hair linen, or alternatively of some soft material such as flannel or duvetyn, are required. 448 shows the three layers of material, which are stitched together by a reversed seam. Several rows of stitching will stiffen the edges; a bias band in the shape of a knot holds the bow together. 449 shows a stiff bow, often made of velvet ribbon; also another bow, consisting of a band joined into a ring with another band tied over.

447

449

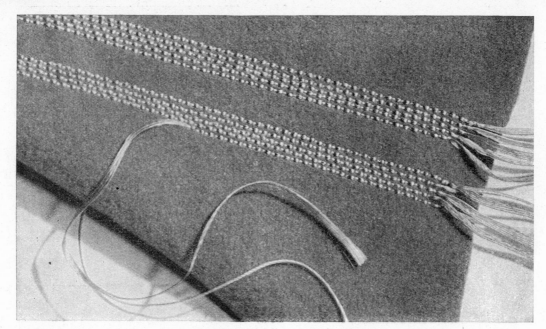

450

451

Ornamental Stitching

Stitching can always be used, in one form or another, for ornamental purposes, whether it be on silk or woollen materials, on sportswear or elegant dresses. The simplest method is to apply rows of stitching; the distance between the rows may be narrower than, or as wide as, the presser-foot. The stitching may be done with ordinary sewing silk of a matching or contrasting shade, buttonhole twist, or braid. If braid is being used, note that the upper thread must be of sewing silk or buttonhole twist, and the lower thread of guimp, as the latter cannot pass through the eye of the needle. To place the guimp on the right side the stitching must be done on the wrong side. For pattern-stitching the design must accordingly, in this case, be drawn on the wrong side.

If the stitching is to be carried out in twist silk, sewing silk should be used for the bobbin thread; this will give the thicker stitches on top a well-moulded appearance.

For ornamental stitching, the machine must be adjusted to give a longer stitch so that the stitches will come out very clearly. The stitching looks particularly attractive if it is carried out on double material, or on material interlining and facing. 452 shows how cord is stitched on.

450. BRAIDED STITCHING is produced with coloured thread (laced braid of artificial silk) which is wound on the bobbin as the lower thread. Various designs may be stitched with twist silk (buttonhole twist) or sewing silk.

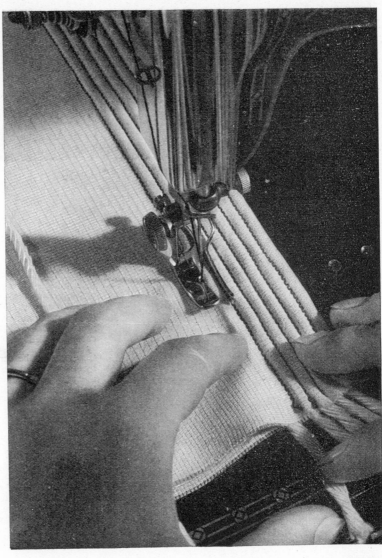

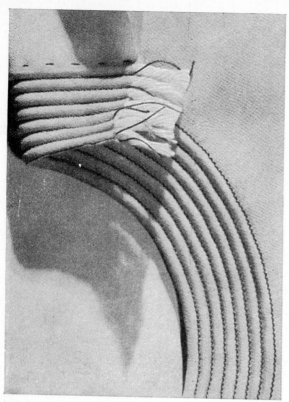

454

455

Cording

Uniform stitching with a very decorative appearance may be achieved by cording or piping. Piping cord—a soft white cotton cord—is sold for the purpose at all drapers'. The thickness of cord to be used depends on the thickness of the material; furthermore, the thicker the cord, the more material will be required, as more material is used to cover the cord.

Cording may be carried out in three different ways : (a) by stitching and then drawing in the cord ; (b) by placing the cord in position and then tacking each stitch line ; (c) by stitching with the corder attachment, this making the previous tacking unnecessary. 453 shows how the corder attachment is used. 454 shows how curved cording is carried out ; this is a much more difficult process, requiring great care. The cord must be tacked in for each row of stitching, or it may be drawn in after the stitching has been executed. 455 shows a thick woollen material underlaid with lining. Each cord is placed in position, the material lightly eased over, and then tacked before stitching. 452 shows how the appropriate machine attachment is used for sewing on cord. This attachment has a groove underneath through which the cord is led. The stitches must lie in the centre of the cord.

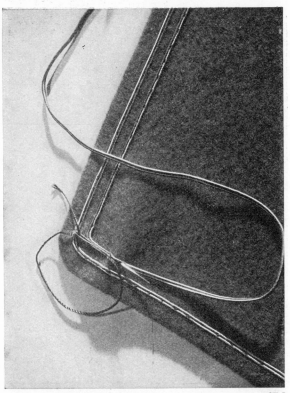

456

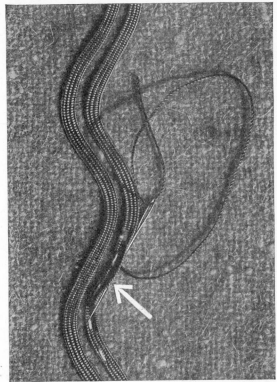

457

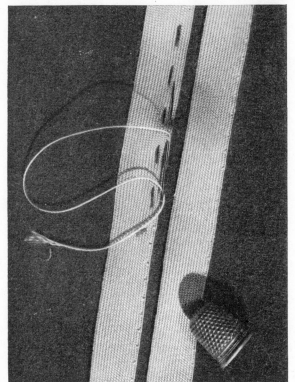

458

How to Sew on Prussian Cord, Soutache, and Military Braid

Prussian cord is often used as an edging; it is sewn on to the fold edge with invisible slip-stitches (459). The ends of the cord should be secured by a knot to prevent them from unravelling.

Soutache differs from other flat woven braids in that it is moulded and has a centre line along which it is stitched by hand or by machine. This narrow braid is very elastic and pliant. The most intricate decorations are often made with it. 456 shows a double soutache edging, sewn on with back-stitches, which have here been made visible for the sake of clearness.

456. SOUTACHE, a silk-covered cotton braid, may be sewn on with the cord-stitching attachment or by hand with back-stitch. It is very suitable for design-stitching.

457. Tubular braid is stitched or slip-stitched on. It is tacked on in straight lines or in a fancy design, and by lifting the edge a little can be sewn on from the inside with small stitches.

139

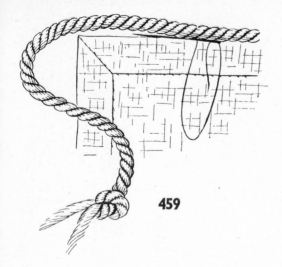

459

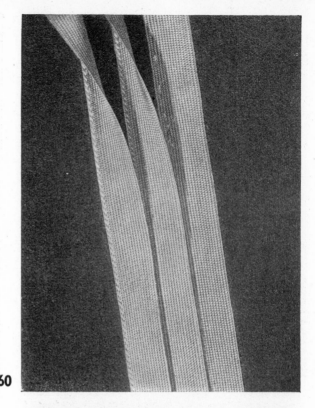

460

Tubular braid (457) is woven, as the name implies, in the shape of a tube. It is sewn on with invisible slip-stitches. The braid then looks as if it has been laid on and not stitched. It may also be stitched on with the seam along the centre.

Flat braids are made in various widths. They may be sewn on in rows close together or far apart, side by side or covering or crossing each other, or they may be used as a binding. They must be sewn on with great care (458), since they are woven on the bias and may therefore easily be sewn on in a wavy instead of a straight line.

The lines along which the braid is to be set should be marked. The braid is then tacked on, care being taken not to stretch it or hold it in, so that the width remains even throughout and the edge which remains loose runs exactly parallel with the next line. A sewing silk to match the exact shade is used to sew on the upper edge of the braid with tiny invisible back-stitches.

460. When setting on several rows of braid to overlap, the loose edge of each row covers the edge of the next. The rows may also be set under one another in graduated widths.

461. BRAID BINDING may be sewn on in various ways. It may either be set on by hand and then felled over to the wrong side, or it may be stitched on reversed and then felled over to the wrong side.

461

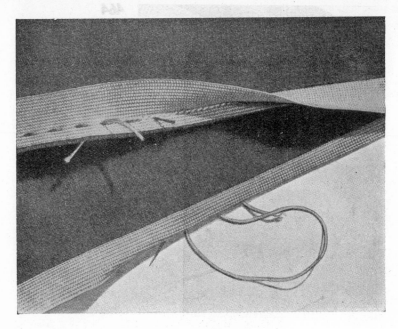

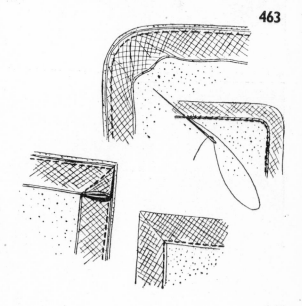

Braid as Trimming and as Binding

Braid is useful for hiding seams which become prominent when altering, in particular lengthening garments. Simple silk braid is easier to use than the more delicate waxed or ciré braid, which must not be creased or scratched, or it will lose some of its sheen. For the same reason waxed braid must not be pressed with a hot iron. Braid should never be dampened; watermarks will show easily.

To stitch on braid by machine it must first be tacked into position. The line of stitching must lie close along the edge and run perfectly parallel with it; in the case of braid in particular the least unevenness will show up prominently.

Braid may be applied in various ways as a binding. In the case of very thick materials, it is best to sew the braid on the inside and on the outside by hand (461), as machine-stitching would draw it too much into the material. For thin fabrics the braid may be machine-stitched on, the open end then being felled over the line of stitching on to the wrong side. When turning the braid over it will be seen whether the seam has been stitched unevenly or perfectly in line with the woven edge of the braid.

The braid must be eased on rounded corners so that its even width may be maintained, even after turning (463). For edge-binding the braid is stitched on reversed; the corners mitred and the braid stitched down on the right side (463).

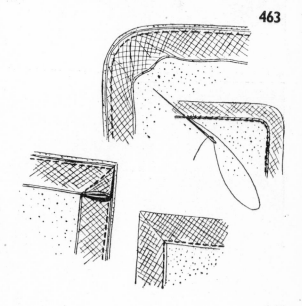

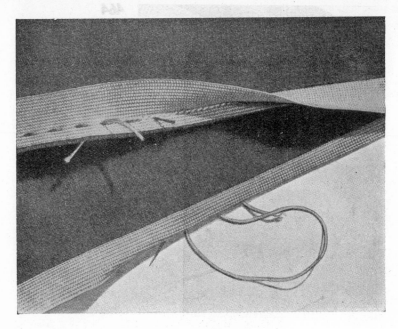

462

463

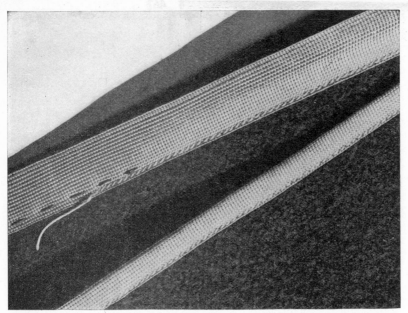
464

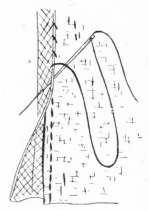
465

466

467
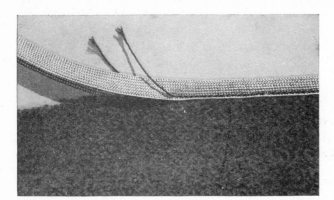

Braid Binding

Besides hemming on and setting against, another usual method of securing braid is to stitch it on. The distance from the edge of the material to the edge of the braid must be exactly half the width of the latter, so that there will be the same amount of binding on both sides. A line of stitching running exactly along the edge of the braid is used to fasten the braid either on the right side of the material (for method of felling over the edge see 465) or on the inside. If the braid has been stitched on on the inside, it is tacked over so that the seam is covered by the turning, which must also be stitched down.

The simplest way to bind the edge is to stitch down both braid edges simultaneously. For this, the braid must be folded double lengthways and pressed, so that the lower half projects about $\frac{1}{12}$ in. beyond the upper edge. The stitching is done on the upper edge, and the lower edge stitched through at the same time (467).

Braid piping may be placed between a seam or applied as an edging. To form a piping the braid is folded double and pressed so that the fold edge forms the piping. As it is almost impossible to achieve accuracy when stitching the

464. When applied as a binding the braid may be stitched on from the right side and felled over, or from the wrong side, folded over, and then stitched down on the right side beside the seam.

467. BRAID PIPING may consist of folded braid stitched under, or stitched on reversed and felled over, as a neatening.

468

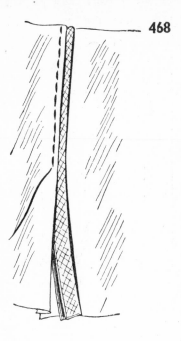

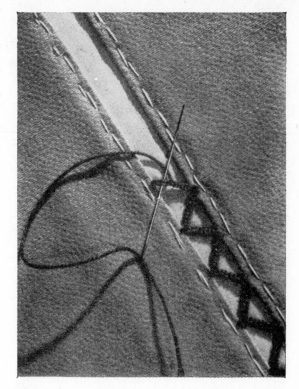

469

Braid Binding *(continued)*

piping between the seam reversed, a stitched-over seam is used (468).

For piping edging the braid is stitched on right side to right side and tacked over with a narrow edging. The edge of the braid is hemmed on or stitched down so as to cover the folded turning.

Decorative Stitching : Tassels

For a joining stitch resembling hem-stitching, two sections of material are tacked on to a paper strip (469); the distance between must be even. A double thread is stretched from one to the other zigzag fashion, and in going backwards, worked over with buttonhole-stitch. Such bars are less stiff if carried out in fine cotton or sewing silk, but on the other hand naturally do not wear as well.

Three of the simplest and most frequently used embroidery stitches (471) are chain-stitch, fly-stitch, and feather-stitch. They form a quickly worked and very pretty decoration for children's garments, and may also be used as a fastening stitch for turned-in hem edges. The method is clearly illustrated. By working several rows of the stitching or by drawing out the individual stitches, variety may be obtained.

To make even balls or bobbles requires a little practice. In 470 all the details of the method are shown. Two discs, of the same diameter as the ball tassels it is intended to make, are cut out of

470

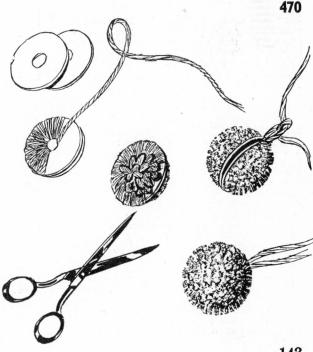

471

472

473

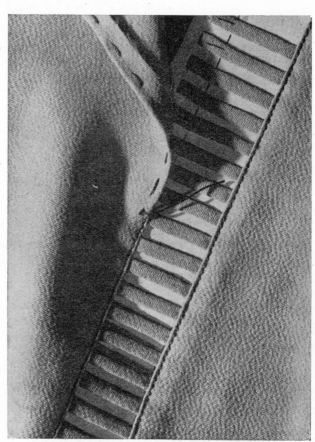

Decorative Stitching : Tassels (*cont.*)

cardboard and a circular opening made in their centre. Strands of wool, the longer the better, are wound closely round the two discs and then cut open round the edge. A thread is passed in between the two discs, which will keep the strands together in the middle, and serves later to fasten the tassel. The cardboard discs must be removed by drawing them outwards carefully, and the ball is ready.

For tassels too the silk, cord, braid, or wool is wound evenly over a rectangular piece of cardboard. The strands are bundled together at the upper end—that is, the looped ends of wool should be kept firmly together in one piece—and cut open at the lower end. The tassel is again wound round at the top (472).

Appliqué :
French Knots : Dots

We must begin by explaining the ornamental seam shown in 473. Narrow straight bands are used to join the two sections of material. The bands are tacked on to tissue paper and the sections stitched on. When the stitching is completed, the tissue paper can be removed carefully. This effective ornament may be carried out in bands of various widths, or with braid or ribbon.

Appliqué is the term employed when cut-out designs of material are sewn on, or when two sections of material are joined so that they overlap. A different method is employed according as the material is non-fraying (leather or cloth, for instance) or fraying; the former may be

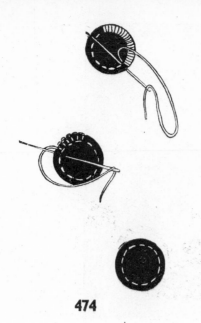

474

Appliqué (*continued*)

stitched on with open edges, or secured with blanket- or buttonhole-stitch, whereas the latter will have to be fastened securely with turned-in edges. The machine zigzag seam is very useful for appliqué, as it covers and fastens the cut edges of the material very firmly.

Sections or edges of material which have been cut out, or larger pieces on which the design has been marked, can be tacked quite close to the edge and stitched down, the material beside the stitches being then cut away. The method employed depends entirely on the pattern and the material. Dots are frequently applied (474).

The so-called Paris stitch is very effective when used to join two pieces of material (476). The facing should be cut out and tacked on with the edges turned in. It is then sewn on to the upper material with the stitch, which closely resembles hem-stitching.

The size of French knots depends on the number of times the embroidery thread is wound round the needle (475). Embroidered dots are made fuller by padding them with satin-stitches.

476

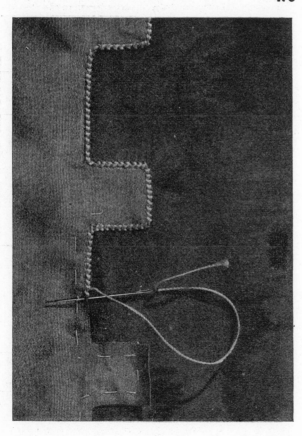

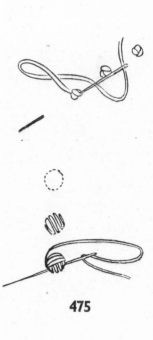

475

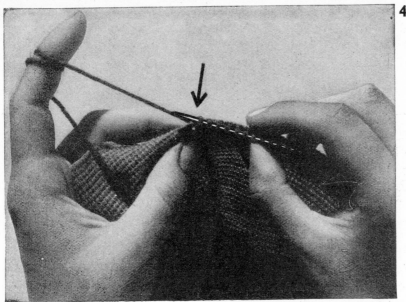

477

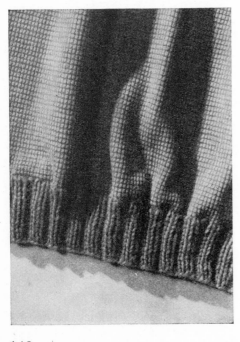

478

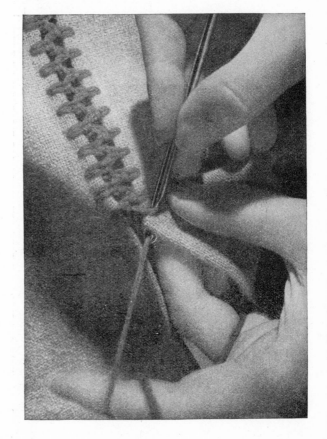

479

Knitted and Crocheted Finishes

A knitted border, two plain and two purl stitches alternately, is useful for lengthening tricoted and woollen materials. The edge of the material must be fairly wide, for although the knitting will " give," it will draw the material in to a certain extent when not stretched (478). For this reason the knitted border is particularly useful for finishing off blouses and sleeves, but it may also be used for extending the edges of knickers. If the fabric is sufficiently loose, the first row of stitches is taken up with the knitting-needle or with the crochet hook by passing the needle from the front to the back through the turned-over edge of the material (477). The stitches must be placed at an even depth and distance, so that the onset of the knitting comes out clearly and neatly. The border must not be made too wide, or it will look as if it had been " pieced " on.

Crocheting serves to conceal unwanted joins, as, for instance, when a child's frock has been lengthened. It provides at the same time a pretty trimming. The edges of the material must be hemmed narrowly, or just turned in so that the crocheting has sufficient hold in the double material. Each section may be edged with a plain row of crochet to begin with, and the two edges afterwards joined by crocheting the meshes together; the joining may also be carried out in one process (479). As this illustration shows, the crochet needle enters the upper and the lower edges of the two sections alternately and carries out one stitch and two chain each time. The chain meshes serve as the uniting bars, and by reason of the alternating stitch form a zigzag pattern. With the help of contrasting colours and materials, crochet work of this kind can achieve good effects.

480

481

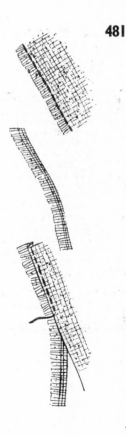

482

Fringe Edging : Knotted and Drawn

To make a hand-knotted fringe, use silk, lacet ribbon, or tubular braid. The material is wound round a rectangular piece of cardboard and pieces are cut off as required. They should be a little more than twice the length of the fringe, and of course should all be the same length. The edge of the material, if single, must be turned in. The threads or braid are then drawn half-way through, so that the same length hangs down on each side, and fastened with a little knot, which should be pushed close up to the edge of the material and drawn tight (480). To finish off, the ends of the fringe are trimmed off evenly.

Fringed braid is stitched on or placed between two edges of material.

Straight edges, if the fabric is suitable, can be frayed out and secured by a row of stitching. Narrow strips can also be frayed out and stitched on as a fringed braid.

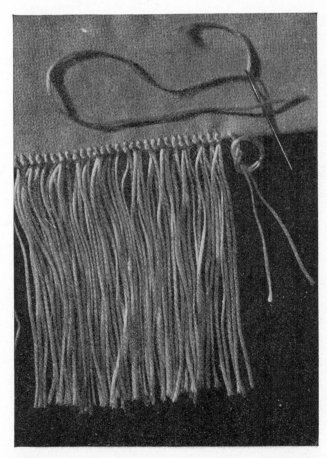

483

PART THREE

Lingerie
Underwear
Etc., Etc.

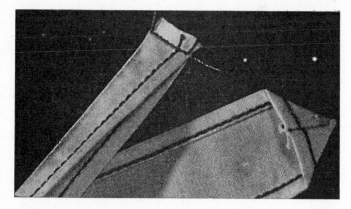

484

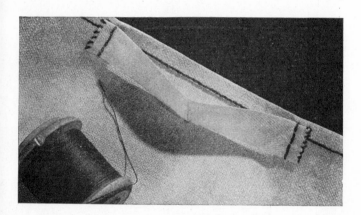

485

484. To make a shoulder strap, fold a narrow piece of ribbon or material lengthways with the right side inside. The ends are stitched straight across so as to form a point when the band is opened out. In the case of shoulder straps made of double material, the ends are mitred, turned in against each other, and neatened.

485-487. Hangers made of tape are stitched on flat by hand. The ends are turned in and hemmed on, and neatened by back-stitching. A loop-hanger is stitched into the hem of the article and then stitched over.

487

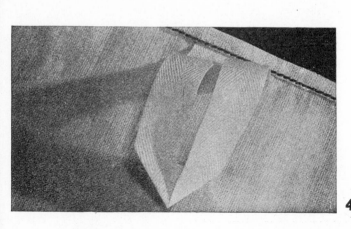

486

488

489

490

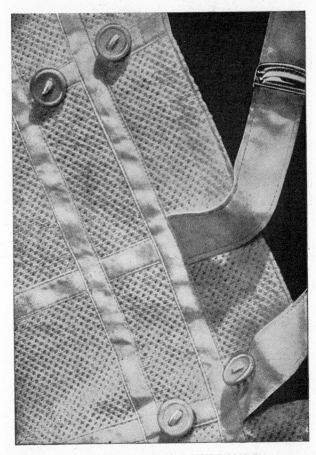

488-491. A CHILD'S STAY BODICE may be cut from used cellular (e.g. Aertex) garments. The material, which is elastic, is strengthened with bias-binding and bands, which are set on crosswise; these serve at the same time as a support for suspenders and buttons.

492. The seams connecting the sections of the bodice are directed to the right side and covered with bands. Then the remaining bands are stitched on lengthways. The shoulder straps consist of two strips of material folded double and placed together with the folds touching. They are held together by bands stitched across.

491

492

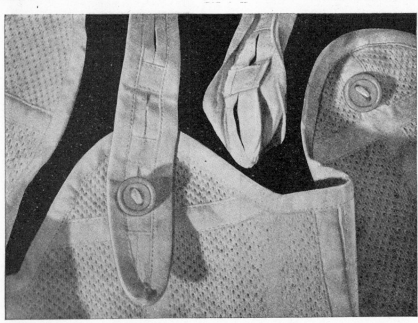

493. The buttonholes or the back fastening are made of faced or double bands held together with binding. A wide underlap and buttons threaded on narrow tape are stitched on in one seam which is afterwards covered with a band.

494. This illustration shows clearly how the buttonhole lap is made. The lower edge of the bodice is neatened with a bias-strip set on like a hem, while the upper edge and the shoulder straps are bound with bias-strips set on the wrong side and stitched down on the right side.

495-496. BRASSIERES are made in various designs. For simple models, washing-net, cotton, art silk, or silk stockinette can be used, while brassières for out-size figures are often made of strong batiste or cotton material. The style here illustrated has been made up of charmeuse used in conjunction with sateen. The cellular fabric sections are stitched one on top of the other (as with a flat fell seam). The same silk corded ribbon which is used for the shoulder straps is stitched inside the upper cellular fabric edge. The shoulder straps are adjustable in front. The set-on belt is tacked on to the lower edge of the cellular sections and secured with batiste bands ⅜ in. wide; these are also used to neaten the other belt edges. Buttonhole elastic is used for the back fastening.

493

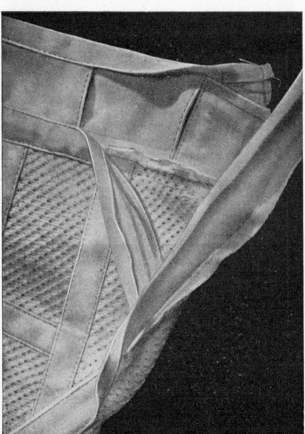

494

495

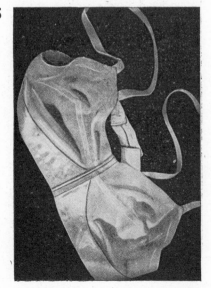

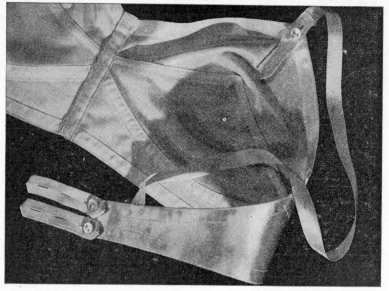

496

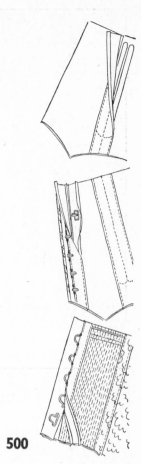

498

500

497-500. CORSETS, too, may be made in various shapes and of various fabrics according to fashion and figure requirements. Often, as in our model, sateen is used in conjunction with elastic belting. The sections made of fabric are lined with batiste. The front section is often reinforced with fabric; here only two steel " whalebones " have been worked into band slots on each side to give abdominal support. The fabric sections are underlaid with lining and edge-stitched together; the elastic sections being set on at the sides, or set in by single seams. Two wide bands are stitched on to the inside of the front section, one on each side, and divided down the centre by a row of stitching; these bands take the whalebones. Hook-and-eye fastenings are set and all the edges are neatened with set-on binding.

497

502

501

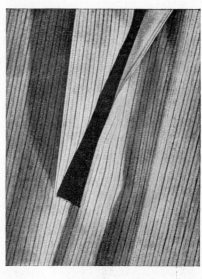

499

501. TUNIC SHIRT with hidden centre pleat. When cutting out, about 3 in. will have to be allowed for the fastening and pleat below the wrap. The slit is cut in; it should be about 16 in. long and ⅜ in. to the right of the front centre. A slash across the end of the slit will make it easier to set on the facing strip.

504

504. The right edge of the slit is faced with a strip of the shirting about 1½ in. wide, and the left edge with a strip of linen of the same width, which is intended to reinforce the buttonholes.

503

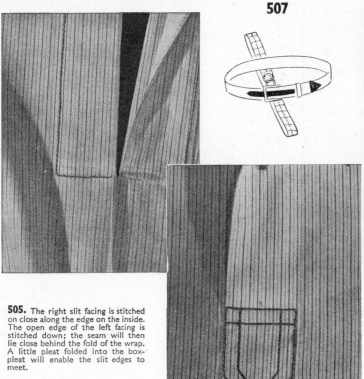

505. The right slit facing is stitched on close along the edge on the inside. The open edge of the left facing is stitched down; the seam will then lie close behind the fold of the wrap. A little pleat folded into the box-pleat will enable the slit edges to meet.

508. TUNIC SHIRT with set-on wrap: A strip 1¼ in. wide is set on the right slit edge for the underlap, or it may be allowed for when cutting out. On the left edge a strip a little longer than the slit and with a pointed end is stitched on for the wrap. A strip of linen should be laid in for strengthening.

506. The overlapping wrap and the pleat are fastened simultaneously by double stitching which runs into two points. The pleat makes the slit end perfectly neat on the inside. The illustration shows how far away the first of the three or four buttonholes should be from the end of the slit.

511

510

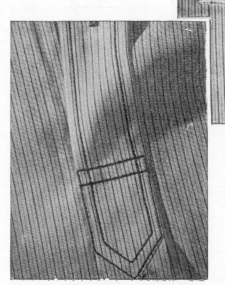

509. The right slit facing is stitched down and also the wrap, a correspondingly wide turning being provided. The box-pleat in front is now laid; the fold on the right should be somewhat wider than that on the left.

510. Slit end and pleat are secured with stitching, which should end with two rows across about 2½ in. above the point. This type of shirt is used chiefly for sports shirts, whereas the one with the hidden centre pleat is more suitable for smarter wear.

512. SHIRT with set-on pleated front.   The front section of the shirt is cut out square and the trunk pleat laid in. Front sections of linen are cut out and set into the opening with the seam directed to the right side.   They overlap in front, corresponding with the fastening.   The tucked fronts are set on to the front edges of the facings by reversed seam.   The seam must lie a little hehind the fold when turning over the edges.

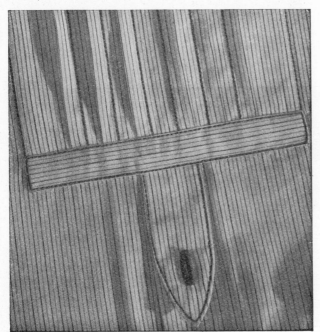

513

514

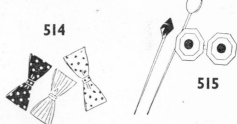

515

513. The edges of the opening are stitched in the width of the tucks and the side edges stitched over the fastening close to the edge.   A band ½ in. wide conceals the lower cross-edge of the front inset and secures at the same time the trunk pleat and the tab, which is pushed under.   The tab should be the same width as the trunk pleat, and made of double material.

In addition to the hidden centre pleat (American style), the set-on centre pleat, and the pleated front, the shape of the front and the grouping of the tucks may be varied in other ways.

516

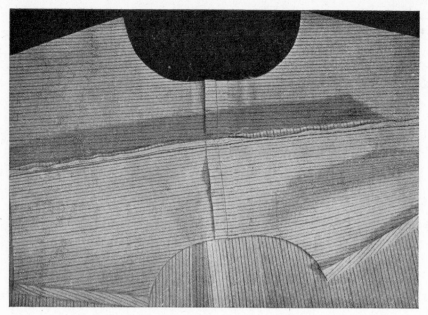

517. THE YOKE: The back section is reduced to the width of the yoke by gathering or pleats. For economy of material, the yoke may have a centre seam. The back section is stitched between the two layers of the yoke with a reversed seam. The yoke is turned up and the seam stitched through once more close to the fold edge. The shoulder edges of the front sections are also stitched between the yoke: shoulder seam and under yoke are joined by reversed seam, and the upper portion of the yoke is stitched over close to the edge so as to cover the first seam. The same method is adopted for a nightshirt with a yoke.

518

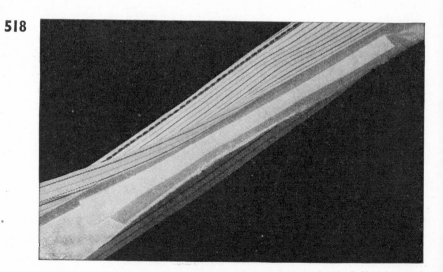

519

518-519. THE NECKBAND: This consists of double material and an interlining of linen. In addition a strip of linen about 4 in. long is laid in at the back for the neckband pocket. The outer part of this neckband pocket is afterwards finished with a buttonhole for the collar-stud. A reversed seam is used to join the two layers of material with the long and the short interlinings, and the strips are then folded over so that the linen sections lie on the inside. The fold edge is stitched close to the edge.

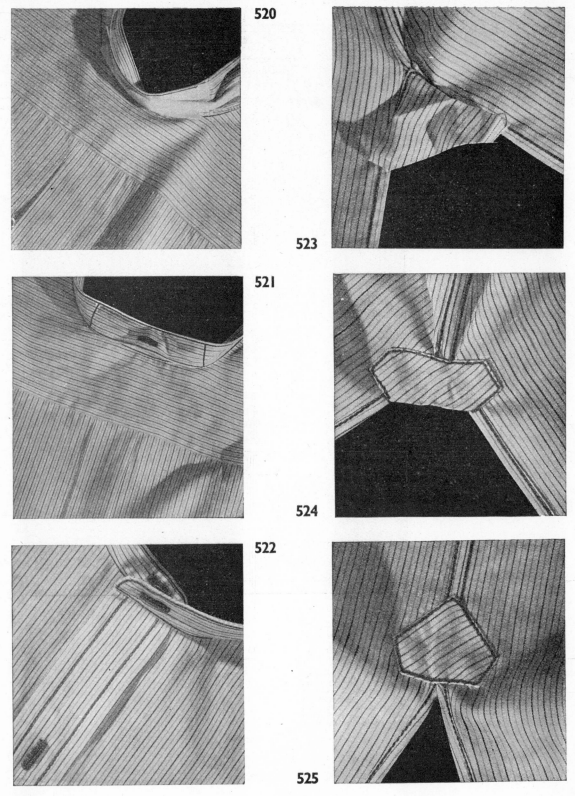

520

521

522

523

524

525

520-522. The edges of lining and interlining of the neckband are stitched on. The inlaid strip is stitched over the neck edge at the middle of the back. The outer material and short inlaid section are stitched together and the open edge of the neckband stitched down.

The neckband pocket is closed at the sides by vertical seams. The rounded ends of the neckband overlap in front and are furnished with buttonholes.

523. GUSSETS at the end of the side-seams, which are left open for the slits, will prevent tearing. The gusset is made by setting in or on a triangle of material.

524. The triangle is folded over in half, stitched on to the slit edges on the right side, and then stitched over to the inside. The bias fold ensures a certain amount of " give."

525. Another method of securing the ends of the slit is to cut off two points of the triangle and stitch it on from the inside; on the right side only the stitching will then be visible.

526. The slit on the shirt sleeve is finished with a narrow underlap binding and a wide onset for the overlap. A continuous seam coming to a point at the end of the slit fastens both strips on the wrong side.

527. The strips are turned over, the first seam of the underlap forming the fold edge. When finished, the overlap should be ⅜ in. wide. It is stitched over close to its first seam, the mitred end covering the end of the slit.

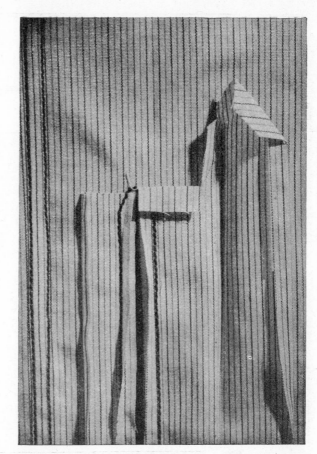

526

527

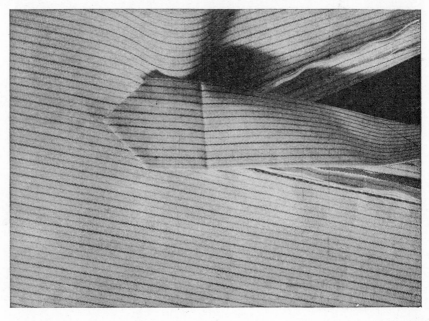

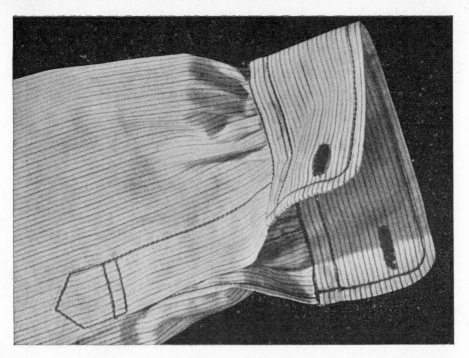

528-529. CUFFS : Cuffs are either single or double, and may be square or rounded. The single cuff belongs to the sports shirt, which usually has a collar attached.

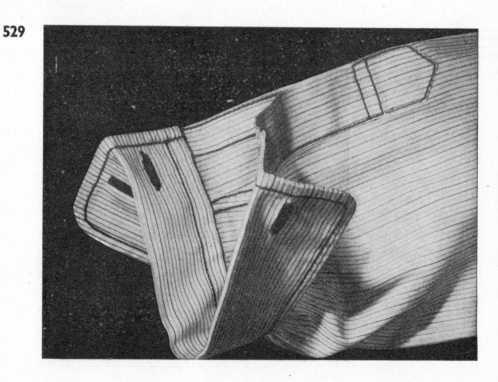

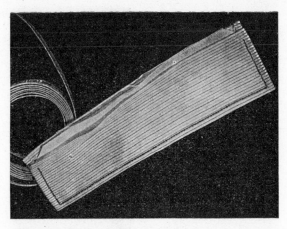

530. The cuff consists of a double layer of material and an interlining of linen. The three layers are joined together by a reversed seam. The upper edges of the interlining are cut away at the corners, so that the seam remains flat.

531. The cuff is turned and the seam well smoothed out. Beginning ½ in. away from the upper edge, the cuff edge is stitched about ⅙ in. away from the edge. The upper edge is turned in about ¼ in.

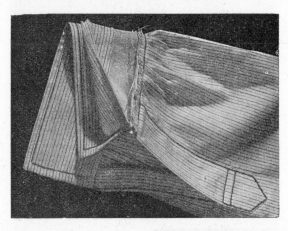

532. The edge of the sleeve is gathered into even pleats (the pleats should be pushed over to the side, so that the sleeves remain smooth on the outside). Set on the lining and interlining of the cuff and turn the underlap in.

533. The onset seam is smoothed out towards the cuff and covered by the cuff section which is stitched over. Another row of stitching is carried across about ⅖ in. away.

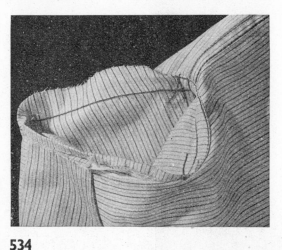

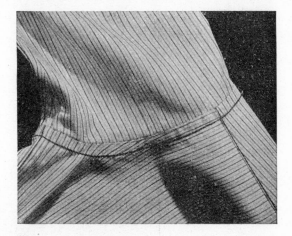

534

535

534-535. When setting in the sleeve the seam should be directed to the inside; the edge of the sleeve must project sufficiently so that it can be turned in narrowly and stitched over close to the edge.

536. COLLAR: If the collar is to be made of thin shirting, an interlining is inserted in the neck portion and into the outer portion which is folded; in thicker materials the interlining will be required only for the neck portion. The three layers of the outer part are stitched together on the three outside edges, turned, and stitched again close to the edges. The outer part is then placed between the layers of the inner part and secured with a reversed seam.

538-539. The layers of the neck part are turned in at the open edges still remaining and stitched. Continuing the seam, the joining seam must be stitched over to enclose the seam edges within the line of stitching.

The rounded ends of the collar are not of the same length, the left end overlapping the right end so that the collar cannot gape in front. The collar is finished by working in three buttonholes.

538

537

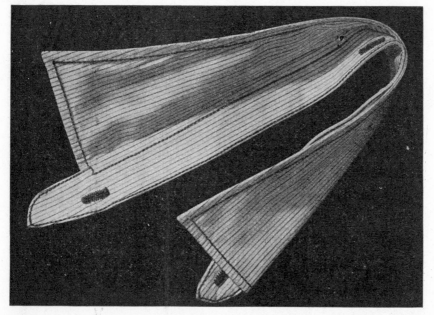

164

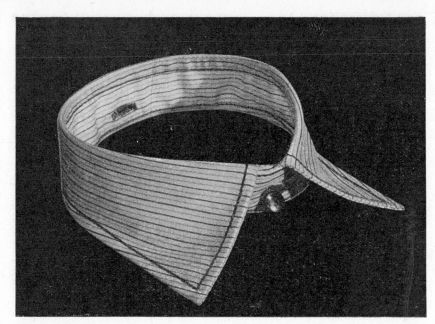

539

540

541

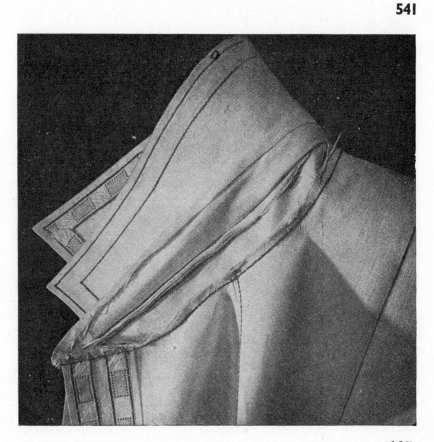

541-542. NIGHTSHIRT: In this, too, the shirt sections are joined by a double yoke. Overlap, sleeves, and collar are trimmed with washable guimp. The guimp is set on to the neck part of the collar with its corners sharply mitred, and the turnover, which should be made of double material, is then set into the neck part. The collar section is stitched to the neckline from the inside and its upper part stitched over on the right side. The middle seam and ends of collar are stitched at the same time. Buttonholes are then worked.

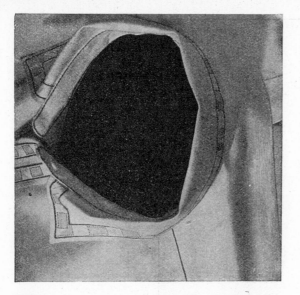

542

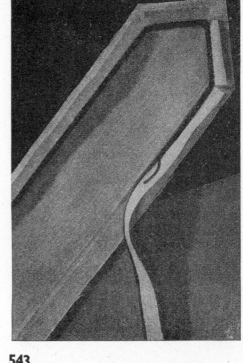

543

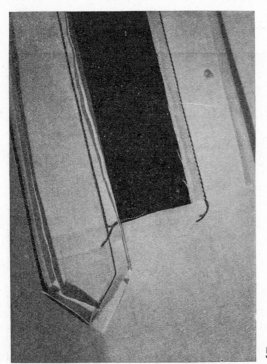

545

544

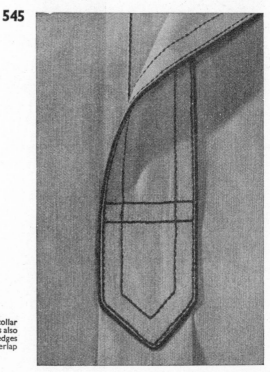

543-545. Coloured piping provides a pretty trimming for nightshirts. On collar and sleeve band the piping is stitched between the outer seams, and piping is also stitched on to the overlap. Overlap and underlap are stitched on to the slit edges and both turned over to the right side. With the piping in the fold the overlap is turned over and secured with a double row of stitching.

546

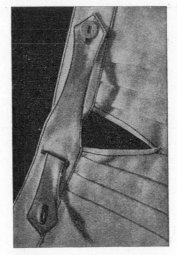

549

550

547

546-548. BUTTON FASTENING ON PANTS:
An underlap about 1-1½ in. wide is cut out on the right front edge, and a facing strip set against the underlap. 1½ in. should be allowed on the left side; this is turned over to the wrong side and a double band laid under its back edge, which is then stitched down. The slit end is secured by stitching. Finally, the waistband is joined on, buttonholes are made, and buttons sewn on.

549. THE ADJUSTABLE BAR
on the waistband is made by lengthening the waistband ends, which should be neatened by being sewn into a point. The right bar is drawn through a slit like a large buttonhole, which is worked into the left waistband. The buttons are set on as required.

550-552. PYJAMAS:
Pyjama trousers have a girdle drawn through the slot at the upper edge. The slot is made by stitching on a strip of material 1-1½ in. wide. The front edges are arranged for concealed button fastening. The left front edge of the facing remains open and forms the slot for drawing in the girdle. On the right side the girdle is led through a buttonhole which is worked into the outside material.

551

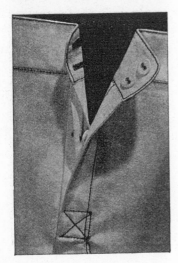

548

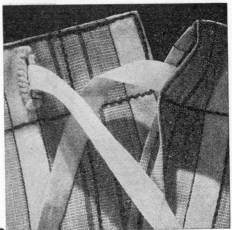

552

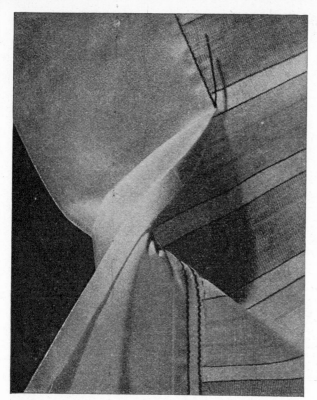

553

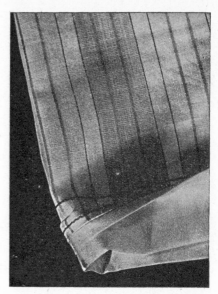

554

553-554. THE TROUSER ENDS can be furnished with turn-ups. These are made of material about 3 in. wide closed into a ring and set on to the bottom edge of the trouser leg. The trouser leg must be cut with allowance for the turn-up.

Both seam edges are stitched on with open edges; the facing is turned over to the inside so that the fold lies about ⅛ in. above the seam. The inner edge is stitched on and the turn-up folded over.

556

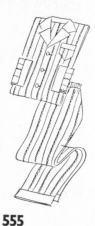

555

556. PYJAMA JACKET collar and revers: A wide facing is laid on the front edges. It may be cut of contrasting material as far as the first button, and from there to the lower edge of self material. The back edge of the facing is stitched down close to the edge. The under collar is set on with a reversed seam, the outer part stitched over with a hanger inserted, and the edges of the collar and front edge-stitched.

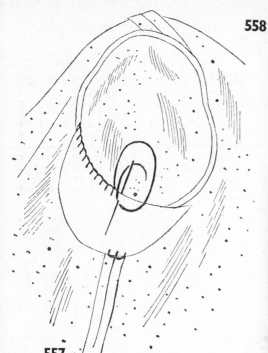

557

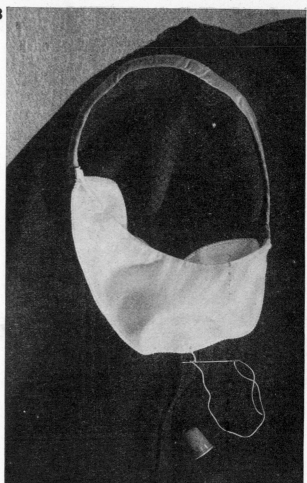

Dress Preservers

Dress preservers, or shields, are obtained in various colours, styles, and sizes. They should be selected as soft and thin as possible, so that they do not bulge too much. The double shield is not always convenient—in a very short sleeve, for instance, it would be visible. Single shields are obtainable which are sewn only on to the bodice. A dress shield must be sewn in to cover only the front part of the armhole, and at the back it must not reach more than about 2 in. beyond the side seam.

The single dress shield is fastened with widely spaced blanket-stitches on the sleeve-hole seam (see sketch above) and on the side seam. The double shield is sewn on only at the outer point: its open edges are fastened to the side seam and sleeve seam by French tacks (558).

Dress shields covered with silk lining to match may also be sewn into coats and jackets (559).

A more perfect protection is obtained by means of a slip bodice made of net or batiste and provided with dress shields; the loose halves of these shields being fastened with a press-stud to the sleeve seam of each garment.

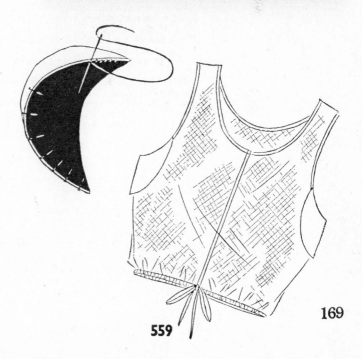

559

F*

169

Lingerie, Day and Night

WOMEN'S KNICKERS. Knickers may be flared, cut French style, or knee-length. Of these three styles the French knicker is most popular. The material is cut on the cross to provide softly falling folds while fitting snugly across the hips and round the waist. In fitting the pattern measure the waist, the hips, and the side length. There will be some stretch across the front through the " give " in the material, and this must be corrected by placing darts at intervals round the waistline. In most patterns the lower edge is curved, but where the knickers are to be finished with a facing, or with embroidery, it is best to cut the lower edge straight across. Full-length waist-to-knee knickers have a centre gusset and a yoked waistband. For fuller figures the gusset is made larger and higher than for the normal, and the height of the back must be carefully adjusted in fitting the pattern. The yoke may be a small flat one in front of the knickers only, or a wider one carried farther round the side. The latter is the better type for the full-fronted figure. Where the yoke is made larger than is allowed for in the pattern, a dart should be taken out in the seam equal to the extra allowance of waist size. In testing the size note whether the garment still slips on easily over the waist. If there is any tension, the back should be let out a little in the centre waistline. The back of yoked knickers is usually completed with an elastic to draw in the waist. This is made by sewing a facing of the knickers material or bias-tape from one end of the yoke to the other across the back, and threading elastic through this. Another method is to shape the knickers to fit the waist by means of darts, facing this with matching material or binding with braid (see 462–466). Or a band to match the yoke in front may be mounted over the darted waist at the back, with an opening at each side, with buttons and buttonholes for fastening. For evening knickers the flat yoke in front and a darted and bound waistline at the back, with tiny buttons and button-holes down each side, is neater and lies more snugly under an evening frock. Careful pressing will ensure that the garment lies smoothly around the hips, while the bias-cutting will give leg fullness without bulkiness.

CAMI-KNICKERS can be adapted from a good French knicker pattern used in con-junction with the top half of a princess-slip petticoat pattern. Mark off the waistline on the latter by placing pins at intervals, trace off the outline of the pattern on brown paper, cut this out, and lay on the material with the knicker pattern. As this garment goes on over the head the tab gusset will have a fastening. The gusset is cut with a V-shaped end. The straight end is attached to the centre of the knickers at the back, and the pointed end, which should have three buttonholes worked in it, is brought to the front. Mark a place on the centre front of the cami-knickers to correspond with the buttonholes, and sew on three small pearl buttons of the same colour as the material. Care must be take to allow plenty of length for movement. A tab gusset, 8 in. in length, is a good average for a 34-in. size cami-knicker, allowing 3 in. for the overlap of the tab in front for buttoning. Finish off the bodice with lace (see 223–232), and shoulder straps of the material itself, made of narrow " tubes " of bias-cut fabric. If an invisible tab fastening is desired, make two tabs, each measuring 2 or 3 in., and fell these to the inside of the back and front of the centre hem of the cami-knickers. Work two or three small buttonholes in one, and sew on two or three small pearl buttons to correspond on the other. In these, as in other intimate garments, it is best to sew entirely by hand, using French seams.

NIGHTDRESSES. These may be magyar, shaped at the waist, with a full, straight-hanging skirt ; in this case the length from shoulder to hem will be about 54 in. After cutting the pattern, arrange the front fullness for tucks, gauging, or smocking. Allow the full width of the material in front for the two latter forms of trimming. In the case of a lace-topped nightdress apply the lace *before* shaping (see 223–232 for method of applying lace). The back will have to be cut full length unless the lace is to be applied at the back as well as the front. Leave about 2 in. longer in front than in the back to allow for the amount taken up from the length by the bust. Increase this amount according to the bust measurement. Have the underarm point about 10 to 11 in. below the shoulder, and measure off the depth of the V-neck on the centre line of the folded material, having folded the front in half on the centre line. If a fitted, princess line is desired, arrange darts or tucks at the waistline, first marking these off with pins (see 72–74 for method of pin-tucking). A centre seam will make the shaping of the bust in front easier.

BED OR DRESSING JACKET with Squared Revers and Pockets.

Tack, stitch, and press the front shoulder darts, on the wrong side. Stitch a single turning down the inner edge of each front facing—the longer edge. Tack to the fronts with right sides touching and stitch ⅜ in. inside the level raw edges. Turn to the inside, press, and tack together the raw, slanting edges. Join the shoulders, sides, and sleeves with French seams. To make a French seam, stitch on the right side, just inside the level raw edges. Press, fold at the seam to cover the turnings, and stitch on the wrong side, just below the turnings. Hem the bottom of the jacket and slip-stitch the facing ends, turned in, over the hem. Narrowly hem the pocket top and work with blanket-stitch. Turn in the raw edges and tack, then stitch in position to the right front. Hem and blanket-stitch the outer edges of the collar. Stitch the raw edge to the neck, with right side of collar touching inside of jacket. Trim the jacket turning to $\frac{1}{8}$ in., turn in the collar turning over it, and stitch. Turn back the collar on to the jacket. Seam each cuff into a circle by the notched ends. Hem and blanket-stitch the upper edge and stitch the inner edge to the wrists as you have set on the collar, and turn back. Catch to the sleeves at the seam. Make a buttonhole in the right front just below the collar and sew a button to the left front to fasten.

PRINCESS SLIP. In making a princess slip remember :

1. To try the pattern against the figure and make any necessary adjustments.
2. To study the diagram and place all pattern pieces on the material before beginning to cut.
3. To notice notches (V), perforations (O), and wheel-tracings. When making up place notches to notches and perforations over perforations. Wheel-tracings are always explained on the pattern.

For turnings, allow $\frac{3}{8}$ in. turnings on seams, none on bound edges, and 2 in. at hem. Cut the shoulder strap double the width of pattern. Mark all turnings and notches with tack lines as a guide for stitching the slip together. Seam the centres to side pieces, then the sides of the slip. Press and oversew together the turnings. Bind the top of the slip. Cut the binding 1 in. wide on the cross ; stretch under a warm iron, and tack to the slip with right sides touching. Stitch $\frac{1}{4}$ in. inside level raw edges. Press binding over turnings to the inside, turn in, and fell the raw edge at the back of seam.

If a lace motif is used, tack this in position to the centre front, oversew it to the material with satin-stitch, and cut the material from the back of the lace (see 223–232).

Fold each shoulder strap lengthways and seam the side. Turn right way out and press. Stitch and fell the straps in position under the top of the slip. Hem the lower edge.

PYJAMAS (WOMEN'S). For the plain coat variety with yoked trousers.

Press a turning along the lower edge of each pocket facing. Lay it wrong side up on the inside of the pocket, upper raw edges level, and stitch along the top ; turn over the facing to the right side and machine the prepared edge into place. Fold and press the turning allowance on sides and bottom and stitch one to each front—the correct position will be indicated by perforations on the pattern. Then join on the front facings, stitch first on the right side, then turning to the inside and machining into place—the stitching to show through. Work three buttonholes on the right front. Flat felled seams join the shoulders, sides, and sleeves ; follow these by neatening the jacket edge with a hem. Seam the four cuff pieces into rings and pair them, right sides together ; stitch along their upper edges, turn right way out, and run and fell to the wrists. Set the sleeves into the armholes with centre tops and seams exactly together. Pin the two collar pieces right sides together and stitch along the top and each end ; trim the turnings before changing it over to the right side, and press well. Stitch the upper collar edge to the neck and top of the revers, leaving the under collar loose to fell over and neaten the join. Start at the centre back and run to each end separately. Seam the trouser legs and join the ankle strips into rings. Along the upper edge press a turning, then slip the facing inside the leg, stitch along the lower raw edges, turn facing to right side, and machine. Join the centre front and back seams and make a $\frac{3}{4}$-in. wide hem across the top of the back, stitching it at top and bottom. Join the two yoke pieces together across the top and press a turning round all the edges. Tack the yoke front into position, then insert the elastic through the back hem, and adjust it to fit. Stitch the yoke into position, machining in the ends of the elastic at the same time, and fell the lining inside to cover all joints.

DRESSING GOWN. To make up a reversible dressing gown, tack, stitch, and press the front shoulder darts, on the wrong side. Seam the shoulders and press open the turnings.

Seam the centre back of the collar, cut in one with the fronts, and stitch by its notched edge to the back of neck, with right sides touching.
Seam the sides of the gown and press open the turnings.
Hem the pocket tops, turn in the raw edges and tack, then stitch in position to the side fronts of gown.
Seam the sleeves, tack them into the armholes, and if they set well, stitch by machine. Press, and snip the turnings where necessary.

Make the lining to match, and place gown and lining face to face and stitch round all but the lower edge and wrists, ½ in. inside level raw edges.

Turn right way out through the lower edge, slip the sleeves one into the other, and press. Turn in and slip-stitch together the lower and wrist edges, and turn back the sleeves at trace-line to form a cuff.

Place the belt layers face to face and stitch the sides and one end. Turn right way out, close the open end, and press. Sew a button to this end and make a buttonhole in the other.

Sew a narrow slot of the material or make an oversewn slot over each side seam at the waist, to thread the belt through.

DRESSING GOWN WITH CONTRASTING FACINGS. Dart the front shoulders. Seam the shoulders, using French or lapped seams, and join the centre back of the collar with a single seam pressed open. Stitch by notched edge to back of neck, with right sides touching.

Seam the centre back and stitch the ends to the facing, then stitch a single turning round the inner edge. Tack to the collar and fronts with right sides touching and stitch ½ in. inside level raw edges. Turn to the upper side of collar and inside of fronts and press.

Seam the sides of the gown and hem the lower edge. Slip-stitch the facings in position and the ends, turned in, over the hem.

Hem and set on the pockets.

Seam the sleeves and each facing into a circle. Turn in and tack the turning on the upper edge of facings, stitch by raw edge to the sleeve with right sides touching, and turn to the inside and press. Fell the prepared edge to the inside of sleeve at trace-line, and turn back to form a cuff.

Tack the sleeves into armholes, try on, and if they hang well stitch by machine, matching seams.

Seam the belt into one length, fold, and stitch the side and one end.

PART FOUR

Tailored Clothes

560

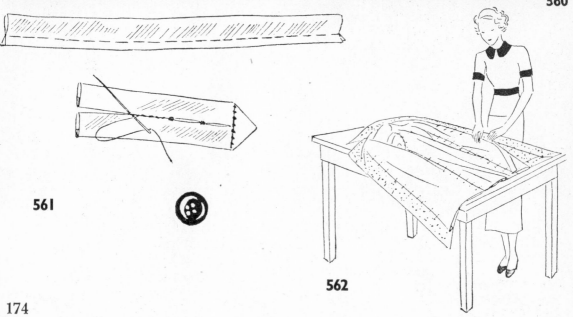

561

562

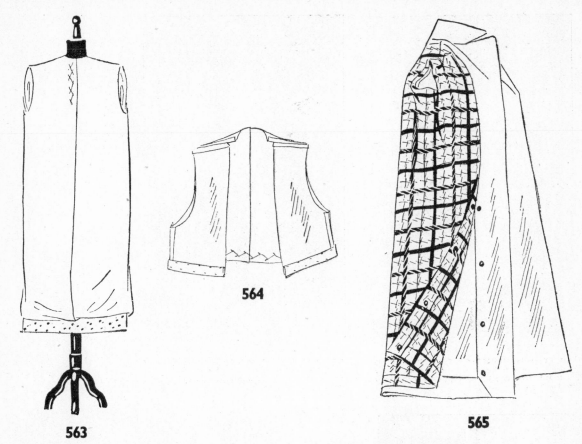

564

563

565

How to Line Coats and Jackets

Linings made of pure silk, though very elegant, are not very hard-wearing. The most serviceable lining is a union material of artificial silk and cotton. The lining should match the coat material, unless it is sought to obtain a special effect by means of a contrasting shade.

The lining is carried out before the sleeves are set in. The coat pattern is used for cutting out, though of course no material need be allowed for the front facings. One inch should be allowed at the fold edge of the back section; this provides an ease pleat. This pleat may be tacked in through the whole length before pinning on the pattern, and ironed afterwards.

The sections of the lining are often machine-stitched together for the sake of simplicity, but this is not a " professional " method. As the effect and appearance of the completed garment depend greatly on a well-fitting lining, it is worth the trouble to hem on all lining seams by hand. Turn the coat inside out and pin in the lining, beginning at the front section. Darts opening out (i.e. not stitched throughout) should be provided to correspond with the outer garment. The easiest way to put in a lining is to use a tailor's dummy. The darts, shoulder seams, neckline, and armhole edges in particular should be pinned on the dummy, while the rest of the work may be done upon a large table. Begin by basting the side-seam edges of the lining with large stitches to the seam edges of the dress material. The front shoulder edges are also tacked on lightly. The front edges are then pinned on to the facing. The middle pleat of the back section is placed upon the tacked centre line at the back of the garment; its shoulder

and side-seam edges are turned in so as to overlap the front sections. All pinned edges can now be basted unless you wish to save yourself this trouble by hemming on straightway all the pinned edges. But before this is done the lining round the armholes is basted on so that the sleeve may be set in. The sleeve lining is stitched together by machine so as to make it more hard-wearing. Sleeve and lining are turned inside out, their seam edges tacked together, and the lining is then pulled over. The lining is basted through about 4 in. below the top edge and tucked on at the lower seam edge, its length being eased somewhat. The sleeve is now tacked in with the lining folded back and stitched on. At the top the lining is then eased over the seam and hemmed on (560).

The hem edge of the coat lining must also have ample allowance for turning, so that when the garment is finished the lining hangs loosely, thus preventing all drawings and stretching (563).

The whole of the lining is now hemmed (felled) together. Then, beginning with the side seams at the shoulder, these are hemmed all round (in direction of arrow, 560). A band of lining for buttoning on the underlap is sewn on under the lining of the right side seam (561); its buttonholes (produced by leaving open the edges of the two bands which are placed side by side) fasten on the button of the left coat edge.

Coats are often only half lined, the lining remaining loose at the lower edge (564). Raincoats can be fitted with detachable woollen lining. This is attached to the coat by press-studs or buttons; it has no sleeves and remains loose at the hem (565).

175

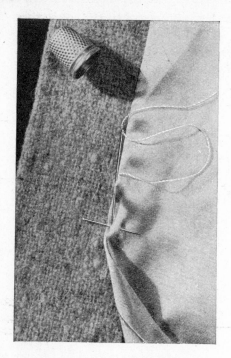

566. THE HEMMING OR FELLING in of the lining is done with close invisible slip-stitches. Of the outside material only the turning (facing or hem) may be taken up.

567. THE COAT LINING may have a pocket of lining on the right side. If desired, the pocket opening can be finished with a ruche which is stitched on to the upper edge.

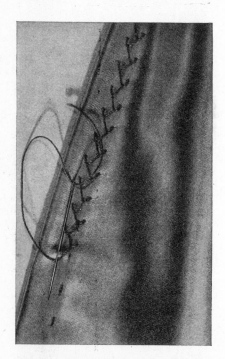

568. LOOSE-HANGING LINING HEMS, e.g. in the case of half-linings, are not finished with simple slip-stitching. A row of herringbone-stitch on the right side makes the hem more durable and at the same time serves as a trimming.

How to Hem in Lining: Quilting

The hemming in of the pinned or tacked-in lining is also called felling. When felling, the work is always held so that the lining lies in front of, and the edge of the material is turned away from, the person. With a needle as short and fine as possible (special felling needles are obtainable), take up the fold edge of the lining and the material in turn; the stitches lying in between are invisible. Only the turning of the material, facing or hem, must be caught—never the underlying outer material.

A lining pocket is placed on the right side, between the first and second buttons, so that one can get at it easily. An oblong bag is made of lining; its front edges have a short seam at the lower end, and the top is left open for the hand. The bag is rounded at the top, square at the bottom. The upper open edge is either piped or trimmed with a ruche of pleating stitched down, the lower edge is hemmed on to the facing, and the inner edge at the top is sewn on to the lining (567).

If the coat is to be quilted, this is done before the lining. The wadding is generally put in only as far as the waist, sometimes not even as far down, so that the hang of the lower part of the coat is not interfered with. The main object of quilting is to

(cont. on p. 178)

571

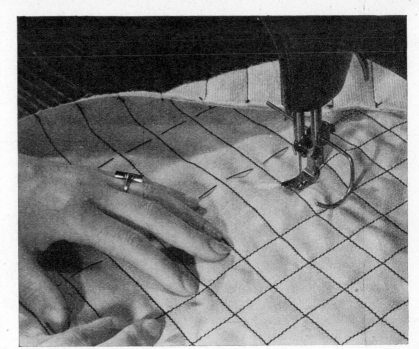

569

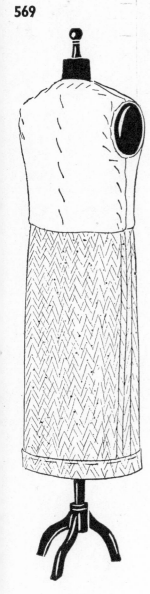

570

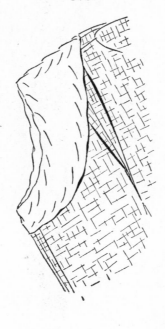

572

573. FOR QUILTING it is necessary to mark the design on the underside and tack it through to the right side. The lines are first tacked, and then stitched through the three layers.

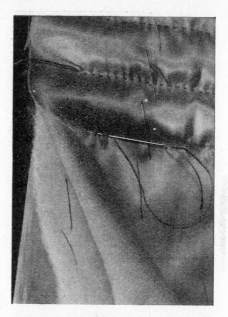

574. HAND-QUILTING is done with small running-stitch. To give it a full appearance, the top lining must be eased slightly when tacking and also when it is being sewn.

575. DIAMOND QUILTING is particularly suitable when a very full effect is sought, as it is stitched on a diagonal grain which allows a more even distribution of the upper layer.

How to Hem in Lining : Quilting *(continued)*

keep the upper part of the body—shoulders and back —warm.

The quilting is tacked in and the seam edges are tacked together by overcasting to keep them flat.

When stitching in the sleeves, the quilting ends in the seam, the sleeves being left unquilted. At the neckline it is afterwards sewn to the base of the collar ; in front the quilting reaches to the edges of the facing. The lower edge of the quilting may be slip-stitched to the dress material, if this is thick enough, so that the stitches do not show through on the outside.

Padding is inserted to conceal defects in the figure. Dropping shoulders, for instance, are disguised by tacking a layer of wadding all round the armhole, narrow underneath but widening out towards the top of the shoulder ; alternatively, two or more layers of interlining wool may be used for the purpose. The padding should be sufficient to make up for the amount of drop in the shoulder. A second or third layer of padding need not go all round the armhole, but only over the shoulder. The edges of the wadding are thinned a little so as to keep the line smooth. The tacked-in padding is sewn in with the sleeve (570).

571–575 show the various methods of quilting adopted. With the help of the adjustable quilting gauge illustrated in 571, rows of stitching may be carried out evenly and at whatever distance apart may be required. 573 shows a lining with flannel underlay. 572 shows a quilted lining consisting of silk, wadding, and cotton lining. For method of execution see illustrations.

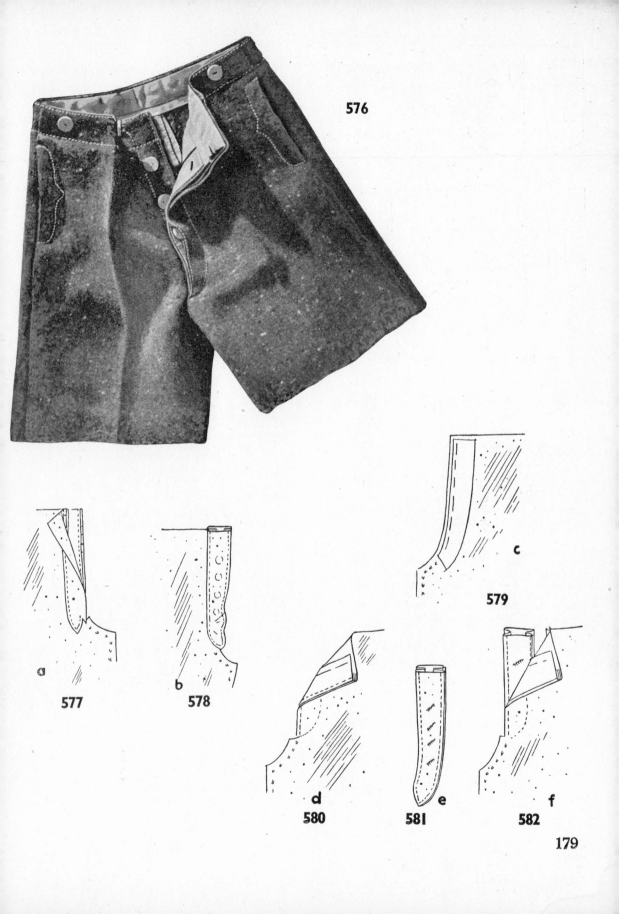

576

a

577

b

578

c

579

d

580

e

581

f

582

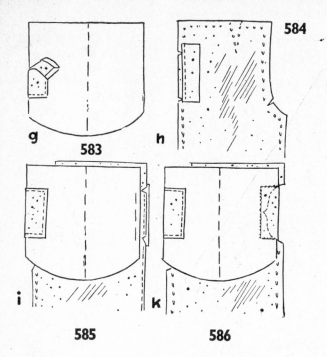

g

583

h

584

i

585

k

586

How to Make Boys' Knickers

Boys' knickers have a fly-opening in front. For this a fly-lap (for buttons) is set on to the right front and a double fly-lap (for the buttonholes) is set under the left front. The button-lap of material and lining is sewn together along the outside edge, right side to right side, and edge-stitched after turning it inside out. Only the dress material is stitched to the right front of the knickers (577); the layer of lining is hemmed on the inside over the seam and the seam top-stitched close to it (578). The slit edge of the left knicker front is faced with a strip of lining, which is set on right side to right side (579) and turned to the inside in such a manner that the material projects a little. The edge is top-stitched close to it (580). The buttonhole-fly, also of material and lining, is stitched together on the front edge, right side to right side, turned inside out, and the edges at the back turned to the inside together and top-stitched along the long edges (581). The buttonholes are best worked in slanting (lower in front), to ensure a smooth appearance when fastened. When stitching the fly from the wrong side, the lining strip is caught in the seam (582). The side pocket of lining is faced with a strip of material at the inner edge of the opening (583). At the side edge of the front a strip of material is set on, right side to right side, for the length of the pocket opening, to serve as a pocket facing (584). The pocket section is tacked on the wrong side (585). The facing is turned to the inside and hemmed on to the pocket, and the opening edge stitched in the shape of a flap (586). The inner edge of the pocket is set on to the back section of the knickers, and the side seams above and below the pocket openings are closed (587). This may be done by single seam, or the front section may be stitched on to the back section with a narrow lap seam.
The inner leg seams are stitched together, and the middle seam sewn from the waist at the back to the fly opening to join the two legs (588).
The knickers may be lined throughout, or merely the

crutch covered with a protective lining. This is cut in the shape of the knicker sections, reaching in front to the fly and a little higher behind. The crutch-lining is fastened along the seams with slip-stitch, and secured all round with herringbone-stitch (590).
The waistline is reduced at the back by darts, in front often by little pleats stitched down close to the edge and opening out lower down. It is neatened with a strip of lining which is stitched on, reversed, and stitched down (591). The leg openings are hemmed with slip-stitch. Buttons are sewn on at the upper edge of the waistline, inside or out, for the braces. If the knickers are to be fastened to a bodice, buttonholes must be worked instead of sewing on buttons. For wear with a belt, narrow belt carriers are sewn on at the back and sides. Very small boys generally wear the knickers buttoned on to a lining bodice, which may be made of single or of double stuff. For the latter, both layers are stitched together along neckline and armhole by reversed seams, the sections are turned, the shoulder seams of the outer layer stitched together and those of the inner layer felled over the seam edges. Along the opening and the lower edge both layers are turned in and stitched together. For a single-material bodice the neckline and armholes are bound with bias-strips. The lining bodice is usually fastened with buttons down the back, but it may be arranged with a front opening. The overlap and underlap on a bodice of single material should have a wide hem to give a better foundation for the buttons, as should also the lower edge to which the knickers are buttoned. It is a very practical idea to sew the buttons at the back on to short strips of elastic, which will "give" to any bending and prevent the material from tearing. It is advisable also to cut the bodice a little longer than necessary, the extra length being taken up by a tuck which can be let out as the child grows. This tuck should be directed to the inside, and the strips of elastic for the back buttons can be stitched on to it.

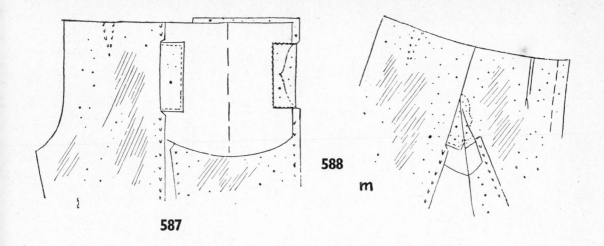

587   588

m

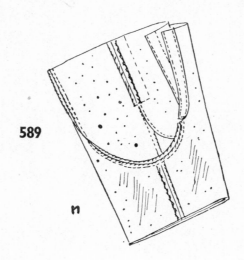

589

n

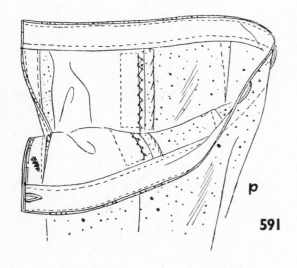

591

p

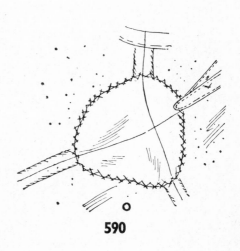

590

o

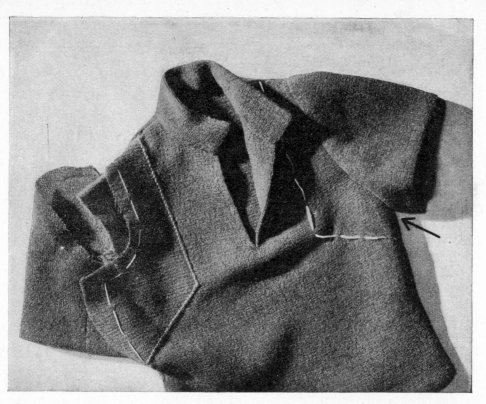

Mending

By mending is generally understood the setting-in of patches; this work has already been described. We need only repeat that the patches must always be set in on a straight thread and that the corners must be worked absolutely cleanly, so that in certain weaves the seam is not visible at all.

This method, however, cannot always be employed when mending dresses and costumes, where it is essential to restore the worn part in a manner that will not be noticeable. A good tip, suitable for blouses which are worn under the arms, is shown in 592. A section of material is set on in such a way as to make it appear that it was part of the original pattern. Mark out first of all the shape of the yoke on the blouse with tack stitches. The dart seam may give the direction for this. Sleeve, side, and shoulder seams are unpicked so that the new section (which should be cut, allowing for turnings, with the old section as pattern) may be tacked on. The yoke is best edge-stitched on and all the seams are then closed. The back section can be renewed in the same way, if necessary.

By slip-stitching on a stitched band, a long sleeve may be mended in a way that is unnoticeable. The band may reach from the wrist edge to beyond the elbow.

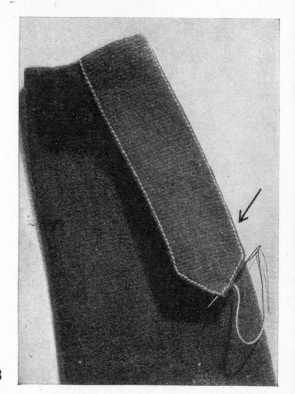

593

594

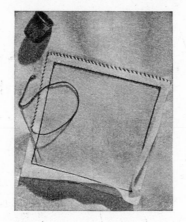

595

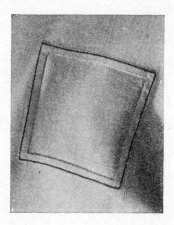

596

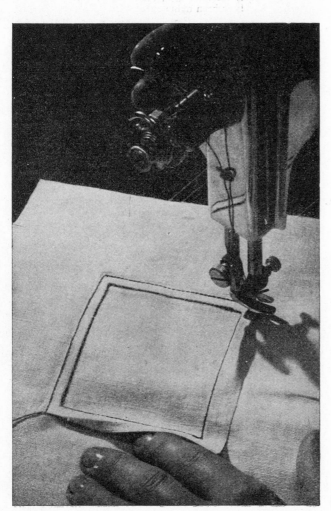

597

594-597. THIN OR TORN PLACES in the fabric are replaced by set-in patches on a straight thread. The material is cut out in a square or rectangle all round the worn place and the patch cut to fit, adding double the width of the seam and the turn-in, i.e. $\frac{3}{8}$ in. must be allowed. The corners of the cut-out must be notched $\frac{1}{8}$ in., so that the edge of the material can "give." In order to obtain particularly clean and neat corner seams, leave the needle in the material when turning it to work another edge. The turning of the patch is hemmed over or stitched down.

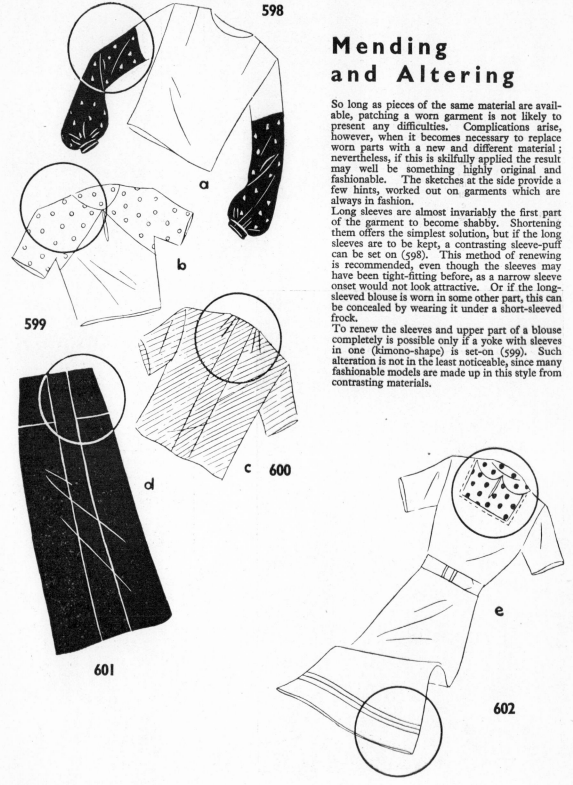

Mending and Altering

So long as pieces of the same material are available, patching a worn garment is not likely to present any difficulties. Complications arise, however, when it becomes necessary to replace worn parts with a new and different material; nevertheless, if this is skilfully applied the result may well be something highly original and fashionable. The sketches at the side provide a few hints, worked out on garments which are always in fashion.

Long sleeves are almost invariably the first part of the garment to become shabby. Shortening them offers the simplest solution, but if the long sleeves are to be kept, a contrasting sleeve-puff can be set on (598). This method of renewing is recommended, even though the sleeves may have been tight-fitting before, as a narrow sleeve onset would not look attractive. Or if the long-sleeved blouse is worn in some other part, this can be concealed by wearing it under a short-sleeved frock.

To renew the sleeves and upper part of a blouse completely is possible only if a yoke with sleeves in one (kimono-shape) is set-on (599). Such alteration is not in the least noticeable, since many fashionable models are made up in this style from contrasting materials.

Mending and Altering (continued)

If the back section is to be widened (600), the material used should be the same, if possible. The insertion need not consist of one long strip; several pieces may be skilfully joined together, with a point stitched over. Such a strip can only be used to widen the back section, but if the back is torn by the armhole, the shoulder, armhole, and side seams are unpicked, the strip is set into the middle of the back section, and the extra width so obtained may be sufficient to allow the worn part at the side to be cut away. The shoulder seam will have to be moved to correspond with the alteration.

If the neckline has become too wide, it can be reduced by putting in a few dart pleats.

To alter a skirt, the same material will be required, if it is a case of widening or lengthening (601). A worn jacket of the same material may serve very well for the purpose. A widening strip is set into the middle of the front, if necessary into the back as well; the strip may consist of several pieces joined together, and it should be as long as the skirt after the yoke sections have been joined at the sides. The depth of the yoke will depend upon the amount of lengthening that is required. A narrow yoke strip is often sufficient, and may be quite invisible if the blouse is worn over the skirt. The skirt may also be lengthened by setting on a hem-strip of the same material. The seam can be concealed by several narrow tucks.

If it is desired to alter a low-necked frock to one with a round neck, a contrasting collar vest can be set in (602).

607

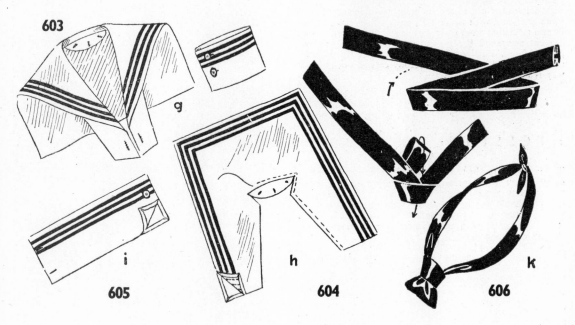

603

g

i

605

h

604

606

k

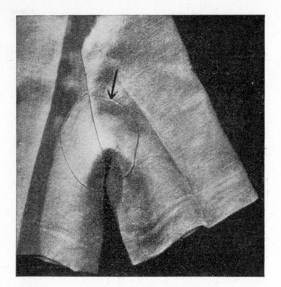

608

How to Mend Boys' Knickers

607–608 show a very practical method of mending worn knickers. Middle seam and inner leg seam are un-picked as far as necessary, and the outline of the part to be mended is marked with tack thread. Sections of material are cut out to the shape of the marking in the same grain and with ample turnings. They are pinned in and tacked on from the right (607). The worn parts are cut away and the seams stitched and thoroughly pressed (608). Finally the leg seams and then the middle seam are closed. Mending carefully carried out in this way is barely visible.

Pressing

The iron must not be too light, so that there may be suffi-cient weight when pressing heavy materials. Those who have to press jackets, coats, and men's suits fre-quently should purchase a second iron for this purpose only. If the iron has no stand, it should be placed on an asbestos mat, with which most ironing-boards are already equipped.

The ironing-board should be pointed at one end so that dresses can be drawn over it easily. The soft ironing-blanket should be protected by a calico cover which can be removed for washing. A cover with a cap, set on with a reversed seam, is very practical (609). This may be tied on with tapes. The sleeve-board (610) is also provided with a washable cover, which is sewn together for half its length so that it may be drawn on like a

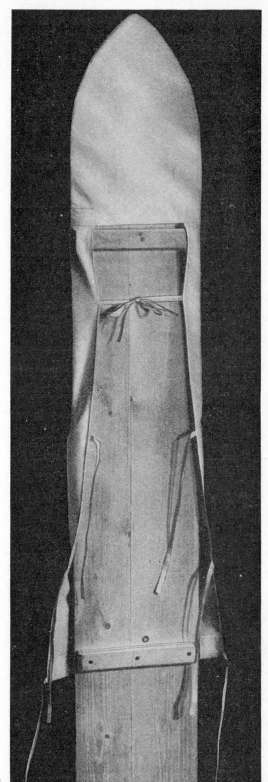

609

Pressing (continued)

pillow slip; the other half has a slot seam with a draw tape. Fairly important, too, are the hand-cushion, the large press-cushion, and the so-called collar-board (611), which is made of hard wood and is used when pressing thick edges of material. The pressing-cloth should be of linen or a non-fluffing cotton material.

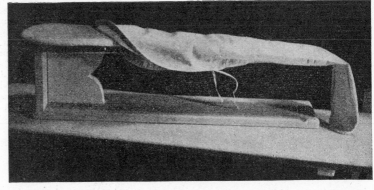

610

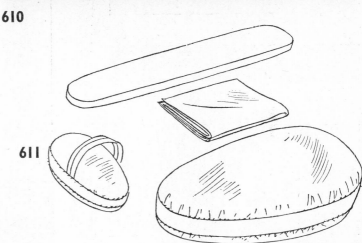

611

How to Iron Shirts and Collars

The sports shirt remains soft. The tunic shirt is half starched, i.e. the neckband, front, and cuffs are starched. The same applies to collars. Sports collars remain soft; the ordinary shirt collar is slightly starched, and the stiff collar is thoroughly starched.

The neckband is ironed first: it should be laid down flat, the inside uppermost, ironed on a little, turned, ironed fast, and rounded like a collar. Next the yoke (612) and the folded sleeves (613). The cuff, too, is ironed on the inside and then ironed fast on the right side; on a double cuff, the fold is dampened, and when the cuff has been turned

back so that the buttonholes meet, the fold is ironed fast. When rounding, the cuff is drawn once under the iron, and then the outside (614) (right and wrong sides in turn) is pressed, working the iron towards the centre; finally, the folded cuff is ironed over again. The back section comes next: to iron this, the shirt may be drawn over the ironing-board. The lower front section follows, and then the shirt front. The front fastening must close up exactly. The left front is done first; all little wrinkles are smoothed towards the outer edge (615).

The collar is held with the left hand and ironed lightly

612

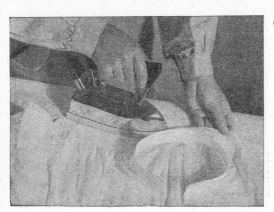

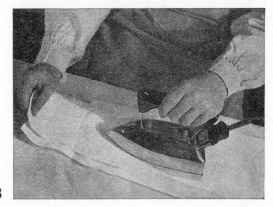

613

614

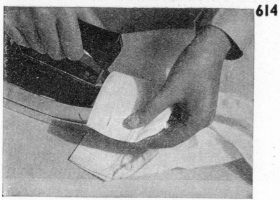

This procedure is repeated from the right ; the collar is drawn under as far as the middle and the end turned inwards (616). Finally, in the case of a wing collar, the fold lines for the wings are dampened and the corners bent over by hand and ironed over (617). The turn-over collar must be well dampened in the fold. When ironing it over, a soft flannel cloth is laid in (618) and the lower part ironed again. When the collar has been ironed dry and ironed over again from the outside, it is rounded.

615

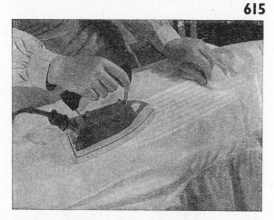

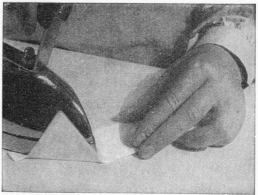

617

616

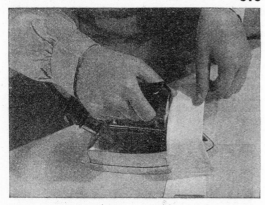

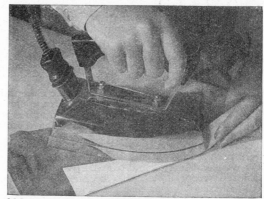

618

Ironing (continued)

on the wrong side. It is then turned to the right and all little creases smoothed quickly, working towards the outside edges. The ironing is done lightly at first, then continued with increasing pressure. The buttonhole is opened with the folder. To round the collar it is ironed lightly on the inside, then the iron is set on at the left buttonhole, and the collar drawn quickly to the right with the left hand.

619

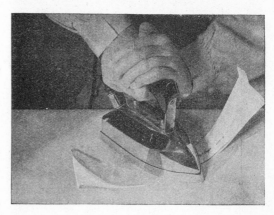

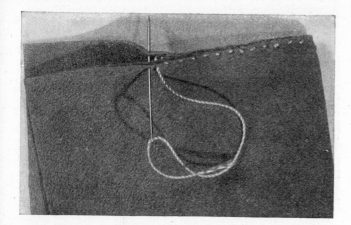

620. Two leather edges can be joined by stitching up and down, thus producing a running-stitch. The stitches should be carried out with a special leather-needle and must be placed close together and drawn tight.

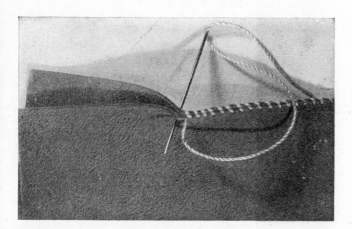

621. Leather may also be sewn together by overcasting. This gives a flatter seam than the running-stitch. If carried out with thread in a contrasting shade, the row of overcasting forms a pretty trimming.

Leather Work

Thin, soft leathers may be worked like cloth; though in the case of chamois leather due attention must be paid to the grain. There is no need to make any allowance for the natural elasticity of the leather when cutting it out for trimmings and facings, since these will not be called upon to stand hard wear or strain. For belts, however, the leather must be so cut that it does not stretch in use. Leather gloves must be able to stretch across, but should not have any " give " lengthways. If you have a whole skin at your disposal, you will find that its stretch is across, and only to a very slight extent lengthways.

If the skin is not perfectly smooth and flat, it must be stretched. For this purpose the back of the skin is dampened so that the leather can be stretched and then nailed upon a board. The skin must be allowed to dry in the air (never near a fire). The pattern can be drawn or transferred upon it while still upon the board. The cutting out is done with scissors, but in the case of a thick skin a razor blade is used (622) so that smoother-cut edges can be produced. Skins or pieces of skin that are a little too small can be enlarged by alternately dampening and stretching.

Leather can be sewn by hand or by machine. The latter should be used only for thin, soft leathers in order to avoid straining the machine. For sewing by hand, a special leather-needle is required, with a triangular point which will pierce the leather like a little knife. Buttonhole twist should be used for thread; it is drawn through tailor's wax to render it more hard-wearing and enable it to glide more easily through the leather without its becoming frayed or untwisted. Cut fringes at the edges of leather sets (623) look very attractive.

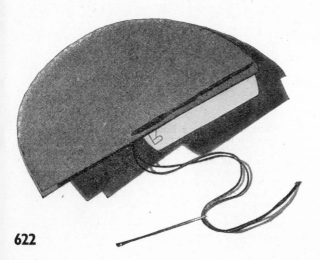

622

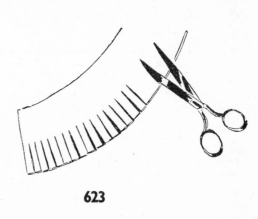

623

624

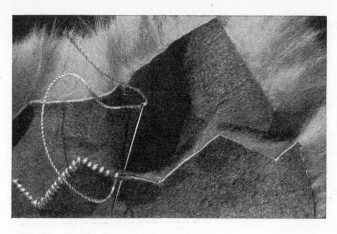

624. WHEN JOINING PIECES OF FUR, overhanding stitches are used. Lamb's wool interlining makes the fur soft and warm. The fur edge is neatened with binding tape set on reversed and catch-stitched to the interlining.

625

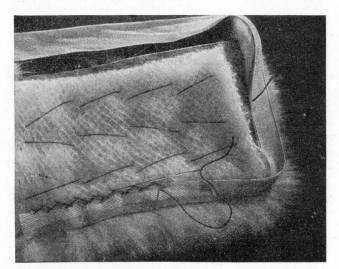

Fur

A fur skin is smoothed out like a leather skin, by dampening and stretching; before this is done, any tears or holes in the skin should be sewn up. For dampening use a rag, or a so-called cloth sponge made up of a number of strips of cloth tied together by another strip (626). The skin—fur-side down—is nailed on to a board with small tacks and must be stretched at the same time. It should be allowed to dry in the air, as artificial heat will make it hard and brittle. When the skin is stretched and dry, the pattern can be traced upon it (627). If several pieces of fur have to be joined to make up a large section, the direction and colour of the hair must be carefully matched. This requires great skill and practice, and difficult work should therefore be left to the expert. A join is less noticeable if carried out in a

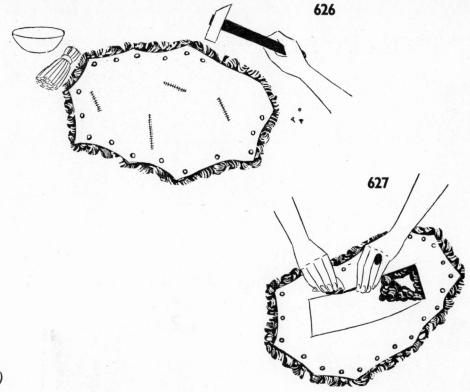

626

627

Furs *(continued)*

zigzag line (624), but for all curly pelts a simple straight over-handed seam is sufficient. When sewing, the hair should be stroked inwards.

In the case of thick leathers, a Polish seam will wear particularly well. This is made by working a second overhanding seam over the first.

The cutting out is done with a furrier's knife, or, as a makeshift, with a sharp razor blade sewn between two pieces of cardboard (622). The hair must not be damaged when cutting out.

Fur is always interlined ; muslin, flannel, or lamb's wool is used for the purpose, depending on the fur, whether it is flat or full, intended merely as a trimming or to give warmth. 625 shows how the inter-lining is basted on with large stitches ; the set-on tape makes it an easy matter to neaten the edges.

The fur is lined with silk (628), or hemmed on with slip-stitch, as in the case of the cloth collar with linen interlining (629).

628

629

G

PART SIX

Knitting

Knitting Hints

One of the features of good knitting is its evenness, which may be obtained by working *steadily*, whether quickly or slowly. It is usually found, however, that the quicker one knits the easier it is to attain the desired evenness. Always complete a row before leaving your knitting, otherwise a loose stitch is formed by the dragging of the needles.

You will find it a help to mark decreasing, increasing, or any place from which you have to count up the rows, by knitting in a tiny piece of coloured thread. This can be easily drawn out afterwards.

Knitting, unless it has a decided surface pattern, is greatly improved by pressing. To do this, first pin out the work to the required shape and size, right side downwards, on an ironing-board, then place over it a damp cloth and press thoroughly with a warm iron, redampening the cloth as necessary. Garter-stitch, moss-stitch, and similar raised patterns do not require such heavy pressing as do stocking-web and most open patterns. Ribbing loses its elasticity if pressed too heavily, and is sometimes better left unpressed.

How to Cast on Stitches

All knitting is begun from a single loop on the needle, which is made thus : Hold wool between thumb and first finger of left hand, the " tag " hanging down in the palm. With the right hand, twist wool round into ring (630), which hold in position with the left-hand thumb ; let the wool from ball pass over the tag end with ball on the right. Pull the wool from the ball up through the ring (631), then let the ring gradually slide up this wool and so form a loop.

Pass this loop on to a needle.

Hold the needle with the loop on it in left hand, ★ take second needle in right hand, hold it between thumb and first finger exactly as a pen would be held, the wool over the first finger, under the second and third fingers and over fourth finger. Pass the point from front to back through the upper thread of the loop on left-hand needle, when the left needle will be on top (632).

633 shows how the hands hold the needles, the wool being regulated and passed over the right-hand needle by the first finger of the right hand.

Now bring the wool up at back of both needles, then over point of right-hand one, as 634, and draw it upwards through the loop on the left-hand needle. There is now the original stitch on the left-hand needle, and the new stitch on the right-hand needle. Pull the stitch on the right-hand needle out until it is an inch or more in length, as 635, then insert the point of the left-hand needle into this extended loop (see 636). Both needles are now in the same loop. Slip out the right-hand needle, and so add a new stitch to the left-hand needle, which gently pull up close to needle. Continue in this manner from ★ until the specified number of stitches are all on the left-hand needle (see 637).

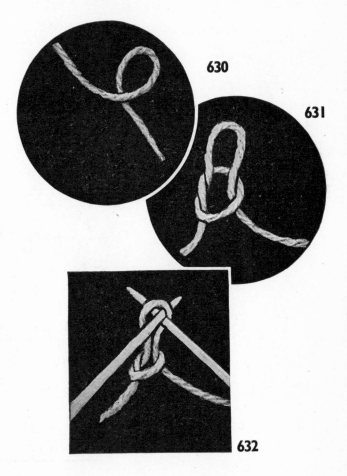

630

631

632

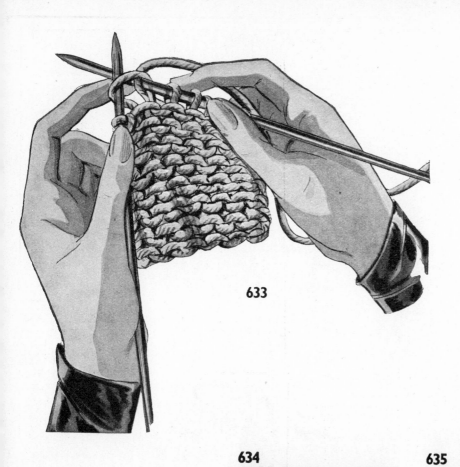

633

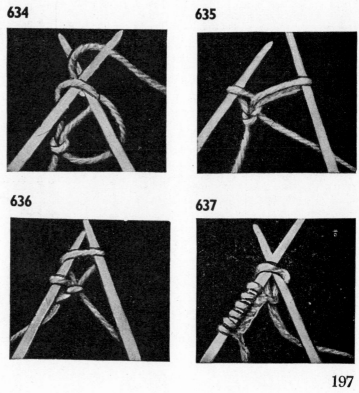

634

635

636

637

Simple Stitches

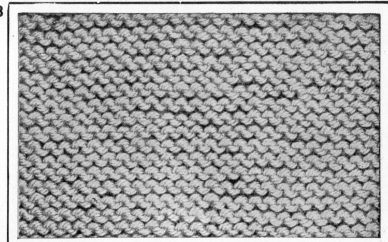

Begin garter-stitch by casting on any required number of stitches, then take the needle with the cast-on stitches and hold it in the left hand, with its point between the thumb and first finger. Take the other needle between the thumb and first finger of the right hand and hold it as shown in 633, then insert the point of the needle from left to right through the first stitch on left-hand needle. With the first finger of right hand pass the wool round the point of the right-hand needle (first under and then over), keeping the wool now, and always, at the back of the work, draw the wool on the needle through the stitch to front of knitting, slip the old stitch off the left-hand needle, and keep the new stitch on the right-hand needle ; continue in this way until all the stitches are worked. Now reverse your needles, hold them as at first, and continue to work each row in exactly the same way, for length required.

Stocking-stitch consists of one row of *plain* knitting and one row of *purl* knitting. Cast on any required number of stitches and knit first row as for garter-stitch. The second row is a purl row and worked thus : Hold the needles as before, the full needle in the left hand and the spare needle in the right hand (for this row always keep the wool in front of the work), pass the point of the right-hand needle under the wool and insert it from right to left, through the first stitch, bringing the needle in front of the left-hand needle. With the first finger of the right hand pass the wool over the point, then under the needle to the front again, then draw the

638. GARTER-STITCH, sometimes referred to as plain knitting, is the simplest kind of all and is alike on both sides.

639. STOCKING-STITCH, which shares the honour equally with garter-stitch, these two being the basic stitches of practically all knitting.

640. Here is shown the reverse side of stocking-stitch, and this is the one that faces the worker when the purl rows are in progress.

wool on the needle through the stitch, to the back of the work, slip the old stitch off the left-hand needle and keep the new stitch on the right-hand needle ; continue in this way until all the stitches are worked off. Repeat these two rows for length required.

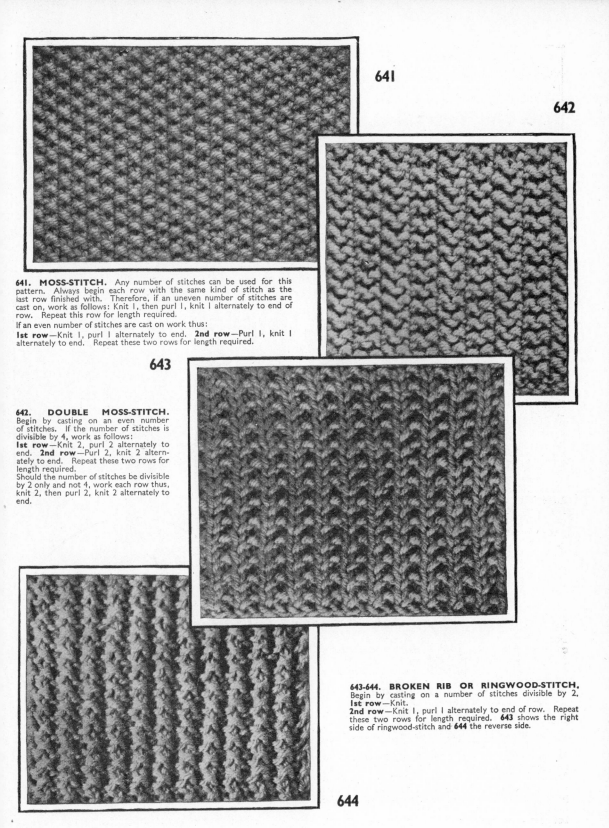

641. MOSS-STITCH. Any number of stitches can be used for this pattern. Always begin each row with the same kind of stitch as the last row finished with. Therefore, if an uneven number of stitches are cast on, work as follows: Knit 1, then purl 1, knit 1 alternately to end of row. Repeat this row for length required.

If an even number of stitches are cast on work thus:

1st row—Knit 1, purl 1 alternately to end. **2nd row**—Purl 1, knit 1 alternately to end. Repeat these two rows for length required.

642. DOUBLE MOSS-STITCH. Begin by casting on an even number of stitches. If the number of stitches is divisible by 4, work as follows: **1st row**—Knit 2, purl 2 alternately to end. **2nd row**—Purl 2, knit 2 alternately to end. Repeat these two rows for length required.

Should the number of stitches be divisible by 2 only and not 4, work each row thus, knit 2, then purl 2, knit 2 alternately to end.

643-644. BROKEN RIB OR RINGWOOD-STITCH. Begin by casting on a number of stitches divisible by 2. **1st row**—Knit. **2nd row**—Knit 1, purl 1 alternately to end of row. Repeat these two rows for length required. **643** shows the right side of ringwood-stitch and **644** the reverse side.

645

646

Ribbed Knitting

Composed by alternately Knitting and Purling any set number of Stitches so that upright or horizontal Bands or Ribs are formed.

RIDGED KNITTING (645). Begin by casting on required number of stitches.
1st row—Knit. 2nd row—Purl. 3rd row—Knit. 4th row—Knit. 5th row—Purl. 6th row—Knit.
Repeat these 6 rows for length required.

RIBBED KNITTING (646-647). This type of knitting is mostly used for cuffs, neckbands, and weltings for stockings and jumpers. It is particularly elastic, so that while fitting closely it will stretch to almost any size. For the example shown here, begin by casting on a number of stitches divisible by 4.
1st row—Knit 2 stitches plain, bring the wool to the front of the work between the two needles, and purl the next 2 stitches, pass the wool to the back of the work between the two needles, and knit 2, bring the wool to the front of the work and purl 2. Continue in this way to the end of the row. Knit each row in the same way for the length required.
Wide or narrow ribbing can be obtained by varying the number of stitches in the rib. For instance, knit one, purl one, forms an effective narrow rib, and knit 3, purl 3 a wider one. In each of these cases the purl and plain ribs are of even width.
For a wide and narrow rib as shown in 647 commence by casting on a number of stitches divisible by 6.
1st row—Knit 4 stitches, purl 2 stitches alternately to end of row.
2nd row—Knit 2, purl 4 alternately to end of row.
Repeat these two rows for length required.

BLOCK PATTERN (648). For this pattern commence by casting on any even number of stitches. If the number of cast-on stitches is divisible by 4, work as follows.
1st row—Knit 2, purl 2 alternately to end. 2nd row—As 1st row.
3rd row—Purl 2, knit 2, alternately to end. 4th row—As 3rd row. Repeat these 4 rows for required length. Should the number of cast-on stitches be divisible by 2 only and not 4, work thus :
1st row—Knit 2, then purl 2, knit 2 alternately to end.

647

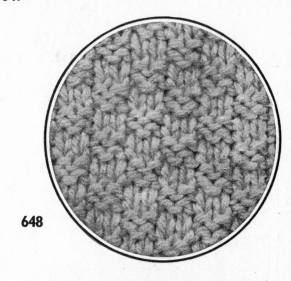
648

2nd row—Purl 2, then knit 2, purl 2 alternately to end.
3rd row—Purl 2, then knit 2, purl 2 alternately to end.
4th row—Knit 2, then purl 2, knit 2 alternately to end.
Repeat these 4 rows for length required.

Increasing and Decreasing

(see overleaf)

649

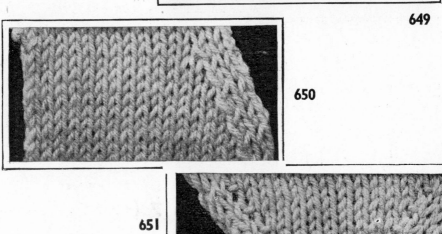

650

651

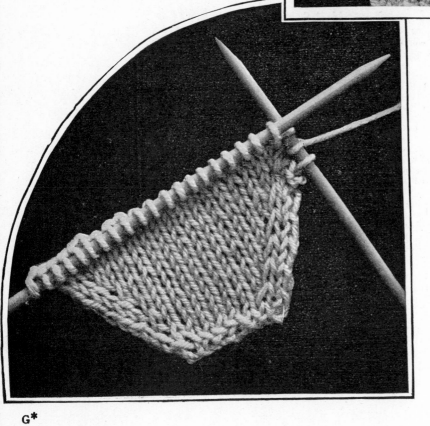

652

G*

Increasing
and Decreasing

DECREASING (649-650). Stitches in knitting can be decreased by either knitting 2 stitches together, or purling 2 stitches together, as the case may be. 649 shows this method of decreasing. Another way is to slip 1 stitch, knit the next stitch, then pass the slipped-stitch over the knitted one. This is shown in 650. To slip a stitch, simply take the stitch from the left-hand needle to the right-hand needle without knitting it.

INCREASING (651-652). To increase, knit 2 stitches into 1 stitch, by knitting into the back, as well as the front of the stitch, before slipping it off the needle (651).

Another very neat way is to knit a stitch into the loop just below the next stitch to be knitted on the left-hand needle, as shown in 652.

These methods are rarely used in openwork or fancy patterns; in the latter the way described overleaf is employed, as the object is usually to make a hole, thus forming the open pattern.

653

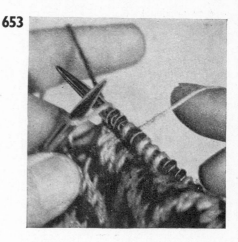

Knitting
with Two Colours

654

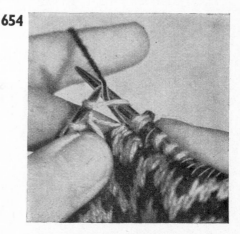

The easiest way to hold the wool when working Fair Isle or jazz patterns in a round, or for knit rows, is as illustrated. This obviates dropping and picking up each colour in turn.

The knitting is held in the usual way and one colour (fawn for instance) is held in the right hand, as for plain knitting. The other colour, say red, is held in the left hand over the middle finger, which holds it out away from the knitting, just as it is held for crochet (see 653).

If a fawn stitch is to be worked, this is done in the usual way, and as the left hand is holding out the red wool the fawn passes over it and thus " strands " at the back. When a red stitch is required, the fawn wool is still retained in the right hand, and the point of the right-hand needle is passed through the next stitch in readiness for knitting, then over the red wool (see 654), and under it from right to left, at the same time pulling the wool through (655). This method does not weave the wools, but merely " strands " them. For weaving, work as follows : Hold the colour to be woven in left hand as shown in 653, then work as just described, but at every alternate stitch, or every second or third if preferred, pass point of right-hand needle through stitch, then under red wool, pass fawn wool over point of right-hand needle, then draw it through stitch, allowing red wool to slip off. The colour to be woven must always be held in the left hand. When weaving in a purl row, the wools are held in the same way, and one stitch is worked under and one over the wool.

655

Casting Off

656. Knit the first 2 stitches, then pass left-hand needle from left to right through first stitch, and pull this stitch over second one and off right-hand needle. Now knit next stitch, and take second one over this and off needle in same way as first stitch. Continue thus until only 1 stitch remains, break off wool, and slip end through last stitch, which slip off needle, and draw end tight. Another method is to knit the first 2 stitches together, slip the stitch on the right-hand needle back on to left one, then knit this stitch together with third one on right needle. Continue thus until only 1 stitch remains, break off wool and finish as in other method.

657

658

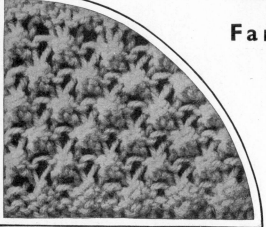

Fancy Patterns

TO MAKE A STITCH (657). This method is generally used in fancy patterns, as, where each stitch is made, a little hole appears in the knitting, also, in most cases, to retain the balance of the stitches, one is decreased either before or after the made stitch. 657 shows the made stitches quite clearly; to work this, cast on any number of stitches divisible by 3. **1st row** —Knit.
2nd row—Purl. **3rd row**—Knit 1, make 1 (by passing the wool round the point of the right-hand needle, first under, then over), knit the next 2 stitches together, now knit 1, make 1, knit 2 together, continue in this way to end of row. **4th row**—Purl. Repeat the 3rd and 4th rows for required length. To make a stitch in a purl row, pass the wool from front of work, first over, then under right-hand needle.

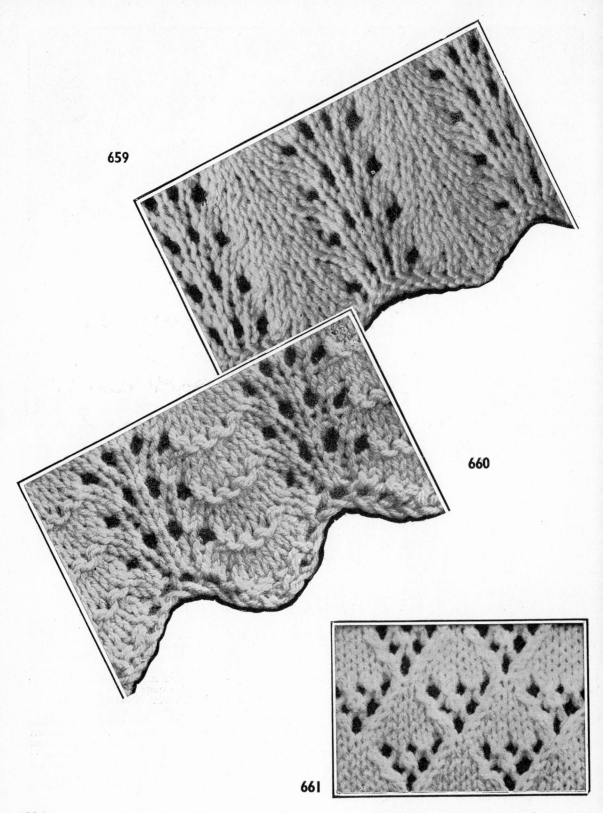

659

660

661

BLACKBERRY-STITCH (658). Begin by casting on a number of stitches divisible by 4, with 6 over. These 6 stitches are for border, 3 at each edge.

1st row—Knit 3, * then knit 1 and purl 1 and knit 1 into the next stitch (thus making 3 stitches), pass the wool to front of work and purl the next 3 stitches together, pass wool to back of work, repeat from * until 3 remain, knit 3.

2nd row—Purl. **3rd row**—Knit 3, * purl the next 3 stitches together, then knit 1 and purl 1 and knit 1 into the next stitch, repeat from * until 3 remain, knit 3. **4th row**—Purl. Repeat these 4 rows for length required.

FEATHER PATTERN (659). Begin by casting on any number of stitches divisible by 12. Knit 1 row, purl 1 row. **1st row**—Knit 2 together, knit 2 together, * make 1, knit 1 alternately 4 times, then knit 2 together 4 times, repeat from * until 8 remain, then make 1, knit 1 alternately 4 times, knit 2 together, knit 2 together.

2nd row—Purl.

3rd row—Knit. **4th row**—Purl. Repeat these 4 rows for length required.

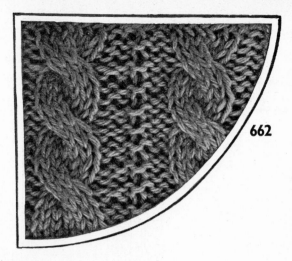

662

RIDGED FEATHER PATTERN (660). Begin by casting on any number of stitches divisible by 12 with 4 over. Knit 1 row, purl 1 row. **1st row**—Knit 2, * purl 2 together, purl 2 together, then make 1, knit 1 alternately 4 times, purl 2 together, purl 2 together, repeat from * until 2 remain, knit 2. **2nd row**—Purl. **3rd row**—Knit. **4th row**—Purl. Repeat these 4 rows for length required.

ARROWHEAD PATTERN (661). Begin by casting on a number of stitches divisible by 8 with 1 over. **1st row**—Knit 3, * knit 2 together, make 1, knit 6, repeat from * until 6 remain, knit 2 together, make 1, knit 4. **2nd row**—Purl.

3rd row—Knit 2, * knit 2 together, make 1, knit 1, make 1, slip 1, knit 1, pass the slipped-stitch over, knit 3, repeat from * until 7 remain, knit 2 together, make 1, knit 1, make 1, slip 1, knit 1, pass the slipped-stitch over, knit 2. **4th row**—Purl.

5th row—Knit 1, * knit 2 together, make 1, knit 1, make 1, knit 2 together, make 1, slip 1, knit 1, pass the slipped-stitch over, knit 1, repeat from * to end. **6th row**—Purl. **7th row**—Knit 7, * knit 2 together, make 1, knit 6, repeat from * until 2 remain, knit 2. **8th row**—Purl.

9th row—Knit 6, * knit 2 together, make 1, knit 1, make 1, slip 1, knit 1, pass the slipped-stitch over, knit 3, repeat from * until 3 remain, knit 3. **10th row**—Purl. **11th row**—Knit 5, * knit 2 together, make 1, knit 1, make 1, knit 2 together, make 1, slip 1, knit 1, pass the slipped-stitch over, knit 1, repeat from * until 4 remain, knit 4. **12th row**—Purl. Repeat these 12 rows for length required.

CABLE-STITCH (662). Begin by casting on any number of stitches divisible by 11 with 1 over. **1st row**—Knit 1, * purl 2, knit 6, purl 2, knit 1, repeat from * to end. **2nd row**—Knit 3, * purl 6, knit 5, repeat from * until 9 remain, purl 6, knit 3. Repeat these 2 rows once. **5th row**—Knit 1, * purl 2, slip next 3 stitches on to spare needle, place them in front of the work, knit the next 3 stitches, place needle containing the 3 slipped stitches to back of work, and knit these 3 stitches (the last 6 stitches from the cable pattern), purl 2, knit 1, repeat from * to end. **6th row**—As 2nd row. Repeat these 6 rows for length required.

DOUBLE KNITTING (663). Begin by casting on an even number of stitches.

1st row—Bring the wool to the front and slip the first stitch purlways, pass the wool to the back, and knit the next stitch plain ; bring the wool to the front and slip the next stitch purlways ; pass the wool to the back and knit the following stitch plain ; repeat thus alternately slipping one stitch and knitting one stitch to end of row. Repeat this row for length required. Always remember that the stitch which was slipped in one row must be knitted in the next row.

663

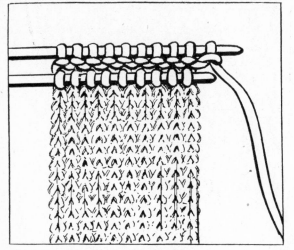

664

How to Graft

When leaving stitches for grafting do not break the wool off close to last stitch, but leave a long end. Thread this into a wool-needle, place the two needles containing stitches together, right side outside, holding work so that end of wool is at the right-hand end of back needle as seen in 664.

Pass wool-needle through first loop of front needle purlways (665), but do not slip loop off the knitting-needle, then pass needle through first loop of back needle as if about to knit, but do not slip loop off (666). * Slip off first loop as if for plain knitting in front row, but keep loop on wool-needle until next loop is worked, pass needle through second loop as if for purling, but do not slip loop off knitting-needle. This is clearly shown in 667. In back row, slip off first loops as for purling, keeping on wool-needle, pass through second loop as for knitting, but do not slip loop off knitting-needle. Repeat from * until all loops are worked off. Fasten off.

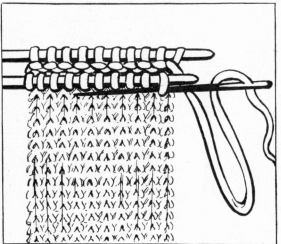

665

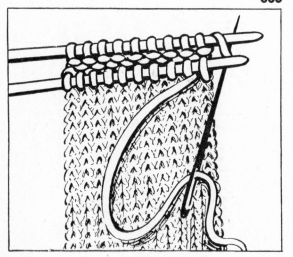

666

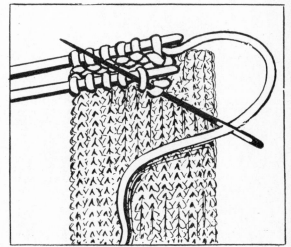

667

Making up Knitted Garments

Pressing must be carefully done, as this can make or mar a garment. Press all pieces on both sides with a damp cloth and warm iron before making up, ribbing excepted. This should be pressed lightly on the wrong side and not stretched. Then each seam should be pressed after being sewn, instead of pressing all together. Use a warm iron and a damp cloth, and lift the iron up and down instead of pushing it along as in ordinary pressing.

Seams can be sewn in several ways. For stocking-stitch garments, or fairly firm patterns, place right sides together and back-stitch $\frac{1}{8}$ in. from the edges with matching wool. Then press the turnings open. For garter-stitch and open patterns the edges should be drawn together with a lacing-stitch. A stitch should be taken into an edge loop, first on one side and then on the other.

Some jumpers with a V-neck are finished off with a ribbed border. To pick up the necessary stitches at the neck for this, hold the V-neck right side towards you. Hold work in the left hand and knitting-needle and wool in the right. Insert the needle through the knitting on stitch from the edge and draw up a loop on the needle to the right side; repeat until you have all the stitches you are directed to have. It is usual to work the ribbing round the neck on much finer needles than those used for the jumper. This also applies to the cuffs.

If you are casting off for the edge of a garment, e.g. on the bottom of a jumper (either back or front, the other edge being cast on), then the cast-off edge should correspond in tightness to the cast-on edge. As casting off is apt to be tighter than casting on, it is a good plan to use a needle two sizes larger for the jumper. If this is not done, you should pull a fairly long loop out for every stitch. Sometimes, of course, " cast off tightly " is directed. In this case draw the stitches as tightly as possible. Cast off on the wrong side if possible, as this gives a better effect.

TO CAST OFF: Knit 2 stitches, * with the point of the left-hand needle lift the first stitch over the second, knit another stitch, and repeat from *.

Note that in casting off a few stitches and leaving other stitches still to be worked on (as in certain parts of a garment), you will be left with one stitch on the right-hand needle, and this has to be counted as one already knitted.

When casting off ribbing, it is best to do so in the rib, as this gives a looser and more pleasing effect : i.e. (suppose it is a knit 1 and purl 1 rib) knit 1, purl 1, put the wool to the back of the needle then * lift the first stitch over the second one; knit 1. Repeat from *. Continue in this way to the end.

The Mark of Good Knitting

Good knitting should be fairly tight, but not so tight that the stitches stick when they are pushed along the needle. Very loose knitting stretches very quickly out of shape and is never satisfactory in wear. On the other hand, too tight knitting is not flexible, as the natural elasticity of the wool is destroyed.

Always complete the garment as quickly as you can. Of course, if you are knitting day in and day out you will always knit at the same tension, but if you only knit for an hour or two at intervals of a week or so, you are liable to vary your tension, and consequently your garment is looser in some places than in others.

Simple Crochet

The beginning of crochet is illustrated in 668–670, the preliminary stitches are sketched in 671–681, and from these basic stitches are worked up all patterns illustrated. The stitches chosen can all be effectively worked in wool, but in cotton crochet, chain, double crochet, trebles, long trebles, holes, small holes, bars, and lacets are the chief ones introduced.

The beginner is advised to use a coarse hook and wool with which to practise the stitches, then when she has learned the actual formation to use finer materials and continue practising until an even tension is obtained.

and pull cotton up, releasing the loop, still holding the tag end to enable the loop to be drawn up close to the hook. Now hold the base of the loop between thumb and finger and cotton in position over fingers as above stated, when there will be a loop on hook. * Pass cotton over hook as in 670, draw through loop on hook, which forms a chain-stitch, and repeat from * until length of chain required is made. Keep all stitches as even in size as possible and do not work too loosely unless otherwise directed. The loops should be just large enough for the hook to pass easily through.

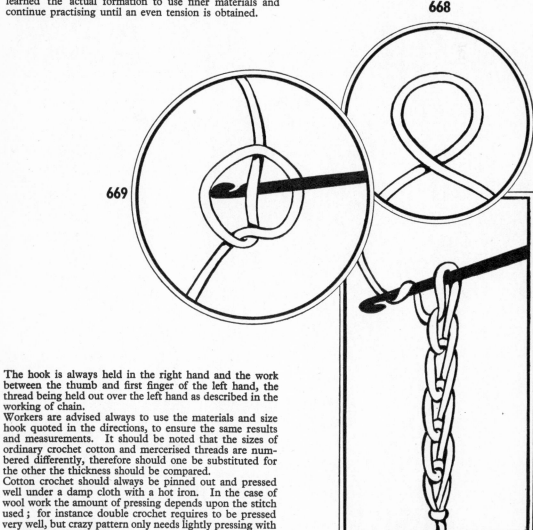

668

669

670

The hook is always held in the right hand and the work between the thumb and first finger of the left hand, the thread being held out over the left hand as described in the working of chain.

Workers are advised always to use the materials and size hook quoted in the directions, to ensure the same results and measurements. It should be noted that the sizes of ordinary crochet cotton and mercerised threads are numbered differently, therefore should one be substituted for the other the thickness should be compared.

Cotton crochet should always be pinned out and pressed well under a damp cloth with a hot iron. In the case of wool work the amount of pressing depends upon the stitch used ; for instance double crochet requires to be pressed very well, but crazy pattern only needs lightly pressing with a moderately hot iron.

Practically all crochet commences with a length of chain for a foundation, and in order to begin, there must be a loop on the hook, so make a loop, as 668, hold the base of loop, where cotton crosses, between thumb and finger of left hand. Let the cotton pass over the first and second fingers, under the third, and over the fourth or little finger. With hook in the right hand, insert it in the loop as 669,

Principal
Stitches

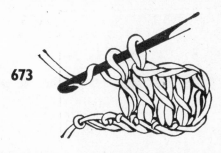

673

TREBLE (673). To work treble, there should be a loop already on the hook, * then wool over hook, insert hook into the stitch to the left, wool over hook, draw through this stitch (3 loops now on hook), wool over hook, draw through first 2 loops on hook, wool over hook, draw through remaining 2 loops, thus making a treble, repeat from * number of times required.

671

SLIP-STITCH (671). Used for passing from one part of the work to another, making an almost invisible stitch. With a loop already on the hook, insert hook into first stitch to the left, wool over hook and draw through the stitch in which the hook was inserted and through the loop on hook, thus making 1 slip-stitch.

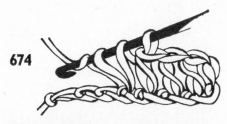

674

SHORT TREBLE (674). With a loop on the hook, * wool over hook, insert hook into a stitch to the left, wool over, draw through this stitch (3 loops now on hook), wool over hook, draw through all loops on hook, thus making a short treble, repeat from * number of times required.

672

DOUBLE CROCHET (672). To work double crochet, there should be a loop already on the hook, * then insert hook into the stitch to the left, wool over hook, draw through this stitch (2 loops now on hook), wool over hook, draw through the 2 loops on the hook, thus making 1 double crochet, repeat from * number of times required.

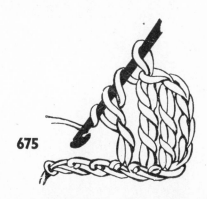

675

LONG TREBLE (675). With a loop on the hook, * pass wool twice over hook, insert hook into the stitch to the left, wool over hook, draw through this stitch (4 loops now on hook), wool over hook, draw through 2 loops on the hook, wool over hook, draw through 2 more loops, wool over hook, draw through 2 remaining loops, thus making a long treble, repeat from * number of times required. **VERY LONG TREBLE.** With a loop on the hook, pass wool 3, 4, or 5 times over the hook, then insert hook into stitch to the left, wool over hook, draw through this stitch, * wool over hook, draw through 2 loops on hook, repeat from * until only 1 loop remains on hook, thus making a very long treble.

211

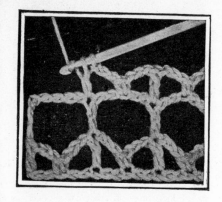

676

LACETS (676). A lacet consists of 3 chain, miss 2 stitches, 1 double-crochet into the middle stitch of bar, 3 chain, miss 2 stitches, 1 treble into treble at end of bar.

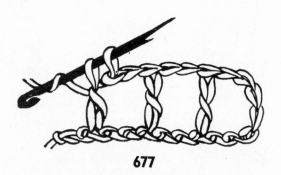

677

HOLES (677). To work holes, first make 1 treble into a stitch, * then make 2 chain, miss 2 stitches, make 1 treble into the third stitch (thus completing a hole), and repeat from *.

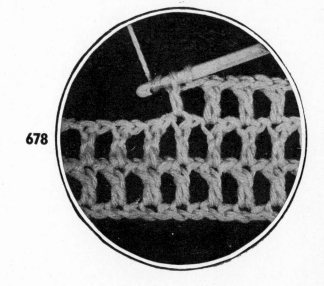

678

SMALL HOLES (678). For a small hole first make 1 treble into a stitch, * then make 1 chain, miss 1 stitch, make 1 treble into second stitch, then repeat from * as required.

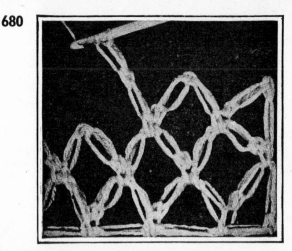

BARS (679). A bar comprises 5 chain, miss 5 stitches or a lacet, 1 treble into next. The treble finishing the last hole, bar, or lacet before a group of trebles, also counts as the first treble of that group.

SOLOMON'S KNOT (680). **1st row**—Loop wool on to hook, then * draw out stitch on hook to form about ½-in. loop, wool over hook and draw through loop, insert hook into back thread of loop, wool over, draw through, wool over, draw through both loops on hook (this completes 1 Solomon's knot), repeat from * for length required. **2nd row**—Miss first 3 Solomon's knots, then work 1 double crochet into knot (see illustration), * 2 Solomon's knots, miss 1 Solomon's knot in previous row, 1 double crochet into knot, repeat from * all along. 2 Solomon's knots, turn. **3rd row**—Miss first 3 Solomon's knots, then work 1 double crochet into knot, * 2 Solomon's knots, miss 2 Solomon's knots in previous row, 1 double crochet into knot, repeat from * to end, 2 Solomon's knots, turn. Repeat 3rd row for length required.

Double Crochet

TO DECREASE (681). *By working two double crochet drawn together.* Insert hook into required stitch, draw wool through, insert hook into next stitch, draw wool through (3 loops now on hook), wool over, draw through these 3 loops on hook at same time.

DOUBLE CROCHET (682). Begin with a length of chain. **1st row**—Miss first chain, then work 1 double crochet into every chain, 1 chain, turn. **2nd row**—1 double crochet into every double crochet of previous row, always working into the 2 top threads of every stitch. Repeat 2nd row.

RIDGED DOUBLE CROCHET. Begin with a length of chain. **1st row**—Miss first chain, then 1 double crochet into every chain, 1 chain, turn. **2nd row**—1 double crochet into every double crochet in previous row, always working into top back thread only of every stitch, 1 chain, turn. Repeat 2nd row.

MOSS-STITCH (683). Begin with a length of chain divisible by two. **1st row**—Miss first 3 chain, 1 double crochet into next chain, * 1 chain, miss 1 chain of the foundation, 1 double crochet into next chain, repeat from * to end, 2 chain, turn. **2nd row**—1 double crochet into first 1 chain space, * 1 chain, 1 double crochet into next space, repeat from * to end, 2 chain, turn. Repeat 2nd row for length required.

SEMI-DOUBLE CROCHET PATTERN (684). Begin with a length of chain. **1st row**—Miss first 3 chain, insert hook into next chain, draw wool through, insert hook into next chain, draw wool through, draw through all loops on hook at same time, this forms first semi-double crochet, * 1 chain, insert hook into next foundation chain, draw wool through, insert hook into next chain, draw wool through, wool over, draw through all loops on hook at same time, repeat from * to end, 2 chain, turn. **2nd row**—Miss first 2 chain, then insert hook into first semi-double crochet in previous row, draw wool through, insert hook into next chain, draw wool through, wool over, draw through all loops on hook at same time, this forms first semi-double crochet, * 1 chain, then work next semi-double crochet thus : insert hook into next semi-double crochet in previous row, draw wool through, insert hook into next chain, draw wool through, wool over, draw through all loops on hook at same time, repeat from * to end, 2 chain, turn. Repeat 2nd row for length required.

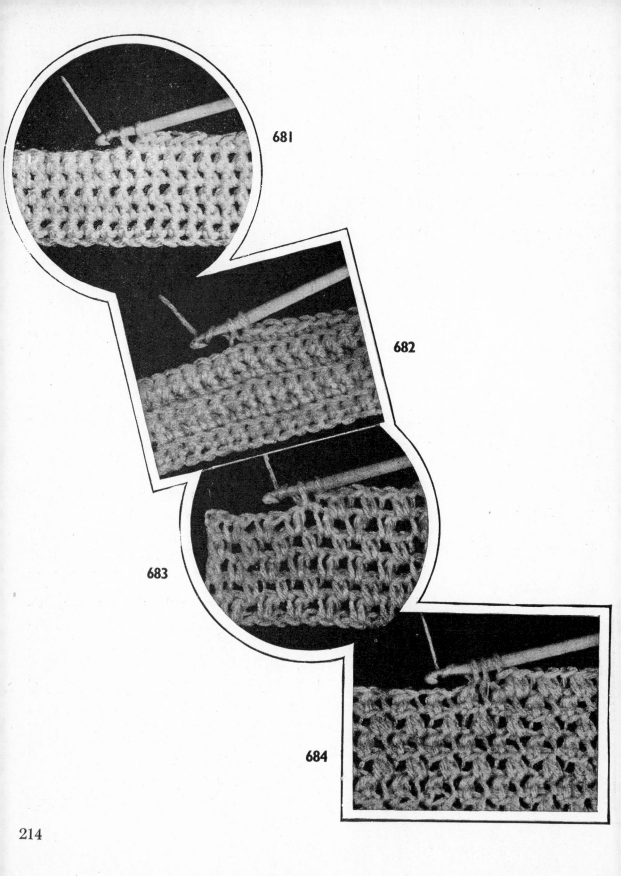

681

682

683

684

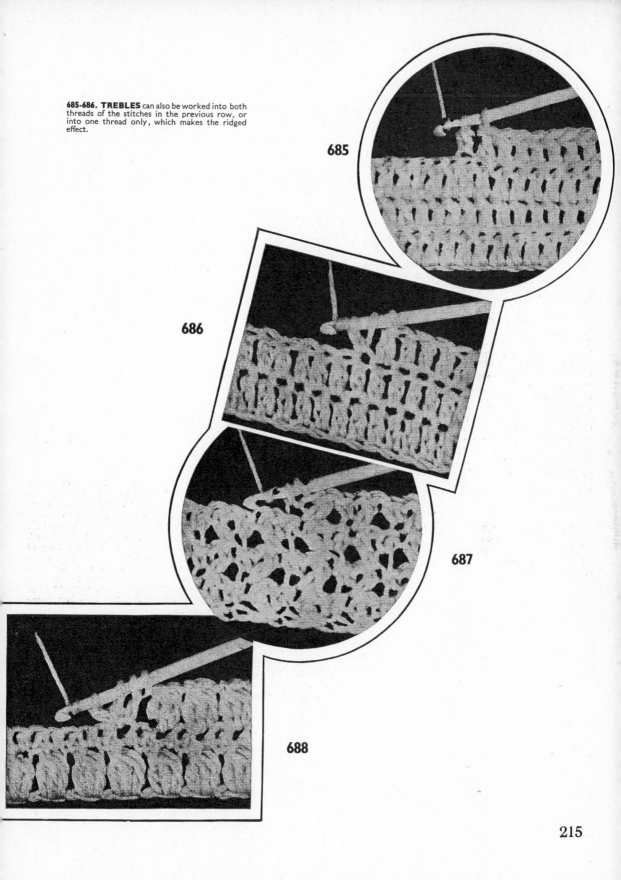

685-686. TREBLES can also be worked into both threads of the stitches in the previous row, or into one thread only, which makes the ridged effect.

685

686

687

688

215

Trebles

RIDGED TREBLE. Begin with a length of chain. **1st row**—Miss first 3 chain, then work 1 treble into every chain, 3 chain, turn. **2nd row**—Miss first treble, then work 1 treble into every stitch of previous row, always working into top back thread only of every stitch, 3 chain, turn. Repeat 2nd row for length required.

A VERY SIMPLE STITCH (687). Begin with a length of chain divisible by three and one over. **1st row**—1 treble into 4th chain from hook, working into both threads of the chain, 1 chain, 1 double crochet into front thread only of same chain, * miss 2 chain, 1 treble into both threads of next chain, 1 chain, 1 double crochet into front thread only of same chain, repeat from * to end, 2 chain, turn. **2nd row**—1 treble into both threads of first treble, 1 chain, 1 double crochet into front thread only of same treble, * 1 treble into both threads of next treble, 1 chain, 1 double crochet into front thread only of same treble, repeat from * to end, 2 chain, turn. Repeat 2nd row for length required.

GROUPS AND DOUBLE CROCHET (688). Begin with a length of chain. **1st row**—Miss first 3 chain, then work one group thus : Wool over hook, insert hook into next stitch, draw wool through, wool over, draw through two loops, wool over, insert hook into same place, draw wool through, wool over, draw wool through two loops, wool over, insert hook into same place again, draw wool through, wool over, draw through two loops, wool over, draw through all loops on hook at same time, * 1 chain, miss 1 chain of the foundation, then work one group as already described into next chain, repeat from * to end, 1 chain, turn. **2nd row**—1 double crochet into every stitch, 3 chain, turn. **3rd row**—Miss first double crochet, then work one group into next double crochet, * 1 chain, miss 1 double crochet, then work one group into next double crochet, repeat from * to end, 1 chain, turn. Repeat last 2 rows for length required.

HALF TREBLE. With a loop already on the hook, * pass wool over the hook, insert into required stitch, draw wool through, wool over, draw through first loop on hook, wool over, draw through all loops on hook at same time, repeat from *.

Fancy Stitches

STAR-STITCH (689). Begin with a length of chain. **1st row**—Miss first chain, * insert hook into next chain, draw wool through, * repeat from * to * 4 times (6 loops now on hook), wool over, draw through all loops on hook at same time, ** 1 chain, insert hook into small hole formed by the one chain at top of star just worked, draw wool through, insert hook into back of last loop of same star, draw wool through, insert hook into chain last worked into of the foundation, draw wool through, repeat from * to * twice, wool over, draw through all loops on hook at same time, ** repeat from ** to ** until 1 chain remains, then 1 chain, 1 treble into last chain of the foundation, fasten off. **2nd row**—Slip-stitch into beginning of previous row, 3 chain, miss first chain of these, insert hook into next chain, draw wool through, insert hook into next chain, draw wool through, insert hook into stitch along side of first star in previous row, draw wool through, insert hook into hole of same star, draw wool through, insert hook into stitch along side of next star, draw wool through, wool over, draw through all loops on hook, * 1 chain, insert hook into hole of star just made, draw wool through, insert hook into back of last loop worked of same star, draw wool through, insert hook into same place as last stitch of previous star, draw wool through, insert hook into hole of star in previous row, draw wool through, insert hook into stitch along side of next star, draw wool through, wool over, draw through all loops on hook, repeat from *, and when working the last star, instead of inserting hook into the stitch along side of star, insert hook into treble at end of row, draw wool through, wool over, draw through all loops on hook, 1 chain, 1 treble into same treble again, fasten off.

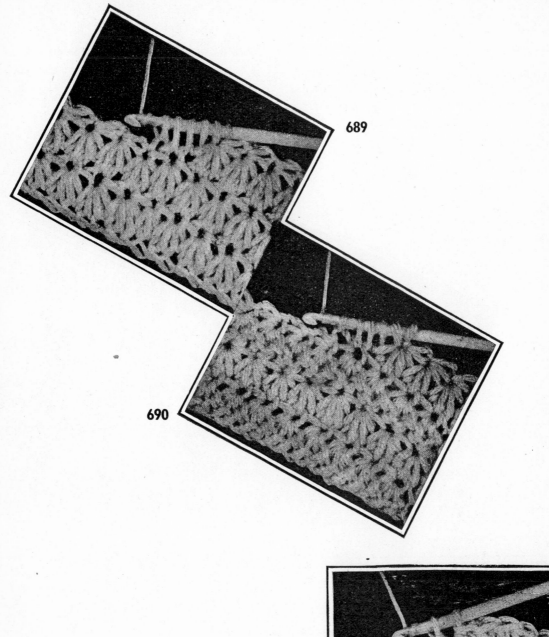

689

690

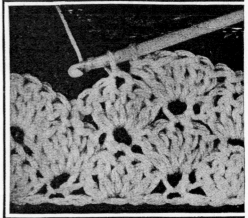

691

217

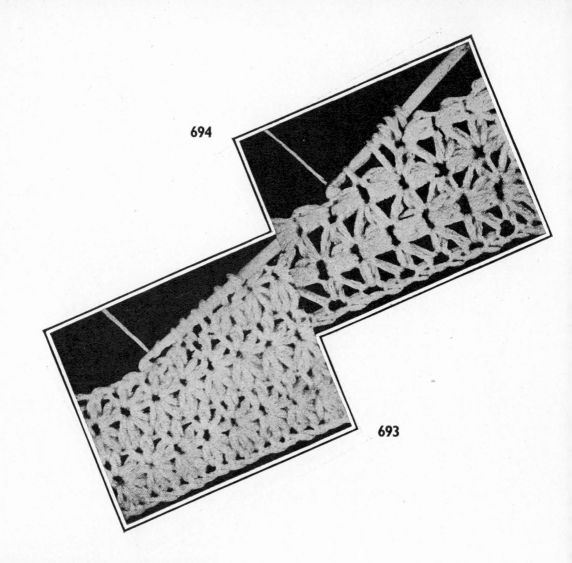

694

693

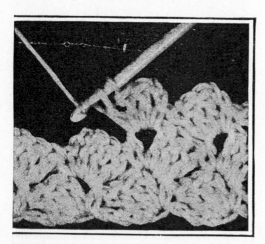

692

STAR-STITCH (690). *Worked in rows backwards and forwards.* Begin with a length of chain.

1st row—Miss first chain, * insert hook into next chain, draw through, * repeat from * to * 4 times wool (6 loops now on hook), wool over, draw through all loops on hook at same time, ** 1 chain, insert hook into hole at top of star just made, draw wool through, insert hook into back of last loop of same star, draw wool through, insert hook into chain last worked into of the foundation, draw wool through, repeat from * to * twice, wool over, draw through all loops on hook at same time, repeat from ** until 1 chain remains, then 1 chain, 1 double crochet into last chain of the foundation, 3 chain, turn.

2nd row—Miss first chain, insert hook into next chain, draw wool through, insert hook into next chain, draw wool through, insert hook into double crochet, draw wool through, insert hook into hole of next star in previous row, draw wool through, insert hook into stitch along side of same star, draw wool through, wool over, draw through all loops on hook, * 1 chain, insert hook into hole of star just made, draw wool through, insert hook into back of last loop of same star, draw wool through, insert hook into same place as last stitch of previous star, draw wool through, insert hook into hole of next star, draw wool through, insert hook into stitch along side of same star, draw wool through, wool over, draw through all loops on hook, repeat from *, then 1 chain, 1 double crochet into extreme end of row, 3 chain, turn. Repeat 2nd row.

SCALLOP SHELL-STITCH (691). Begin with a length of chain.

1st row—Miss first chain, 1 double crochet into next, * miss 2 chain, 5 treble all into next chain, miss 2 chain, 1 double crochet into next chain, repeat from * to end, 3 chain, turn.

2nd row—2 treble into first double crochet, * miss next 2 treble, 1 double crochet into next treble, then 5 treble all into next double crochet, repeat from *, working only 3 treble into last double crochet, 1 chain, turn.

3rd row—1 double crochet into first treble, * miss next 2 treble, then 5 treble all into next double crochet, miss next 2 treble, 1 double crochet into next treble, repeat from *, working last double crochet into top of 3 chain here seen, 3 chain, turn. Repeat last 2 rows for length required.

CRAZY-STITCH (692). Begin with a length of chain divisible by four and two over.

1st row—Miss first chain, then work 1 double crochet, 2 chain, 3 treble all into the next chain, * miss 3 chain of the foundation, then work 1 double crochet, 2 chain, 3 treble all into the next chain of the foundation, repeat from * to end, 1 chain, turn.

2nd row—Work 1 double crochet, 2 chain, 3 treble all into the first 2 chain space, * then work 1 double crochet, 2 chain, 3 treble all into the next 2 chain space, repeat from the * to end, 1 chain, turn. Repeat 2nd row for length required.

This is a light and dainty stitch, very suitable for shawls, matinée coats, and other baby wear, and is easily and quickly worked.

DAISY-STITCH (693). Begin with chain.

1st row—Miss first chain, * insert hook into next chain, draw wool through, * repeat from * to * 4 times (6 loops now on hook), wool over, draw through all loops on hook, ** 1 chain, insert hook into hole at top of daisy just made, draw through, insert hook into back of last loop of same daisy, draw through, insert hook into chain last worked into of the foundation, draw through, repeat from * to * twice, wool over, draw through all loops on hook at same time, repeat from ** all along, then 1 chain, 1 double crochet into last foundation chain, 2 chain, turn.

2nd row—1 double crochet into hole of first daisy, 1 chain and 1 double crochet into hole of every daisy, then 1 double crochet into extreme end of last daisy in previous row, 3 chain, turn. **3rd row**—Miss 1 chain, * insert hook into next chain, draw through, repeat from * once, insert hook into first double crochet, draw through, insert hook into next double crochet, draw through, wool over, draw through all loops on hook at same time, ** 1 chain, insert hook into hole at top of daisy just made, draw through, insert hook into back of last loop of same daisy, draw through, insert hook into chain already worked into, draw through, insert hook into next double crochet, draw through, insert hook into next chain, draw through, wool over, draw through all loops on hook at same time, repeat from ** all along, then 1 chain, 1 double crochet into stitch last worked into, 2 chain, turn. Repeat last two rows.

ANOTHER DAISY-STITCH (694). Begin with a length of chain.

1st row—Miss first 2 chain, insert hook into next chain, draw wool through loosely, wool over, insert hook into same chain, draw wool through loosely, miss 1 chain, insert hook into next chain, draw wool through loosely, miss 1 chain, insert hook into next chain, draw wool through loosely (6 loops now on hook), wool over, draw through all loops on hook, * 1 chain, insert hook into small hole just formed by the 1 chain, draw wool through loosely, wool over, insert hook into same place, draw wool through loosely, insert hook into foundation chain last worked into, draw wool through loosely, miss 1 chain, insert hook into next chain, draw wool through loosely, wool over, draw through all loops on hook, repeat from * to end, 3 chain, turn.

2nd row—Miss first chain, insert hook into next chain, draw wool through loosely, wool over, insert hook into same place, draw wool through loosely, insert hook into first small hole in previous row, draw wool through loosely, insert hook into next small hole in previous row, draw wool through loosely, wool over, draw through all loops on hook, this completes first daisy, * 1 chain, insert hook into small hole just formed by the 1 chain, draw wool through, wool over, insert hook into same place, draw through, insert hook into small hole last worked into in previous row, draw wool through, ** insert hook into next small hole in previous row, draw wool through, wool over, draw through all loops on hook, this completes another daisy, repeat from * until last daisy is reached, then work thus : Repeat from * to ** once, insert hook into extreme end of row, draw wool through, wool over, draw through all loops on hook, 3 chain, turn. Repeat 2nd row.

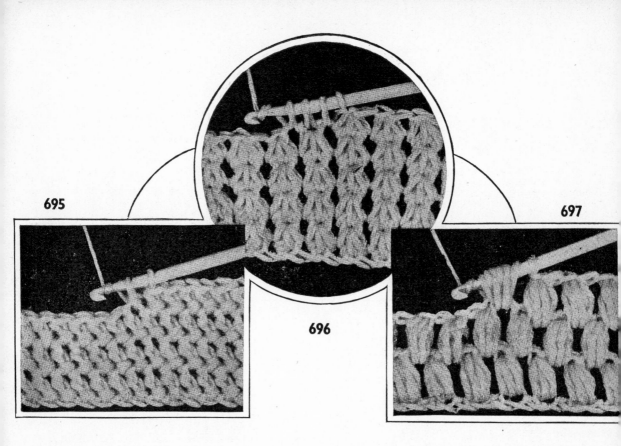

695

697

696

KNOTTED-STITCH (695). This stitch is worked in rows from right to left. Begin with a length of chain. **1st row**—Wool over hook, miss first 2 chain, insert hook into next chain, draw wool through chain and first loop on hook, wool over, draw through the two loops on hook, ★ wool over, insert hook into next chain, draw wool through chain and first loop on hook, wool over, draw through the two loops on hook, repeat from ★ to end, fasten off. **2nd row**—Commence at beginning of previous row. With a loop on the hook, pass wool over hook and insert it into first stitch in previous row, draw wool through stitch and first loop on hook, wool over, draw through two loops on hook, ★ wool over, insert hook into next stitch, draw wool through stitch and first loop on hook, wool over, draw through two loops on hook, repeat from ★ to end, fasten off. Repeat 2nd row for length required.

TRINITY-STITCH (696). *Worked in rows from right to left.* Begin with a length of chain. **1st row**—Miss first 3 chain, ★ insert hook into next chain, draw wool through, ★ repeat from ★ to ★ twice (4 loops now on hook), wool over, draw through all loops on hook at same time, ★★ 1 chain, insert hook into chain last worked into, draw wool through, repeat from ★ to ★ twice, wool over, draw through all loops on hook at same time, ★★ repeat from ★★ to ★★ all along, then 1 chain, 1 double crochet into last chain of the foundation, fasten off. **2nd row**—Slip-stitch into top of chain at beginning of previous row, 2 chain, insert hook into small space here seen before first group, draw wool through, insert hook into top of next group in previous row, draw wool through, insert hook into next stitch, draw wool through (4 loops now on hook), wool over, draw through all loops on hook at same time, ★ 1 chain, insert hook into stitch last worked into, draw wool through, insert hook into top of next group in previous row, draw wool through, insert hook into next stitch, draw wool through, wool over, draw through all loops on hook at same time, repeat from ★ all along, then 1 chain, 1 double crochet into last stitch again, fasten off. Repeat 2nd row for length required.

BALL-STITCH (697). This is worked in rows backwards and forwards, both sides of the work being alike. Begin with a chain the length required. **1st row**—Miss first 3 chain, then wool over hook, insert hook into next chain, draw wool through loosely, wool over, insert hook into same chain, draw wool through loosely, wool over, insert hook into same chain again, draw wool through loosely (7 loops now on hook), wool over, draw through all loops on hook at same time, ★ 1 chain, miss 1 chain of the foundation, wool over hook, insert hook into next chain, draw wool through loosely, wool over, insert hook into same chain, draw wool through loosely, wool over, insert hook into same chain again, draw wool through loosely, wool over, draw through all loops on hook at same time, repeat from ★ to end, 3 chain, turn. **2nd row**—1 ball-stitch into space between first and second ball-stitches in previous row, ★ 1 chain, 1 ball-stitch into next space, repeat from ★ to end, 3 chain, turn. Repeat 2nd row for length required.

Tricot Crochet

For this effective stitch, a tricot hook must be used which is of uniform thickness from the hook upwards. The tricot hook should be if possible a little longer than the width of the work to allow for all the stitches.

PLAIN TRICOT (698). Begin with a length of chain. **1st row**—Miss first chain, insert hook into next chain, draw wool through and keep this loop on hook, * insert hook into next chain, draw wool through and keep this loop also on hook, repeat from * all along, when there should be the same number of loops on hook as the number of foundation chain, then wool over hook, draw through first loop on hook, ** wool over, draw through 2 loops on hook, repeat from ** to end.
2nd row—The loop that remains on hook forms the first stitch of the row, therefore insert hook from right to left through second upright stitch in previous row, draw wool through and keep loop on hook, * insert hook from right to left through next upright stitch, draw wool through and keep this loop also on hook, repeat from * to end, then wool over, draw through first loop on hook, ** wool over, draw through 2 loops on hook, repeat from ** to end. Repeat 2nd row for length required, and finish by working 1 slip-stitch into each upright stitch of the last row worked.
To Decrease
Insert hook from right to left through two upright stitches and draw wool through both of these at same time.
To Increase
To increase at beginning of a row, insert hook from right to left through first upright stitch, draw wool through, then continue along row as for plain tricot until 1 upright stitch remains, insert hook into stitch between upright stitches, draw wool through, insert hook into last upright stitch, draw wool through, and now finish row as described for plain tricot.

FANCY TRICOT (699). Begin with a length of chain. **1st row**—Miss first chain, insert hook into next chain, draw wool through and keep this loop on hook, * insert hook into next chain, draw wool through and keep this loop also on hook, repeat from * to end, when there should be the same number of loops on hook as the number of foundation chain, then wool over hook, draw through first loop on hook, ** wool over, draw through 2 loops on hook, repeat from ** to end. It will be seen that there is a row of small horizontal stitches at the back along top of row, and these are the stitches that are worked into. **2nd row**—Insert hook into horizontal stitch at back of second upright stitch in previous row, draw wool through, * insert hook into horizontal stitch at back of next upright stitch, draw wool through, repeat from * to end, then wool over hook, draw through first loop on hook, ** wool over, draw through 2 loops on hook, repeat from ** to end.
Repeat 2nd row for length required.

PLAITED TRICOT (700). Begin with a length of chain divisible by two. **1st row**—Work in the same way as described for the first row of plain tricot.
2nd row—Insert hook from right to left through third upright stitch, draw wool through, insert hook through second upright stitch, draw wool through, * miss one upright stitch, insert hook through next upright stitch, draw wool through, insert hook through the stitch that was missed, draw wool through, repeat from * until one upright stitch remains, insert hook through this stitch, draw wool through, wool over, draw through first loop on hook, ** wool over, draw through 2 loops on hook, repeat from ** to end.
Repeat 2nd row for length required, and finish by working 1 slip-stitch into each upright stitch of the last row worked.

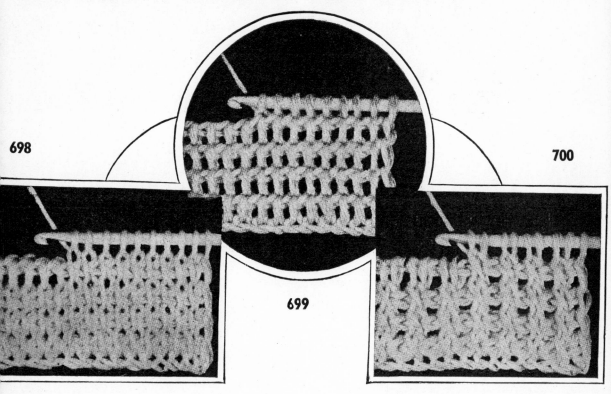

698

699

700

221

Index

The numbers refer to pages, and not to the illustrations

Index